Change and Continuity in
American Politics

CHANGE AND CONTINUITY IN AMERICAN POLITICS

The Social Bases of Political Parties

David Knoke

THE JOHNS HOPKINS UNIVERSITY PRESS

Baltimore and London

The Johns Hopkins University Press, Baltimore, Maryland 21218
The Johns Hopkins Press Ltd., London

Library of Congress Cataloging in Publication Data

Knoke, David.
    Change and continuity in American politics.

    Bibliography: pp. 174–87
    Includes index.
    1. Party affiliation—United States. 2. Voting
—United States. 3. United States—Politics and
government—1945–   I. Title.
JK2271.K56   329'.02   76-14997
ISBN 0-8018-1790-0

For My Parents, Who Showed Me How

Contents

Contents   ix

Figures

Tables

Preface and Acknowledgments

As this book went to press, millions of Americans were participating in the selection of political party candidates for the 1976 elections. Voting is the major activity which activates the parties in the electorate. The collective decision reached in the primary and general elections in large part will shape the character of the parties in government and their legislative outputs. Barring an unforeseen twist of events, the election results should resemble those of the recent past, for the electorate's standing support of the political parties has exhibited only minor variations on a consistent theme.

This book dissects the parties in the electorate along the religious, racial, regional, and socioeconomic fault lines of the post–World War II period. These political cleavages have shown remarkable persistence, despite the tremendous upheavals of the civil rights movement, the Vietnam war, Watergate, and stagflation. Change is not absent, however; it is fully reflected in the growing number of Independents and the general softening of ties between party identifications and voting choices. This mixture of change and continuity has caused some commentators to despair of the parties' responsiveness to voter interests, and others to predict an impending dissolution of the party system. These prognostications are unwarranted projections of short-term conditions.

For the remainder of this century the main domestic and international problem confronting this nation and, indeed, the world is the diminishing supply of cheap raw materials upon which rapid growth industrial society has been built. The first tremors of economic, social, and political dislocation have been felt, and the nation and its political leaders are still groping for solutions. While crises of this magnitude have historically been associated with major transformations of the political party system, there is reason to believe that such conversion will not take place this time. A chronic depression in the 1930's gave birth to the present system in which the Democratic party predominates within the electorate. The chronic economic crises in the years ahead are likely to reinforce the existing structure of political interest representation. The natural constituencies of the Democratic party—blue collar workers, ethnic and religious minorities, intellectuals—will probably continue to find their interests articulated by that party. The Republican party's defense of vested corporate power, at a time when the life styles and living standards of the majority are ground down by inflation and unemployment, will not win sufficient numbers of voters to compete effectively with the Democrats. The past is thus a prologue to the future of American politics, and for that reason the investigation of the mass basis of party support over the past two decades has more than historical value.

The perspective of this book is political sociology, which I take to be the analysis of the social organization of political behavior. Some people see this orientation as reducing politics to a derivative of the larger social structure. I would not deny that the political system is proactive, that authorities are often able to manipulate the polity to achieve their own goals. The legal, institutional, and formal organizational aspects of electoral behavior are topics beyond the scope of this book, however. My purpose is much more modest: to describe in great detail and precision the social group composition of the mass electoral parties and how they have changed or remained stable in the recent past. This investigation is carried out by analysis of national surveys in presidential election years from 1952 to 1972. Secondary survey analysis has achieved a new stature in recent years, assisted by the growth of archiving services. Studies of long-term social change would be impossible without access to surveys conducted many years ago by investigators with other purposes in mind at the time. The secondary data analyst is thus blessed with the fruits of others' labor, but he is also restricted to dealing with those topics and issues which his predecessors felt were important enough to inquire about. Secondary data analysis can never answer all the questions one wishes, but it remains nevertheless one of the few ways of peering accurately into the past.

Readers of this book will confront a great deal of statistical analysis of empirical data. My conviction is that an understanding of the nuances of political behavior can be greatly advanced through the testing of precise hypotheses. I have endeavored to use techniques of quantitative data analysis, which have been used to great advantage in such fields as econometrics and stratification. At the same time, I have tried to make this work accessible to persons who may have an interest in the substantive topic but lack the background to follow all the quantitative derivations. The findings and implications of the data analysis are interpreted in a straightforward manner. I have included an Appendix of basic information about methods which should be sufficient to follow most of the applications in the text. Understanding of the statistical procedures is not an easy task, as I well know from my own experience, but the rewards for persistent effort can be great.

In a project as large and as long in preparation as this one, sorting out all the important influences is difficult. I can only cite some of which I am more aware. To begin with, I owe an enormous intellectual debt to the hundreds of scholars of electoral behavior whose work preceded mine, from whom I have learned a great deal and to whose tradition I hope I have added a small contribution. In particular, my thinking has been heavily influenced by the seminal ideas of *The American Voter*, a classic in its field. Many of the findings and insights of this work, based upon data from only two elections, have proved remarkably durable, and even where circumstances have since changed, the work has been a valuable guide to the relationship of social life and political behavior. My work cannot begin to match the scope, depth, and originality of *The American Voter*, but I am pleased to acknowledge its contribution to my efforts.

Without the pioneering efforts of the University of Michigan Survey Research Center, this book would not have been possible, as most young scholars lack the resources to carry out large-scale primary survey research. The Inter-University Consortium for Political Research has proved to be a valuable asset for persons in a position like myself. I am indebted to the many people in ICPR who made the data archives available for secondary analysis, and I especially want to thank Ronald Weber and Martha Vandivort for their assistance in gaining access to the data at Indiana University. A grant from the Indiana University Biomedical Research Support Committee was helpful in the initial organizing stages of the research. Of course, none of these parties should be held responsible for any abuses of the data which may be found here.

Several scholars deserve special thanks for the interest and concern they have shown for my work. David R. Segal has vigorously encouraged my study of political sociology since my days as an uncertain undergraduate. While he did not see any of these chapters prior to publication, in many ways the book bears his imprint. To Otis Dudley Duncan and Leo A. Goodman I owe most of what little I know about quantitative data analysis. They have given their time freely over the years to instruct me in the tortuous ways of path analysis, regression, and log-linear models and have imparted to me their high standards of excellence in research. In particular, I want to acknowledge their many suggestions, which were not always followed, on the analysis of panel data appearing in Chapter VI. Michael Hout read the first draft of the manuscript and gave many helpful suggestions which improved the later versions. The critical comments of several anonymous reviewers were similarly useful, though the final product surely will not please everyone.

Many people assisted in the production of this book, and without their cheerful cooperation the enterprise would have been vastly more difficult. Kathy L. Carpenter and Debbie F. Adams typed the basic manuscripts with great alacrity. Mary D. Bernetich prepared the tables, and Betty Billman showed me how to make the illustrations.

Finally, but not least, the cooperation of Joann and Margaret Frances Knoke during the months and years spent working on this book is greatly appreciated. Neither played any part in this book except to be the reasons for its existence.

Chapter I

The Roots of
Party Identification

Party identifications are enduring psychological attachments of individuals to the symbols and substance of political parties. The predisposition of the mass electorate to support parties is a major element in the stability of democratic polities. The recognition that party preferences constrain the contest for political office is not recent. Long before the development of survey techniques, students of electoral behavior were aware of the great stability in the voting patterns of aggregate units such as precincts, wards, and counties (Gosnell, 1927; Rice, 1928). Recurrent partisan alignments in election after election reflected the "standing decision" of communities in favor of a particular party. Key and Munger (1959), for example, demonstrated that voting patterns laid down during the Civil War persisted in Indiana well into the twentieth century, long after the original issues had ceased to have meaning to the new participants.

The first major study of the national electorate to use the survey sample discovered that voting was predictably associated with issue orientation, candidate preferences, and party identification (Campbell et al., 1954). Subsequent studies by the Survey Research Center at the University of Michigan (Campbell and Cooper, 1956; Campbell et al., 1960, 1966) used a self-classification of party preference to reveal widespread acceptance of the labels "Republican," "Independent," and "Democrat," as well as varying strengths of attachment. The psychological nature of party identification, rather than a behavioral definition such as voting or campaigning for a candidate, was stressed:

Only in the exceptional case does the sense of individual attachment to party reflect a formal membership or active connection with a party apparatus. Nor does it simply denote a voting record, although the influence of party allegiance on electoral behavior is strong. Generally this tie is a psychological identification, which can persist without legal recognition or evidence of formal membership or even without a consistent record of party support. Most Americans have this sense of attachment with one party or the other. And for the individual who does, the strength and direction of party identification are facts of central importance in accounting for attitude and behavior (Campbell et al., 1960, Ch. 5).

More than 95 percent of adult Americans consistently described themselves as Democrats, Republicans, or Independents in response to a standardized set of questions. The Gallup, Harris, and other public opinion polls
routinely report the distributions among these partisan groups, indicating
widespread understanding and acceptance of these labels by the general
public and mass media.

As surveys and polls accumulated, two central facts about party identification in the immediate post–World War II era stood out. First, the
aggregate distributions of partisans and independents did not greatly change
from election to election despite large swings in the voting percentages.
Democrats held a plurality fluctuating between 45 and 51 percent, and
Republicans just nosed out the Independents in splitting the remainder (see
Flanigan, 1972, p. 33). Panel studies of the same individuals revealed that
while some inter-party movement occurred, much of the stability in the
aggregate figures was due to the temporal stability of party identification
(Campbell et al., 1960, pp. 146–49). Second, party affiliation also appeared
to have a high degree of intergenerational stability. Studies of adults using
their recall of parental party affiliations showed that a large majority tended
to adopt the party identification of the family of origin, especially when both
parents were reported to agree on party (Sorauf, 1972, p. 144). The fact of
high intergenerational correlation was also confirmed in studies of children's
and adolescents' political orientations where parents were directly interviewed (Niemi, 1967; Jennings and Langton, 1969).

Any theory of the causes and consequences of party identification must
deal with the facts of high intra- and intergenerational party stability. The
following sections explore two models which have been proposed to explain
identification in general and party affiliation in particular. These models, the
rational and the traditional, are often viewed as contradictory and irreconcilable images of political man. A closer inspection and comparison, however, does not support this conclusion.

The Nature of Identification

Sigmund Freud's revelations of the human unconscious produced one
model of psychological identification. Initially a sexual bond during infancy,
identification in later life is the expression of an emotional tie with any
person or object with whom a common quality is shared. Since such
emotional bonds may operate below the conscious level, identification can
be irrational or regressive. Identification with political parties, in the
Freudian view, might be largely due to an unreasoning linkage of oneself to
a charismatic political leader or to a set of emotion-provoking symbols, or it
might be a derivative of more primary identifications with parents or social

groups. The family of origin, as the chief agent of socialization, may instill political loyalties in childhood or adolescence through the offspring's emulation of parental behavior. Even the deviation of sons and daughters from the politics of the parents may be viewed as a psychodynamic process of rebellion against parental authority, in which all things identified with the parents are rejected (see Buchanan, 1968; Alexander, 1959; Lane, 1959; Greenstein, 1965a).

An older perspective, receiving one of its strongest expressions in Karl Marx's work, sees political identification as a rational process. For Marx identification with a class and its organized political representation was the inevitable outcome of analysis of one's self-interest. Workers would come to see that their economic, political, and social interests were incompatible with those of the capitalist employers. The rational act would then be to support political parties that would further the goals of the class (Marx, 1956, pp. 191–200). Thus party identification would result from the expectation that collective action would provide a solution to strains inherent in the social structure. Although "false consciousness" was a potential obstacle to correct analysis of interests, party identification, in the rationalist perspective, was basically an instrumental act rather than an emotional reflex.

These two perspectives on party identification implicitly underlie much of the theoretical and empirical work on party preferences and voting behavior. The tendency has been to see the two models as competing and irreconcilable. The Freudian model may depict voters as puppets jerked about by strings attached in childhood, projecting all manner of irrational fears and nonpolitical needs into the political arena. The Marxist model or a modified version of "interest group politics" may portray political man as a coldly rational accountant, cynically selling his political support in the electoral marketplace to the highest bidder, devoid of loyalty and commitment.

As with most caricatures, truth is buried under such distortions and simplifications. Further investigations of more sophisticated versions of psychological identification growing out of the Freudian and Marxian perspectives reveal many points of agreement. To facilitate discussion, the model viewing identification as a process of maximizing interests will be labeled "rational," while the model emphasizing the affective basis of identification will be called "traditional."

The Rational Calculus

In recent years students of voting behavior have developed extensive formal models of rational political behavior. The assumptions underlying these formal models of candidate choice in elections may be extended to the decision on which party to support.

An extreme version of the rational model of political behavior would allow no role for party identification in the United States. Voting, the main or only political activity of most citizens, requires casting ballots for particular candidates in specific races, not for a party slate, as in some European nations. If the rational voter evaluates each candidate solely on his or her merits, then party identification has no function and no reason to exist. Yet this expectation from the extreme rational model flies in the face of reality; more than three-quarters of the electorate *do* profess identification with one of the two major parties. Therefore, a less extreme model of rational behavior must allow persons to choose a party, as well as particular candidates, by the rational calculus described below. Party identification may be viewed as a "standing decision" about which party's candidates to support until the opportunity arises to make an explicit selection of candidates from a ballot. Party identification in the rational model may help organize the citizen's political universe, structure new information, and provide continuity between periods of campaign activity.

The basic assumptions of a rational model of party choice are: a set of alternative actions, such as supporting one of several parties or candidates; a set of possible outcomes resulting from each action, such as election of a candidate or influence over a government decision, and the associated probabilities that the actions will lead to each outcome; and the decision-maker's evaluation, or expected utility (payoff), from an outcome. The postulate of rationality is that a decisionmaker will act *as if* he has calculated the expected utility for each possible act and then chosen the alternative party or candidate which maximizes his payoff. Riker and Ordeshook (1973) provide one of the most accessible recent treatments of the formal theory of rational decisionmaking.

The set of alternative choices are the political parties with which a citizen can identify (including identification with none). The set of possible outcomes are the political consequences, desired or undesired, which may result from the decision. Such outcomes are primarily—but by no means only—the outputs of the party if it attains governmental power. Outputs may be material, as in providing individual and collective goods and services like highways, national defense, or welfare. Outputs also may be symbolic, as in the display of valued goals. For example, a positively-valued symbolic output might be placing of a member of one's own minority group on the judiciary; a negatively valued outcome might be the judicial appointment of a member from a different minority group.

The individual's decision about which party, if any, to support requires him to evaluate the probability that supporting a given party will produce the desired outcomes (and avoid undesired outcomes) and to determine the relative importance (utility) to himself of achieving each of the outcomes. The final decision is achieved by summing these weighted utilities for each party and identifying with the one that yields the biggest payoff. So far, nothing has been said about the admissibility of different types of outcomes in the rational calculus. The most liberal definitions do not restrict the universe of political goals: "Rationality may be interpreted broadly as the ability to choose the more preferred action over the less preferred. In this sense, almost all behavior is rational and the assumption of rationality is close to tautological" (Riker and Ordeshook, 1968, p. 27).

Other authors restrict the set of admissible outcomes to an explicitly political subset. V. O. Key, for example, in his "perverse and unorthodox argument . . . that voters are not fools" (Key, 1966, p. 7), appears to equate rationality in voting behavior with the ability to make evaluations of public policy. By restricting alternatives to evaluation of policy outcomes, the theorist implies that some goals are "rational" (e.g., a foreign policy position) while others are "irrational" (e.g., voting for a "father image" candidate). Such restrictions seem unduly arbitrary; persons who desire outcomes not posited by the observer may nevertheless estimate the utility of identification with one party in a rational manner. Rather than call such behavior "irrational," we shall admit any set of outcomes into the rational calculus. We now seek a system for classifying outcomes so that a comparison of the rational and traditional models of party identification may be made.

In the broad version of the rational model, outcomes may or may not be benefits accruing to the individual. When the individual identifies with a party because he expects to receive personal rewards, such outcomes may be classified as *personal* bases for party identification. Examples include supporting a party in hopes of receiving government employment, tax relief, public welfare support, or government construction contracts. The common element in all these outcomes is the consumption of government benefits (or avoidance of government exactions) wholly on an individual basis, although of course other individuals may likewise benefit. Another set of outcomes are *civic* in nature. They cannot be divided among individuals, nor can some segments of the public be excluded from partaking in the benefits (or disutilities) of such public policies. A party may be supported for altruistic reasons, such as expectations that it will control pollution, provide national parks, increase defense spending, or eliminate bureaucratic waste.

While personal and civic outcomes doubtless occur in the calculation of expected payoffs when choosing parties, they are not the most important set of outcomes for comparing the rational and traditional models. A third category of outcomes relates to the *social group* memberships of decision-makers. An individual identifies with a party based on the expected payoff to the social group(s) to which he belongs. Consumption of government outputs is not direct, as in personal outcomes, nor is it universal, as in civic outcomes. The benefits of government policies may accrue to a group as a whole, often to the exclusion of other social groups in the polity. Such bases of party identification are of great relevance in a pluralistic society. Instances of exclusionary group benefits from government policy are legion, from veterans' benefits to civil rights legislation. Many of the symbolic aspects of politics fall into this category, where actions of the political party may give special recognition to a social group. John Kennedy's election, for example, raised the status of Catholics as a group through the symbol of their co-religionist in the White House. Stokes (1968) made a similar distinction among social group outcomes according to the interest-related, symbolic, or subcultural norm content of their relation to party identification. While the first two criteria seem appropriate to the rational choice model, subcultural norms are considered in the next section as an aspect of the traditional identification model.

The Traditional Model

The traditional model of party choice, growing out of the Freudian perspective on identification, received its sharpest statement in one of the first sociological studies of voting behavior: "a person thinks, politically, as he is, socially. Social characteristics determine preference" (Lazarsfeld et al., 1944, p. 27). This model, often castigated as "social determinism," sees party identification as largely the result of group influences upon individuals to conform to group norms of behavior, including political party norms. Conflicts arise in social life outside the polity and enter into the political arena as group interests. A group member's identification with a party need not be based upon a rational calculus of expected utility to the group from such party support. In the traditional model, noncognitive processes on a subconscious, emotional level can bind the individual to a party as surely as he is bound to his social groups.

The importance of socialization in childhood and adolescence is heavily emphasized in the traditional model. Familial socialization produces non-cognitive identification with many social groupings—race, religion, national origin—and often with a political party, generally one shared by the parents. The traditional model views the process of transmission as inadvertent, imitative identification: "This model has been used most extensively to explain the acquisition of political party preference by children who adopt their parents' partisan outlook. The child may have little understanding of the meaning of party identification, and the identification itself may lack consistent relationship with attitudes toward partisan policies. In this model, attitudes toward a given object are imitated directly from another person" (Hess and Torney, 1967, p. 21).

While the Freudian psychoanalytic approach to political socialization dominated the early inquiries in this area, recent developments in social learning theory have shifted concern from inner personality determinants to external influences on political orientations. A modeling process in which children learn by imitation provides a more parsimonious explanation of parent-child similarities than a postulated complex of subconscious identifications (Bandura, 1971a, 1971b). The basic assumption of social learning theory is that people acquire knowledge about appropriate behavior for given situations by observing others, especially parents and peers, responding to similar situations. For political orientations in particular, a child acquires such attitudes as party identification and sense of efficacy by modeling them on parents' responses to political events.

In the traditional model such political identifications persist largely unchanged into adulthood. The model explains the high intergenerational correlations of party identifications observed in cross-sectional survey studies as the persistence of early socialization outcomes. Children maintain the party loyalties learned from parents because of the accumulated emotional investments in self-identity. Rather than a rational calculation of group benefits to be maximized through party support, party identification is part of a "package" of social identifications passed on from parents to offspring. Deviations from parental or group partisanship, including the absence of party identification and independence, are attributed to poor socialization, apathetic parents, weak integration in social groups, and the like.

Primary groups are the main social structures for preserving traditional party loyalties (Riecken, 1959; McClosky and Dahlgren, 1959; Campbell et al., 1960, p. 77). These face-to-face groups encapsulate most social activity in small networks which filter and interpret the larger society to the individual. The social encounters within friendship circles, work groups, and family units overtly and subtly reinforce group identities and behavioral norms initiated early in life. The message carried by primary groups need not be explicitly stated; it need be only a simple effective reminder that "we" share a common identity and outlook, which also includes support for a traditional party. The primary group influences may be as invisible as the air and just as pervasive.

While the traditional party identification of a social group may have arisen originally as a rational attempt to satisfy group goals, perhaps generations ago, the mechanism for maintaining loyalties does not presume a contemporary rational linkage. In the traditional model, party loyalties can persist well beyond the original issues which gave rise to them. They may even be incompatible with some "objective" analysis of the party payoffs to the group under a rational model. For example, many white southerners maintain nominal identification with the Democratic party, a tradition stretching back to the Civil War, although the national party has undergone a transformation to a more active championing of civil rights.

The major difference between the rational and traditional models of party identification lies in the frequency with which changes in party preferences occur (Oppenheim, 1970, pp. 129–30). The key element in this difference is the impact of new political information on the stability of prior identifications. The rational calculus is a deductive process: given a set of preferred outcomes, what choice of party will maximize an individual's utility? When new information contradicting current beliefs comes to the attention of the individual, will it cause a recalculation of utilities that results in a change in party identification? The problem is one of inductive rationality and has been empirically investigated in voting choice among primary election candidates (Shapiro, 1969).

The rational party identification model contends that the evaluation of new information about parties, such as changes in policy toward various social groups, will not be subject to distortion or misperception. A rational person uses all information believed to be accurate in making the decision whether to continue support or to switch loyalties. If the information substantially changes the estimated utilities of one party relative to another, defection is the rational consequence. Although not all incoming information may be accurate (the assessment of information validity is another question), the rational model posits inductive rationality within the limits of the individual's ability to process new information.

Rational induction of new information is not feasible if new perceptions might create psychological strain by challenging comfortable conventional wisdom. The pioneer study *Voting* (Berelson et al., 1954, p. 220) found that voters' perceptions of a candidate's stand on an issue might be affected by the voters' own preference on the issue. The tendency of partisans to reinterpret perceptions in such a way as to see one's party in a favorable light (assimilation) and the opposition in an unfavorable light (contrast) goes to the heart of the traditional model. Misperception and selective perception of new information is a fundamental psychological mechanism for maintaining traditional party ties. In contrast with the ready defection of the rational partisan when the expected utilities change, the traditional partisan exhibits great inertia in the face of real shifts in party policies. The stronger a person's emotional commitment to a party, the more impervious he is to information that might shake his loyalty.

Reconciling Differences

The rational and the traditional models outlined above posit different and seemingly incompatible causes for party identification. One would presume that an appropriately designed empirical test ought to distinguish which model applies or, in the event that both processes operate, the relative contributions of each to party identification in the United States. Yet despite the analytic differences in the two perspectives, they are too imprecise to generate sufficiently specific predictions to allow a definitive test (this point is stressed by Oppenheim, 1970, p. 130). The two major facts of party identification in the United States, its high correlation between generations and its great stability within individuals, are compatible with both rational and traditional models.

The rational model predicts defection of individuals from a previous choice whenever the relative utilities of the parties change. While the traditional model indicates great inertia of partisanship, it does not prohibit change from ever occurring; selective perception can only go so far in distorting external realities to fit subjective desires. Unfortunately, the two models do not specify how much change is to be expected after exposure to new political information, nor do they predict how rapidly it is expected to occur. Even a model of rational choice conforming to real behavior would not posit instantaneous change. Much past research on the relationship of party identification to voting behavior suggests that party defection is a slow process and is preceded by deviations from the party in voting decisions. The Eisenhower elections of the 1950's exhibited much Republican voting by self-identified Democrats who did not abandon their initial identifications (Campbell, 1966). A similar process may be occurring currently in the South, with lifelong Democrats exhibiting high levels of Republican presidential voting, perhaps as a prelude to substantial realignment in party identification. Whether these patterns are evidence for the inertia of partisanship in the traditional model or evidence of incremental recalculations of utility in the rational model is difficult to determine. A case for either model can be built on the same data.

The traditional model accounts for the observed high correlation between parents' and offspring's party identifications by socialization of an imitative, noncognitive nature. The rational model accounts for the same high correlation by positing that both generations will arrive at an almost identical utility calculation for the parties, and hence will tend to choose the same political party. If the bases for calculating expected utilities are primarily the outcomes which affect social groups, then the rational calculus leads to expectations very similar to those of the traditional model, for the family of origin not only socializes its offspring into a culture, but it provides a set of social groups, many of which are maintained for life, particularly religion, race, ethnicity, and geographic locale (region). Since parents will share many of these membership groups with their children, utility calculations will tend to lead to the same party preference. The party chosen under the rational model would be the same as one chosen under the traditional model; however in the latter the basis for similarity between generations arises from conformity to group norms and the perpetuation of traditional ties. Instances where party affiliations across generations do not coincide because of differences in the social group memberships of parent and child are predicted in both models. For example, if religious conversion occurs in an interfaith marriage, a change in party identification toward that held by the new church may follow. The rational model attributes the change to recalculation of utility for a new membership group; the traditional model attributes the change to adult resocialization in which the political norms of the new group are assimilated. The same outcome is expected under both models.

The apparent incompatibility of the rational and traditional models of party identification may be precisely that—more apparent than real. Particularly when group goals and group norms of political behavior are the primary basis of mass partisanship, the two models lead to almost identical predictions about stability and change in party identification. The two models may be further reconciled by acknowledging that group-based standards of partisanship may often be rational means of achieving goals favored by the group (Goldberg, 1969). Even when initially acquired by affective, noncognitive socialization, such party identifications may serve highly instrumental purposes. Party affiliations rooted in group identification may thus fuse rational goals and emotional commitment into a complex process of identification. The primary interest in this book is not disentangling rational and traditional components of partisanship, an impossible task, given the data at hand. Instead, we will investigate the impact of various social group memberships upon the formation and maintenance or change of party identification. This task requires a conceptual interpretation of social groups and their political goals in a pluralistic industrial society.

Pluralism and Social Groups

The political culture of the United States is an embodiment of the Lockean liberal tradition (Hartz, 1955; Devine, 1972). The polity has achieved basic agreement on the rules and institutions by which power will be attained and used. Within the framework of this consensus occur those disagreements over specific policies and their implementation which give rise to the characteristic cleavage structures of the American polity. The party system, which has not undergone any fundamental change in over a century, contains and channels social conflicts into acceptable modes of political resolution. The great historic social conflicts which created persistent fault lines in the social structure are also crystallized in the mass base of the political parties. Even a century after the Civil War, the South was sharply differentiated from the remainder of the country in the party identifications of its electorate and legislative delegations. Ethnic, racial, religious, and class cleavages originating perhaps generations ago still leave visible imprints on the contemporary parties. The parties' popular images reflect their social group structure as well as their perceived capacities to manage the government.

The multiplicity of social groups in American society, with varying degrees of political involvement, is enormous. They range from highly organized formal entities, like the National Rifle Association, to amorphous "statistical" groups, such as age and sex categories, which only rarely exhibit collective action for political goals. A meaningful analysis of the impact of social groups on party affiliations requires a framework to organize the data.

Two useful dimensions for the analysis of social groups are the structural and the status dimensions. Structural characteristics of groups refers to the type of relationships which members have with each other. The concepts of primary and secondary group affiliations have their roots in the *Gemeinschaft* and *Gesellschaft* (community and association) in classical sociological thought (Toennies, 1957). *Primary* relationships occur in small, face-to-face collectivities organized on affective bases. Families and friendship circles are the most prevalent examples of primary social groups. They often provide the most powerful sources of an individual's psychological identity and intimate satisfactions. *Secondary* groups are characterized by less closely knit relationships among individuals, and direct acquaintanceship is not even possible in larger organizations such as those with a national membership. Secondary groups may organize around a specific set of limited goals, as with most voluntary formal organizations, or may be more diffuse, as with religious and ethnic communities. Obviously many, if not most, secondary groups contain many primary groups within them, as, for example, a manufacturing corporation with small work groups that develop primary ties among their members.

Political parties in the United States are clearly diffuse secondary structures for most members of the electorate. If parties were completely devoid of connection with any other facet of social life, we would expect psychological identifications, if they occur at all, to be very tenuous and constantly changing. The strength of party attachments in the United States does not derive from the party organization itself, since the formal party structure is remote from the lives of most adherents. The viability of party loyalty derives largely from the penetration of the political world into the life of nonpolitical primary and secondary social groups. The "web of group affiliations," in Simmel's apt phrase (1964), ensures that through interaction with other group members individuals will be exposed to and come to adopt the norms of the group—including party preferences—regardless of their rational or traditional origin.

The derivation of party identifications and other political orientations from social group identifications in the electorate was eloquently set out in *The American Voter* (Campbell et al., 1960, ch. 11). The authors emphasized the greater importance of secondary group associations—unions, racial and ethnic communities, religious affiliations—than of primary groups in influencing the voting trends of identifiable social aggregates. Psychological identification with nonpolitical groups varies in degree among those who are nominal members by virtue of having some characteristics in common with other members of the collectivity. But the very fact of sharing some aspects of life chances with other individuals raises the probability that the members of the group will act in ways politically different from nonmembers of the group.

In much of the research reported in this book, adequate measures of the strength of group identification and the political salience of group membership were not available. As a consequence, group membership can only be inferred from the available indicators of an individual's social characteristics. Thus, in classifying respondents as Catholics, blacks, blue-collar workers, or other categorizations we are identifying *statistical* aggregates and social groupings only indirectly. Campbell et al. (1960) have clearly demonstrated that persons subjectively identifying with the secondary group are more likely to behave in politically distinctive ways than persons with the same objective characteristics who do not identify with the group. By locating individuals in the social system according to their objectively shared group characteristics but not by their subjective attachments, we necessarily underestimate the strength of group influence. But by charting the course of a statistical aggregate's political orientation as it changes over time, we gain some indirect indication of the intensity of psychological involvement and structured social interaction within the primary and secondary structures of the group. Clearly, information on social networks, patterns of communication, recruitment and socialization, and reaction to cross-pressures from multiple group memberships with competing claims to loyalty would be desirable to understand better how groups shape the political orientations of their members. Unfortunately, the use of secondary data sources in the study of change over two decades requires one to make do with what is available. While recognizing the limitations imposed by the data, we may still talk of the impact of groups on their members, leaving the precise mechanisms for others to investigate.

Status, the second analytic dimension of social groups, received extensive treatment in Weber's writings (1966). Status is a hierarchical dimension of social relationships, indicating the honor or deference due a social position. Subsequent distinctions have been made between those social statuses which are ascribed and those which are achieved (Mayhew, 1968), and these types will prove useful in the analysis of social group effects in party identifications. Ascribed social statuses generally are not acquired through personal effort but are either present from birth or conferred by ceremony. Status within a family group is an ascribed primary group attribute, obtained only by birth, adoption, marriage, or aging. Secondary group statuses which depend upon ascribed sentiment and belief include race, religion, and ethnicity. Ascriptive statuses frequently involve in-group distinctions, as in the disdain that some racial and ethnic groups have for nonmembers. Because of the intensity of socialization in ascriptive status groups, such groups may exhibit great depths of emotional commitment to the symbols and goals of the group. With roots in kinship, land, and spirit, ascribed status groups may be appropriately called "primordial groups."

Achieved statuses tend to be less fixed and less compelling of emotional commitments. As the name implies, they are obtained by demonstrating the requisite skills and other qualifications. These standards may vary from a simple application to join a voluntary organization to long periods of rigorous training and testing to become a member of a profession. Achieved statuses may occur in both primary and secondary social structures. A primary achieved status might be economic work groups within which specific productive tasks are carried out. Secondary achieved statuses include both formal organizations like unions, corporations, and political parties and even more diffuse collectivities such as hierarchies of wealth, educational attainment, or occupational prestige. Movement up and down the status positions of such groups is more frequent and less circumscribed than change within ascribed status hierarchies. The notion of a "career" is primarily an achieved-status concept.

Although the distinctions between primary and secondary group structures and ascribed and achieved status hierarchies are easy to define analytically, most actual groups do not fall clearly into such neat categorizations. Most persons probably become aware of the secondary groups to which they belong through the mediating involvement with specific primary relationships. Many statuses are not exclusively ascribed or achieved but are probably a blend of the two analytic types.

Given a variety of groups competing for an individual's attention and loyalty, the relative political impact of each upon the party identifications of members is problematic. Ascriptive bases might be expected to produce more intense feelings toward political symbols and party images than would achievement groupings. Lifelong membership and the intense affective socialization of many ascriptive groups, as well as the ability of many primordial groups to form autonomous communities within the society, are likely, when linked with the early socialization of party preferences, to produce stronger group-party bonds than a succession of achieved statuses of shorter duration. Not all ascriptive groupings contain implicit political cues. Age and sex are biologically imperative ascriptive statuses, yet provide less clear-cut bases for party identification than race, religion, or ethnicity. The difference may lie in a lower probability for primary group activity to emerge along age and sex lines than along the latter statuses. Segregation of residential communities along racial, and, to a lesser extent, ethnic, dimensions is a salient phenomenon with important political consequences in the

United States. Age and sex segregation is nowhere nearly as widespread, although the recent attempts to politicize women's roles indicate the dynamic nature of ascriptive status cleavages.

While achieved statuses may generally produce less intense and clear cues for partisanship than ascription does, such relative balance may be situation-specific. In times of economic dislocation, stratification as a political cleavage may emerge and eclipse ascriptive social groups in importance. The experience of the Depression and the postwar decades of prosperity suggest the waxing and waning of achievement criteria, particularly economic group membership, in the formation of party identifications. The emergence of new conflicts in the society, or the resurgence of old antagonisms, may call forth a realignment of party support as the parties attempt to channel the conflict into the institutional structures of the polity. Over time the advantages and/or deprivations to various social groups of the outputs of government and party policies may shift. Party policies will change as parties attempt to satisfy the demands of newly recruited adherents, or the political agenda of a group will shift as it satisfies its original goals. Recent political history in the United States illustrates changing political alignments of the black minority. As increasing numbers of blacks entered the polity through changes in voting registration laws, the Democratic party on the national level made explicit appeals for their support. As black party identification and voting became increasingly Democratic through the 1950's and 1960's, defections of marginal white adherents likewise increased. The tie of blacks to the Democratic party was further reinforced by goal succession, as the initial focus on civil rights legislation gave way to emphasis on black economic problems, both goals supported by Democratic politicians.

The potential for changes in the social system and the party system caution against a static interpretation of the relationship of groups to party identification. Ascriptive groups are not inherently more politicized than are achieved groups. The temporal nature of party cleavages requires an analysis of the relative importance of different social groups for party identification covering a sufficiently long span of time to determine whether alignments are durable or ephemeral. Despite the volumes of empirical studies of the social bases of mass political behavior, many questions remain about the multivariate relationships of social groups to party affiliation, some of which will, I hope, be answered in the ensuing chapters.

The Data

The Survey Research Center at the Institute of Social Research, University of Michigan, has conducted nationwide sample surveys of political behavior at every congressional and presidential election since 1952 except that of 1954. These surveys provided the data for some of the most important monographs and articles on electoral behavior to appear in the past two decades (see especially Campbell et al., 1960, 1966). Through the effort of the Inter-University Consortium for Political Research, the surveys have been deposited in a central archive and are made available at nominal cost to scholars who lack resources for conducting comparable original large-scale political research. The high quality of the sampling and interviewing, combined with their unique historical value, make the SRC surveys an unparalleled time series for investigating the social structure of party identification in recent American history.

The samples represent the voting-age, noninstitutionalized population of the United States. A stratified cluster sampling framework was employed in which the twelve largest Standard Metropolitan Statistical Areas (SMSAs) were drawn with certainty to represent themselves while the remainder of the country was placed into several sampling strata from which area probability samples were drawn. In the presidential year surveys, interviews were conducted with the same respondents during October and again in the weeks after the election. Details of the sampling procedures, wording of the questionnaire items, and descriptions of the coding of responses may be found in the published codebooks for each survey, available through the ICPR. An additional advantage of the SRC surveys is that the 1956, 1958, and 1960 surveys contain a panel study in which more than 1,100 respondents were interviewed as often as five times over a four-year period, thus allowing analysis of individual change over time.

The analyses in the following chapters concern the six presidential year surveys from 1952 to 1972. While the particular items in the questionnaires differ from year to year, many have remained the same, thus allowing comparison of relationships over time. The standard "face sheet" items on respondents' sex, race, size of place, age, and so forth, were either recorded identically in every year or made identical through recoding procedures. Several important sociological variables were not consistently coded across all six surveys, most notably religion and occupation. Recoding of categories made the variables as similar as was feasible. In some instances, the analyses are confined to those years in which the surveys contain the necessary detailed information.

The SRC measure of party identification was asked in identical form throughout the series. It always appeared in the pre-election interview, usually following a series of open-ended probes about the respondent's likes and dislikes of the major parties and presidential candidates and attitudes towards specific political issues. Although the question asks for the respondent's party identification in a general context, individuals may conceivably hold different identifications depending upon the level of governmental system—national, state, or local. One study which investigated multiple-party identifications using an Ann Arbor, Michigan, sample and the 1958 SRC survey found that inconsistent patterns most often involved an Independent identification and a party affiliation at another level, rather than combinations of Republican and Democrat at two or more levels. For the national sample, which involved only national and state levels of politics, inconsistent identifications were present in only 5 percent of the sample (Jennings and Niemi, 1966).

The initial question is: "Generally speaking, do you think of yourself as a Republican, a Democrat, an Independent, or what?" Among those selecting a party, the follow-up question is: "Would you call yourself a strong (Republican, Democrat) or not a strong (Republican, Democrat)?" The self-classified Independents were asked: "Do you think of yourself as closer to the Republican or Democratic party?" The resulting distribution contains seven partisan categories, not including the small number of apoliticals and nonresponses. The present study uses two versions of the item requiring fewer categories. A three-category variable uses responses to the first question without information from the follow-ups. The second version is a five-point scale assumed to be an interval level measurement, thus permitting the use of linear models. The five-point party identification scale is constructed from the full seven-point item by collapsing the categories of "not a strong (Democrat, Republican)" with the Independents reporting themselves closer to that party. The scale is coded from one for strong Democrats through five for strong Republicans.

The interval assumption is a strong one which may not be strictly correct. The party dimension is assumed in this book to be bounded at each extreme by the strong adherents of the two major political parties. The nonaffiliated Independents occupy the center, with the weaker partisans and leaning Independents to either side. This scheme, in addition to implying equal distances between positions, assumes that the two parties are much farther apart from each other than from the Independent position. While this assumption may hold for most persons (and evidence in favor of this assumption is presented in Chapter VI), it may be unrealistic for some. Some Independents are apolitical and uninvolved in politics, while others may occupy positions at the ideologically extreme left or right of the major parties, rather than intermediate to them. However, the evidence suggests that such Independents are a small minority (see Hikel, 1973). Thus, while for particular cases the interval assumption may result in a misclassification, the overall distribution in a large sample will be fundamentally accurate. Nevertheless, the possible limitations on the assumption of interval scaling indicate that the results should be treated with caution. Fortunately, the findings based on the three-category nominal scale of party identification generally agree with the findings using the interval assumption. The advantages of an interval measure for multivariate analysis warrant making the assumptions required.

Plan of the Book

The next seven chapters present findings based on analyses of the six presidential year surveys from 1952 to 1972. Chapters II through IV focus upon specific ascribed and achieved social statuses: religion, race, region, place of residence, and socioeconomic status. Sample respondents in the various statuses of these dimensions are compared on their party identifications over time, often controlling for the effects of other social variables. In Chapter V, the relationships from the previous chapters are integrated into a causal model of the party identification process, which is replicated for each survey. Chapter VI turns to the question of individual change in party preferences, using both cross-sectional surveys and the 1956–1960 panel study to investigate the interaction of party preference and voting for president over time. Chapter VII delves more deeply into the role of party identification in voting for national candidates. It considers the controversy over realignment in the party system or the possible fragmentation of a system which has prevailed for the past several decades. Finally, Chapter VIII pulls together data on the aggregate trend in party identification and its role in congressional elections and offers some speculations on the future of the two-party system.

This book was written on the assumption that readers know or wish to learn the fundamentals of multivariate data analysis. However, the manuscript does not presuppose an extensive familiarity with the techniques of linear regression and log-linear models. I have taken pains to interpret the findings so that they are accessible to persons less comfortable with these methods. To help the reader, an Appendix is included at the end of the volume which describes the basic data analysis techniques, with particular emphasis on log-linear models. This relatively recent innovation is rapidly becoming a major tool for analysts of categoric data. I hope that the usefulness and importance of the log-linear method for testing hypotheses about contingency tables will become apparent to the readers of the following pages.

Chapter II

Religion

Religion has played a major role in American politics since the founding of the republic. This chapter does not intend to present a detailed chronicle of religious conflict and cleavage in the United States, but any understanding of contemporary religious cleavages in the electorate must acknowledge the major contours of history. Much of what follows is indebted to the work of various scholars of religion and politics, most notably Seymour Martin Lipset (1968a).

Brief History

The early American colonies were settled by predominantly English-speaking people of dissenting religious faiths. Despite the official disestablishment of the church by the early decades of the nineteenth century, Protestants of these denominations continued to dominate the economic, political, and social institutions of the eastern seaboard states (Dahl, 1961; Baltzall, 1964). The Congregationalists, Episcopalians, Presbyterians, and other high-status nontraditional faiths, such as Quakers and Unitarians, tended to support the parties of the status quo, initially the Federalist and later the Whig and Republican parties, in most areas. The evangelical Protestant sects—Baptists, Methodists, and fundamentalist and pietistic groups—originally drew a preponderance of their memberships from lower socioeconomic groups disposed to support politically the party of change, the Democratic party.

The rise of mass immigration by Catholics came in two waves, beginning with the Irish in the mid-nineteenth century and culminating in the eastern and southern European influx of Poles, Slavs, and Italians by the end of the century. The absorption of these immigrant groups into the American stratification system, largely at the bottom of various economic and status hierarchies, pushed the collective memberships of several Protestant sects into higher statuses.

Differences in cultural backgrounds and disagreements over the role of government in formal religion and public morality produced enduring social conflicts which were eventually organized into sustained political cleavages. The electoral polarization between the Puritan moralism of the high-status Protestant denominations and the cultural pluralism of the immigrant Catholics structured the party system between the Civil War and the turn of the century. Specific conflicts flared over temperance, prohibition, Sunday blue laws, state support of religious education, and restriction of immigration. But behind the specific issues lay fundamental differences over whether the government or the church would be responsible for enforcing morality and devoutness—the "liturgical-pietist" cleavage. In the North at least, the Republican party was viewed as the political base of pietists who demanded that "the government actively support the cause of Christianity by abolishing the sinful institutions that stood in the way of revivals" (Jensen, 1970). The Democratic party obtained majorities among Catholics and the liturgical German Lutheran groups. The Democratic party went into a secular decline with the election of 1896 as the result of agrarian revolt, economic depression, and the Bryan revivalist appeal to rural Protestants, which alienated much Catholic support (Sundquist, 1973; Jensen, 1971).

Republicanism was not a real option for Catholics. Increasing concentration of immigrants in the newer waves in the large metropolitan areas allowed them to make spectacular gains in political control of local and state party organizations. The base was usually the Democratic party except in cases like New Haven, where the old-line Irish controlled the party, leaving newcomer Italians no viable entry except through the Republican organization (Dahl, 1961). In such instances the political party choice was more clearly a matter of ethnic origin than of religion per se. However, evidence based on contemporary American political identifications exhibits little impact of national origins once religious group membership has been controlled (Knoke and Felson, 1974).

Religion figured importantly in the election of 1928 in a largely symbolic manner. The candidacy of Catholic Al Smith signaled a resurgence of the dormant religious polarization between the big-city Catholic vote and the rural, small-town, and southern Protestant areas. While many scholars contend that the 1928 election did not represent a wholesale realignment of party loyalties but was a deviating election in which voters crossed party lines to cast presidential votes, the realignment of the Roosevelt New Deal saw Catholics and Jews attached more firmly than ever to the Democratic standard (Fuchs, 1956). This cleavage along religious lines has persisted well into the postwar era.

The contemporary religion-party association thus has roots in another century. Catholics and Jews have generally looked to the Democratic party (at least outside the South) as a guardian of civil liberties against Protestant efforts to restrict immigration and legislate a public morality not shared by these religious minorities. The question arises as to whether these motivations continue to play an important part in maintaining the traditional religious-group party affiliations. One component of the linkage is group and family tradition passed down from generation to generation, reinforced by daily contact with co-religionists sharing the same political identifications. A second possible component is the theological content of the religious doctrines, insofar as such theologies provide a secular, political orientation to the faithful. Is the American pulpit a powerful source of political direction in the same way as many European churches actively support the Christian Democratic parties against the secular and socialist parties? Unfortunately, the evidence available in the present study is largely indirect. Disentangling doctrinal from social group influences on party identification is next to impossible. We will be able to investigate whether participation in religious activity, which brings like-minded persons into interpersonal interaction, tends to reinforce party loyalties.

Contemporary Research

Religious identity (Protestant or Catholic) was one of the three components of the Index of Political Predisposition, a major construct to emerge from the Columbia voting studies (Lazarsfeld et al., 1944; Berelson et al., 1954). In both Erie County, Ohio, and Elmira, New York, Catholics voted Democratic in substantially greater proportion than did Protestants. This relationship was observed on a national scale in the Eisenhower years. Although a majority of Catholics voted for Eisenhower, the rate was lower than for the rest of the nation, and Catholic party identification remained considerably more Democratic than did Protestant affiliation (Campbell et al., 1960). John Kennedy's Catholicism created strong defections among Republican Catholics and Democratic Protestants, who voted for the opposite party's candidate (Converse et al., 1961; Converse, 1966a). Given the conceptual distinction between voting and party identification, such voting patterns could be short-term defections that leave the underlying party loyalties of Catholics and Protestants unaltered. Analysis of aggregate voting data for 1964 and 1968 implies that the 1960 vote was a short-term departure from a secular trend toward greater Republican voting by Catholics on the presidential level (Phillips, 1969).

Apart from the question of differences between Catholics, Protestants, and Jews in party affiliation, an important topic of recent research is whether internal differences occur along socioeconomic lines and whether between-group differences might be partly or wholly attributable to differential placement on the stratification dimensions. The preceding historical section noted that most high-status Protestant denominations supported the Republican party, and that as members of low-status sects became upwardly mobile they gravitated away from support of the Democratic party. Catholics from more recent immigrant stock who enter the labor force at the lower occupational and income levels might remain Democrats more from socioeconomic position than from any explicitly religious motivation.

Several recent research findings point to persistent differentials in the relative stratification positions when denominational distinctions are made within the broad Protestant group. Net of education, occupation, race, region, and size of place, one study found Jews, Episcopalians, and Congregationalists substantially above the average family income of the sample, while Baptists, Mormons, and minor Protestant sects fell below (Gockel, 1969). Another review of findings indicated that most researchers had "found that with regard to educational attainment, occupational achievement, and income the Jews, Episcopalians, Congregationalists and Presbyterians rank at the top; Baptists are at the bottom; and Catholics, Methodists, Lutherans, and other religions are in the middle" (Warren, 1971). Such socioeconomic rankings, with the exception of Jews, parallel the rank ordering of propensity to identify with the Republican party, an observation of great age in political sociology (Allensmith and Allensmith, 1948). Lipset used a manual-nonmanual-rural class measure and a Protestant-Catholic religious dichotomy among non-southern whites to provide "rough and relative measures of underlying social forces." While he found it "impossible to reach any definite conclusions" about the relative impact of class and religion on party voting from 1936 to 1964, he concluded that "the Catholic-Protestant difference has been somewhat more important than the manual vs. nonmanual cleavage" (1968, pp. 272, 276). Close inspection of Lipset's Table 8-2 reveals that the magnitude of his indices of class and religious voting are roughly comparable in magnitude and possibly not significantly different in several years. The difficulty in reaching a definite conclusion lies in part in the crudeness of his measures, as Lipset acknowledged. For two large surveys taken in the early 1950's, he found greater variation in party support when he controlled for social class position and membership in separate Protestant denominations, but he was still unable to integrate these findings to arrive at a definite conclusion.

Additional evidence on the effect of detailed religious categories on partisanship comes from Laumann and Segal (1971). Separate multiple regressions of party identification upon years of education were presented for fifteen groups of white males in the Detroit area classified by religion and national origin. The slopes were not significantly different (no interaction effects), but differences in intercepts were noted: "With respect to political and social attitudes, Jews and Catholic groups of the recent "new migration" generally tend to be more heavily Democratic in party preference than 'old migration' Protestant and Catholic (e.g., French and Anglo-American) groups." Although this finding came from a community rather than a national sample, it suggests that when stratification is controlled, religious groups may still differ significantly in their political preferences.

Major Religious Groups

The analysis begins with an examination of the political party identifications of four major religious categories. These are the familiar Protestant-Catholic-Jew trichotomy (Herberg, 1955) and a residual composed of other religions and nonreligious persons. The gross relationships observed here will serve as a benchmark for the more detailed investigation, including controls for stratification, in the next section. For the two surveys before 1960, a further breakdown of religious membership was impossible because the SRC did not code religion in sufficient detail. Table 2.1 presents the percentages of Democrats, Republicans, and Independents among the four categories for white respondents only. In addition, the large Protestant group is separated by region. Region serves as a surrogate denominational difference, since Baptists and fundamentalists are disproportionately represented in the South while the high-status (Presbyterian, Congregational, Episcopal) denominations are overrepresented in the non-southern states. A regional breakdown of Catholics and Jews is not attempted because more than 90 percent of their adherents reside outside the South (Glenn and Hyland, 1967). "The South" refers to the census South, including border states.

Only in 1972 does the percentage of Catholic party identifiers fall below 50 percent Democratic, and the Jews fall below only once, exceeding the Catholic proportion in four of the remaining five years. Although Protestants are more Democratic than Republican in every year, Protestants are also the most Republican of the four religions. Among non-southern Protestants the Republicans preponderate, approaching 40 percent or more in all but the last year. Roughly similar levels of Independent identifiers occur in each of the three major groups in any year, although exceptions are noted below. The "Other" group shows markedly more fluctuation in percentages over time, but since they are a heterogeneous lot, no further attention will be given to them.

Although the relative positions are fairly stable for the three major groups over the twenty-year period, marked changes appear. Several of these changes may be attributable to reactions to the particular presidential candidates so prominently in the news during the October interviews. The two Eisenhower years may be taken as a criterion level, both because they are the earliest surveys and because no evidence exists that religious sentiments were directly involved in the candidacies or campaigns of either national candidate. The percentages in 1952 and 1956 are very close, with

TABLE 2.1.   PARTY IDENTIFICATION BY MAJOR RELIGIOUS GROUP, FOR
             WHITES, 1952-1972

RELIGION AND PARTY	YEAR					
	1952	1956	1960	1964	1968	1972
Protestants:						
Democrat	43.6	40.8	41.3	47.2	37.6	33.7
Independent	22.1	23.8	21.7	21.0	30.9	34.8
Republican	34.3	35.4	37.0	31.8	32.5	31.5
(N)	(1092)	(1118)	(1168)	(940)	(944)	(1581)
Northern Protestants:						
Democrat	31.1	27.6	27.5	37.6	31.1	27.0
Independent	25.9	27.6	24.5	23.1	26.9	37.9
Republican	43.0	44.8	48.0	39.3	42.0	35.1
(N)	(758)	(737)	(708)	(615)	(597)	(988)
Southern Protestants:						
Democrat	71.9	66.4	62.4	64.3	48.7	44.9
Independent	13.8	16.2	17.3	17.5	35.5	29.8
Republican	14.3	17.4	20.3	18.2	15.8	25.3
(N)	(334)	(381)	(460)	(325)	(347)	(593)
Catholics:						
Democrat	54.5	52.2	62.8	58.1	51.4	48.3
Independent	27.0	27.0	21.7	24.6	32.4	36.9
Republican	18.5	20.8	16.5	17.3	16.2	14.8
(N)	(374)	(351)	(339)	(330)	(309)	(600)
Jews:						
Democrat	69.7	58.9	48.3	54.3	52.3	51.7
Independent	30.3	26.9	46.6	38.3	42.9	38.4
Republican	0.0	14.2	5.1	7.4	4.8	9.9
(N)	(56)	(56)	(58)	(44)	(54)	(60)
Others:						
Democrat	34.8	44.3	44.0	35.0	44.5	27.3
Independent	45.6	16.7	30.6	48.4	37.0	59.0
Republican	19.6	39.0	25.4	16.6	18.5	13.7
(N)	(46)	(36)	(134)	(60)	(54)	(117)

only the Jewish percentage of Republicans varying by more than ten points,
a value probably within the range of sampling error, given the small size of
the Jewish subsample.

With the 1950's taken as a norm, the 1960 election manifests a dramatic
shift in the party identifications of both religious minorities. The Catholic
Democratic proportion increases by 11 percent, about equally reducing the
Independent and Republican categories, while the Jewish Democratic rate
falls off sharply with an even larger increase in Independent declarations.
Both movements can probably be traced to the impact of John Kennedy on
the Democratic tradition. His Catholicism became a major issue of the

campaign for many voters and apparently was instrumental in shifting many weakly tied Independent and Republican Catholics in the direction of the Democratic party (White, 1961; Dulce and Richter, 1962). At the same time, uncertainty about the implications of Kennedy's success may have led many Jews to question their traditional ties to the Democratic party. A declaration of independence may be an indication of a wait-and-see attitude. On the other hand, the percentage of Jewish Independents remains high over the next four elections, when no Catholic ran for president, implying that the Kennedy candidacy may be only coincidentally related to a shift in the distribution of Jewish party identifications begun in 1960.

It is interesting that the proportions of Protestant party identifiers do not change markedly in 1960, even when broken down by region. Studies of presidential voting in 1960 revealed quite dramatically that Protestants, particularly those in the South and those strongly identified with the church, were repelled by the prospect of a Catholic in the White House. Converse (1966a, p. 97) demonstrated that despite attempts by political elites to downplay the importance of religion as an issue, "It has become clear that religion played a powerful role in shaping voting behavior in the 1960 election." The effects consisted of both attraction among Catholics and repulsion among anti-Catholic voters. Such defections apparently occurred mainly in the polling booth and not in the psychological identities of northern and southern Protestants, at least as far as one can tell from aggregate net percentages. Changes in the gross distributions of the Protestant groups do not appear until the following elections.

In 1964, with Barry Goldwater heading the Republican ticket, Protestants exhibit a five percent drop in Republican identification and a comparable increase in Democratic identification. Non-southern Protestants are the primary source of the change; the southern Protestant shift was only 2 percent. A further breakdown within region might pinpoint much of the 9 percent decrease in Republicanism outside the South in the Northeast and New England areas (Burnham, 1968). Traditionally the seat of Republican liberalism, these areas seem to have responded to the conservative appeals of Goldwater by loosening their ties to the Republican party. The magnitude of the partisan change for all Protestants is obscured by the greater appeal of Goldwater in the southern and southwestern regions. Voting defection in the 1964 election was much greater than change in party identification. Although a comparison of Catholics in 1960 and 1964 suggests that they moved away from the Democratic party, the effect is an artifact of the particular attractions of 1960. The more appropriate comparison of 1964 for Catholics is the two Eisenhower elections; clearly, Catholics also were pulled in a Democratic direction in 1964 when the 1950's are used as a benchmark.

The outstanding feature of the 1968 election is the sharp drop-off in Democratic identification among Protestants, particularly in the South. From a pre-1968 average of above 60 percent, southern identification with the Democratic party plummets to less than half the electorate. The Republicans did not benefit from this defection, since the main increase is a doubling of Independents to a total of one-third of the southern respondents. A possible explanation again lies in the presidential candidates. George Wallace headed the American Independent Party ticket nationwide but had his strongest electoral showing mainly in the Deep South and border states. The term "Independent" that year in the South may have signaled not nonaffiliation with either major party but support for the Wallace movement. Glenn (1972), using Gallup polls, documented a massive shift in party identification from Democrats to Independents between 1966 and 1968, located primarily in the South and largely temporary. Although he did not break down the analysis by religion, he argued that the change was a reaction to the national Democratic party's civil rights stand, as personified by Hubert Humphrey. By 1971 a majority of the southern Independents who returned to the major parties apparently became Democrats rather than Republicans.

The SRC surveys do not reveal a resurgent Democratic loyalty following the 1968 election. Four years later the percentage of southern Protestants calling themselves Democrats is lower than at any previous time, while southern Republicanism rises to an all-time high of one-fourth of that electorate. While it is too soon to tell whether this trend is an enduring or short-term reaction to yet another unpopular Democratic presidential candidate, the 1972 figures may presage the long-anticipated partisan realignment of the South following many years of Republican voting on the presidential level (Converse, 1963). The southern racial cleavage, which figures so importantly in this regional realignment, is explored in the next chapter.

The major change in the party preferences of the major religious groups over the past twenty years has been the increase in Independents. All groups show fewer Democrats in 1972 than in 1952, and northern Protestants and Catholics also had a decline in percentage of Republican identifiers. Relative position remains unchanged among religious groups outside the South, and the case of southern Protestants probably has little to do with religion per se. Fluctuations of the major groups over the two decades are not spectacular and may be short-term effects of the attractiveness or unattractiveness of a given presidential candidate. We next turn to an investigation of the impact of detailed religious group membership on party identification, net of stratification.

Religion and Stratification

The four surveys beginning in 1960 asked Protestant respondents to name the specific denomination to which they belonged. These were recoded into nine groups which, with the Catholic, Jew, Other, and None categories, produced thirteen detailed religious categories for analysis of party identification. (An earlier version of this analysis appeared in Knoke, 1974b).

The specific groups are: (1) Presbyterian and Congregational; (2) Episcopalian and Dutch Reformed; (3) non-traditional: Mormon, Christian Scientist, Quaker, Unitarian; (4) pietistic: Disciples of Christ, "Christian," etc; (5) Methodist; (6) Lutheran; (7) none; (8) general Protestant: no specific denomination given; (9) neo-fundamentalist: Churches of God, Pentecostal, Seventh Day Adventist, Jehovah's Witnesses, etc.; (10) Baptist; (11) other: non-Christian, non-Jew; (12) Catholic: Roman and Eastern Orthodox; (13) Jew. The detailed religious groups are shown in Table 2.2.

Since no rank ordering of religious denomination has yet been established, let alone an interval scale, a dummy-variable analysis with the thirteen religious groups as categoric independent variables was appropriate. In order to adjust the expected values of the religious groups on the five-point party identification scale for the effects of differential socioeconomic stratification, three independent variables were used, on the assumption that they approximated interval scales. These measures were Duncan's (1961) socioeconomic index (SEI) of major occupational categories for the head of household; the exact number of years of formal schooling of the respondent; and the previous year's total family income scored as the midpoint of the coded dollar interval. When the thirteen religious dummies and the three continuous stratification variables are entered into a linear equation to predict the respondent's party identification on the five-point scale, the following analysis of covariance equation results:

$$Y_{ijkl} = \alpha + \Sigma\beta_i R_i + \beta_j O_j + \beta_k E_k + \beta_l I_l \, .$$

Estimation of the β parameters was accomplished by the ordinary least squares method, with the large Catholic dummy variable omitted to permit statistical identification of the religious set. The religious parameters were then transformed into "structural coefficients" (Melichar, 1965) which are deviations from the grand mean of the sample. Since the three stratification variables were included in the linear regression, these coefficients are the effects of religion on party with occupation, education, and income held constant.

The most striking pattern across all four samples is the wide variation among the nine Protestant denominations. The range in some years is almost a point and a half, or better than one standard deviation (1.35 points) of the party identification variable. The denominations tend to be arrayed in the same relative positions in each year, indicating stability within the Protestant category similar to that found between the major religious groups in Table 2.1. In each year the top position is occupied by either Episcopalian,

TABLE 2.2. STRUCTURAL COEFFICIENTS FOR REGRESSION OF PARTY IDENTI-
FICATION ON 13 RELIGIOUS GROUPS, NET OF OCCUPATION,
EDUCATION, AND INCOME, FOR WHITES, 1960-1972

RELIGIOUS	YEAR			
GROUP	1960	1964	1968	1972
	Structural Coefficients			
Presbyterian	.83	.61	.55	.46
Episcopalian	1.16	1.08	.39	.43
Nontraditional	.75	.29	.52	.29
Methodist	.23	.17	.25	.30
Lutheran	.16	.20	.12	.20
Neo-fundamentalist	.27	.00	.01	.04
None	.25	-.10	-.18	-.60
Pietistic	-.09	.58	-.01	-.13
General Protestant	-.23	-.03	.31	.02
Other Religions	-.07	-.59	-.04	-.03
Baptist	-.30	-.33	-.02	-.01
Catholic	-.62	-.31	-.35	-.36
Jew	-.54	-.67	-.97	-.87
Grand Mean	2.83	2.62	2.80	2.97
	Percentage Distributions			
Presbyterian	10.8	8.9	8.3	8.8
Episcopalian	4.0	3.8	3.0	3.2
Nontraditional	1.0	2.1	2.1	2.5
Methodist	16.3	15.7	15.8	12.4
Lutheran	7.8	8.5	8.3	9.6
Neo-fundamentalist	5.2	6.2	2.7	6.3
None	1.1	3.5	7.9	0.5
Pietistic	2.2	2.7	3.2	1.8
General Protestant	3.7	3.7	3.6	4.7
Other Religions	6.8	0.4	1.4	4.6
Baptist	17.7	16.9	17.7	17.7
Catholic	20.0	24.5	23.1	25.4
Jew	3.5	3.2	3.0	2.5
Total	100.0	100.0	100.0	100.0
(N)	(1764)	(1399)	(1388)	(2397)

Presbyterian-Congregational, or "non-traditional" Protestant groups. That these groups are the most Republican of all religions, even when their stratification position is controlled, reflects their historical position as Establishment churches. The large Methodist and Lutheran groups are less heavily Republican than the high-status Protestant churches but exhibit great stability in their ranking. The minor Protestant sects—grouped here as pietistic, neo-fundamentalist, and general Protestant—show greater fluctuations over the years in their deviations from the sample average. These deviations may reflect sampling errors more than real changes in partisanship. The only major Protestant denomination to show an affinity for the Democratic direction is the Baptist. The pro-Democratic showing in the national sample may be largely due to the heavy concentration of this denomination in the South. By 1968 and 1972, however, Baptists were only at the sample mean in party preference.

The most consistently Democratic deviations in each year are, as expected, the Catholic and Jewish groups. The Catholic net deviation in 1960 is much larger than in the following years, revealing again the special attraction of Kennedy in altering the usual party alignments of his co-religionists. The Jewish deviation is the most Democratic of any religious group, largely because of the virtual absence of Republicanism in this group. The deviations for Jews exhibit an unusual pattern. For almost all the other religious categories the estimated mean party identification with stratification controlled is closer to the grand mean than is the observed group mean. This reduction in variation occurs because some portion of the partisanship of each group derives from its relative advantage or disadvantage on the three stratification dimensions. The Jews, however, are an extremely high-status social group with overwhelming Democratic leanings, in contrast to the usual preference among high-status persons for the Republicans. As a result, with stratification controlled, the expected value of party identification for Jews is *more* Democratic than the observed value. In 1968, for example, the observed mean for Jews was 1.98, but the expected value was 1.84. The interpretation is that if the Jews occupied a position in the stratification system comparable to that of the population as a whole, they would be even *more* Democratic than they are now. By contrast, if the other religious groups were adjusted to identical stratification positions, they would tend to alter their partisanship to be *less* Republican or Democratic than they actually are.

The impact of stratification on partisanship, relative to the impact of religious group membership, can be assessed quantitatively through a partitioning of the explained variance. The result for each of the four years is shown in Table 2.3. The combined additive effect of religion and the three stratification variables accounts for between 5 and fourteen percent of the variation in the five-point party identification scale. The overwhelming bulk of that explained variance can be clearly allocated to the religious dummy variables. Occupation, education, and income contribute by themselves less than 4 percent, dropping in 1972 to an abysmal 0.8 percent. These multiple R^2's are not just artifacts of using thirteen degrees of freedom for religion and only three for the stratification variables. If the three stratification vari-

TABLE 2.3. PROPORTION OF VARIANCE IN PARTY IDENTIFICATION
            EXPLAINED BY EDUCATION, OCCUPATION, INCOME, AND
            RELIGION, FOR WHITES, 1960-1972

INDEPENDENT	YEAR			
VARIABLES	1960	1964	1968	1972
R^2 Education, Income, Occupation	.015	.039	.034	.008
R^2 for 13 Religious Groups	.129	.097	.068	.044
R^2 for Stratification and Religion	.136	.121	.099	.053

ables are also each coded as six-category dummies, the explained variance increases somewhat since nonlinearities are picked up as contributions to between-group sums of squares. However, even when occupation, education, and income are measured as categoric variables, the *increment* due to religion is still more than half the total of the explained variance (see Knoke, 1974b). During those four years religion was a much more important source of cleavage for party identification than was stratification.

Effects of Church Attendance

Religious groups may maintain their cultural and political distinctiveness in the absence of overt religious issues through their members' interactions in primary groups and secondary associations arising from the formal church organization. Previous research on this point has been sparse and contradictory. The systematic study of national samples undertaken here may reveal one of the processes by which political differentiation of religious groups occurs.

Lenski's (1963, p. 174) seminal empirical study of the religious factor in Detroit in 1957-58 indicated that church attendance (which he called "associational involvement") was positively correlated with Republican party preference among both middle- and working-class white Protestants. The hypothesized correlation of greater church attendance and Democratic preference emerged for black Protestants but not for white Catholics. With region of birth controlled for white Protestants, differential effects of church attendance on party preference were observed. Among the non-southern-born, high attendance rates were associated with Republican preference, while among southern-born Detroiters high attendance produced greater Democratic affiliation. Lenski believed that this pattern resulted from attendance at different churches by the southern-born, where behavior peculiar to southern Protestants was reinforced through conformity to group political norms more strongly among the more faithful than among the marginal members of a congregation.

Other studies of the impact of church attendance on political behavior among Protestants indicate a possible transmission of ideology from the pulpit. A study of Eugene, Oregon, found that, even with social class controlled, attendance at churches with a theologically liberal minister tended to produce Democratic party preferences (Johnson, 1962). However, these findings were not replicated in a study of several Illinois counties (Anderson, 1966), and a later reanalysis of the Oregon data cast doubt on its statistical significance (Summers et al., 1970).

A national study bearing on the relationship of attendance rates to presidential voting was carried out with the same 1960 SRC data used in the present study. Among Protestant Democrats, the rate of defection to the Republican candidate was greatest among those who attended church regularly or often. The defection rates of southern Protestant Democrats were parallel to but higher than the rates for non-southerners. These strong correlations of vote and church attendance within Protestant categories were thought to be a short-term effect resulting from the unique features of the 1960 race (Converse et al., 1961). Converse's analysis of political preferences within the Catholic community in 1960 also revealed that the group of regular church attenders was more likely to exceed the expected "normal vote" for the Democratic candidate than was the group of less frequent church attenders. Such correlations had not been observed in previous elections (Converse, 1966a). The relationships were attributed not to explicit religious exhortations from the pulpit but to group processes indicated by church attendance.

The effects of church attendance on partisanship can best be studied by use of the log-linear models for cross-tabulated data. In addition to asking the respondent's religion, the surveys asked how often the individual attended church. The variable for Attendance (A) was dichotomized into high (regular and often) and low (seldom and never) categories. To avoid many small cell frequencies in the religion variable (R), only white Protestants and Catholics were retained for analysis. Region (S) was the census non-South versus the census South, as previous studies had suggested regional variation in church attendance rates and party affiliation. The party identifications were coded as Democrat, Independent, and Republican. Because of the rapid depletion of cell entries when further variables are used in a multivariate cross-tabulation, and because interpretation of systems with large numbers of variables becomes difficult, additional independent variables that might affect the church attendance-politics relationship were not included in the present study. Occupational status was not included for this reason; however, other researchers have suggested that the patterns observed may well be similar among both upper and lower status groups (Johnson, 1962; Converse, 1966a). Race has also been eliminated because most blacks are Protestants and their inclusion would upset the symmetry of the multivariate cross-tabulation.

The data for the log-linear analysis is presented in Table 2.4. The table displays the percentages of party identifiers in the five-way cross-tabulation of attendance by region by religion by party by time (ASRPT), as well as the N's upon which the percentages are based. Church attendance has its most noticeable effect upon the party preferences of non-southern Protestants. In each year except 1972 the high attenders are at least 10 percent less Democratic and about 15 percent more Republican than the low attenders. Among non-southern Catholics the pattern is irregular, with high attenders more Democratic than low attenders in four of the six years but more Republican in half the elections. Likewise, southern Protestants exhibit inconsistent relationships over time, while the small cell frequencies among southern Catholics render difficult the detection of a meaningful pattern.

The basic strategy in ferreting out the impact of church attendance on party identification is to compare the entire five-way contingency table to various log-linear models in which relationships among certain variables are taken as given. The results of these analyses are displayed in Table 2.5. The first model allows all relationships among variables except between church attendance and party identification, since this is the association of interest. Two sets of fitted marginals, (ASRT) and (SRPT), are used to estimate the expected cell frequencies to be compared to the observed data by the likelihood ratio χ^2. This model may be conveniently referred to as the "baseline" model because it represents a null hypothesis against which the subsequent models positing more complex relationships can be compared. As the analysis shows, the baseline model does not adequately account for the relationships in the data. Clearly, church attendance and party identification are related. The subsequent models attempt to improve the fit to the data by incorporating additional relationships between attendance and party, including interactions with religion, region, and time.

Model 2 asserts that the association between church attendance and party identification is direct and is the same within all combinations of the other variables. By giving up two degrees of freedom, a substantial improvement in χ^2 is obtained, but the model still differs significantly from the observed data. Models three through nine add various combinations of three-way interactions, involving specifications of the attendance-party association (AP) by third variables. For example, model 3 includes an (ASP) marginal table indicating that the attendance-party association differs between regions. This model and the others provide significant improvements over model two, indicating that each of the three-way interactions is signi-

TABLE 2.4.   PARTY IDENTIFICATION BY RELIGION, CHURCH ATTENDANCE,
             AND REGION, FOR WHITES, 1952-1972

REGION (S):	NON-SOUTH				SOUTH			
RELIGION (R):	Protestant		Catholic		Protestant		Catholic	
CHURCH ATTENDANCE (A):	High	Low	High	Low	High	Low	High	Low
YEAR (T) AND PARTY (P):								
1952								
Democrat	25.1	36.2	55.1	50.0	71.8	71.8	71.4	60.0
Independent	24.3	26.8	25.5	32.6	14.4	13.0	28.6	20.0
Republican	50.6	37.0	19.3	17.4	13.9	15.3	0.0	20.0
(N)	(354)	(403)	(274)	(86)	(202)	(131)	(14)	(5)
1956								
Democrat	22.0	32.5	51.6	57.1	68.7	62.9	53.3	33.3
Independent	22.3	33.3	28.2	18.4	13.8	21.2	33.3	0.0
Republican	55.7	34.1	20.2	24.5	17.5	15.9	13.3	66.7
(N)	(359)	(378)	(287)	(49)	(246)	(132)	(15)	(3)
1960								
Democrat	19.9	36.6	62.4	62.2	60.9	64.2	55.6	100.0
Independent	21.2	28.4	21.9	15.6	17.8	17.0	37.0	0.0
Republican	58.9	35.0	15.8	22.2	21.4	18.8	7.4	0.0
(N)	(377)	(331)	(279)	(45)	(281)	(176)	(27)	(1)
1964								
Democrat	30.1	46.2	58.8	53.3	63.0	65.7	67.6	42.9
Independent	23.9	22.5	24.0	33.3	16.9	18.7	14.7	28.6
Republican	46.0	31.3	17.2	13.3	20.1	15.7	17.6	28.6
(N)	(322)	(275)	(233)	(60)	(189)	(134)	(34)	(7)
1968								
Democrat	25.8	35.7	56.0	44.2	51.8	45.8	55.0	14.3
Independent	23.6	29.2	28.4	37.7	33.5	37.3	35.0	71.4
Republican	50.6	35.1	15.6	18.2	14.7	17.0	10.0	14.3
(N)	(271)	(319)	(218)	(77)	(191)	(153)	(20)	(7)
1972								
Democrat	26.6	27.2	50.6	40.7	47.9	41.1	70.1	48.4
Independent	34.9	40.2	32.0	46.7	26.4	34.4	20.9	41.9
Republican	38.5	32.5	17.4	12.6	25.7	24.5	9.0	9.7
(N)	(444)	(547)	(322)	(199)	(307)	(282)	(67)	(31)

ficant. In fact, model nine, in which all three such interactions are present, provides a statistically significant fit to the observed data ($\chi^2 = 31.1$, d.f. = 32). This model is the most parsimonious representation of the data. However, a question remains as to whether we have omitted any relationships which could significantly improve the fit over that obtained in model

TABLE 2.5.   LOG-LINEAR MODELS FOR CHURCH ATTENDANCE, REGION,
             RELIGION, AND PARTY IDENTIFICATION, FOR WHITES,
             1952-1972

MODEL	FITTED MARGINALS				DEGREES OF FREEDOM	LIKELIHOOD-RATIO χ^2
1	(ASRT)	(SRPT)			48	179.8
2	(ASRT)	(SRPT)	(AP)		46	104.3
3	(ASRT)	(SRPT)	(ASP)		44	82.1
4	(ASRT)	(SRPT)	(ARP)		44	82.3
5	(ASRT)	(SRPT)	(APT)		36	80.7
6	(ASRT)	(SRPT)	(ARP)	(APT)	34	62.8
7	(ASRT)	(SRPT)	(ASP)	(APT)	34	58.9
8	(ASRT)	(SRPT)	(ASP)	(ARP)	42	48.9
9	(ASRT)	(SRPT)	(ASP)	(ARP) (APT)	32	31.1
10	(ASRT)	(SRPT)	(ASRP)	(APT)	30	30.8
11	(ASRT)	(SRPT)	(ASPT)	(ARP)	22	26.2
12	(ASRT)	(SRPT)	(ARPT)	(ASP)	22	9.4

nine. Model ten, for example, tests whether the four-way interaction involving region and religion (ASRP) specifies the relationship of attendance and party identification. In comparison with model nine, which does not contain this interaction, the two additional degrees of freedom used reduce the χ^2 by an insignificant 0.3. Similarly, in model eleven the four-way interaction (ASPT) uses up ten degrees of freedom to reduce χ^2 by only 4.9. But model twelve, which asserts that religion and year together affect the attendance-party relationship, brings about a significant improvement over model nine ($\chi^2 = 21.7$, d.f. = 10). Thus, while model nine provides an acceptable fit to the data, it omits a statistically significant interaction in the data.

The preceding analysis discloses that the relationship of church attendance to party identification over the two decades is fairly complex. The relationship is separately conditional upon region, religion, and year of election, as well as upon the joint combination of religion and year. A better understanding of these interaction effects can be gained by inspecting the standardized effect parameters (λ) for the additive cell-frequency model presented in Table 2.6. Only those parameters of model 12 which involve the attendance-party relationship are included, to save space.

The first set of effects refers to the two-way association between church attendance and party identification (AP). Only the parameter values for the high attendance category are shown, since the effects for low attendance are the same in magnitude but opposite in sign. High attendance is associated with increases in both Democratic preference (+1.12) and Republican preference (+.23) and with decreases in Independent preference (−1.26) when the conditional effects of region and religion are ignored. These effects

TABLE 2.6.   λ EFFECTS (STANDARDIZED) IN MODEL 12 FOR CHURCH
             ATTENDANCE (A)- PARTY IDENTIFICATION (P) RELATIONSHIP BY
             REGION (S), RELIGION (R), AND TIME (T), FOR WHITES,
             1952-1972

| | TWO- AND THREE-WAY RELATIONSHIPS | | |
	(AP)	(ASP)	(ARP)
PARTY (P)			
Democrat	1.12	-2.47	-2.84
Independent	-1.26	.04	- .33
Republican	.23	1.95	2.56

| | THREE- AND FOUR-WAY RELATIONSHIPS | | | | | |
YEAR (T):	1952	1956	1960	1964	1968	1972
	(APT)					
PARTY (P)						
Democrat	-.04	-.49	-.66	-.35	.91	1.29
Independent	-.01	.73	.93	-.39	-.61	-1.78
Republican	.03	-.32	-.30	.67	-.26	.50
	(ARPT)					
Democrat	-.12	.78	-.15	-.54	-.56	.73
Independent	.57	-1.68	-.91	1.19	.58	1.45
Republican	-.37	1.07	.93	-.70	-.00	-1.74

are shown in the next two columns, where the parameter values for (ASP) and (ARP) apply when non-southern and Protestant categories pertain, respectively. Among non-southerners high attendance diminishes Democratic preference (−2.47) and increases Republican preference (+1.95). High attendance among Protestants has a similar effect on party identification, with the reverse effect of attendance among Catholics. Both of these interactions operate independent of the year of observation.

Presentation of the interactions involving time (T) is somewhat more difficult because both party identification and year are multi-category variables. A total of eighteen standardized effect parameters are required. In the (APT) interaction, the parameters apply to the high category of attendance, while their opposite values apply to the low category. A pattern is not readily discernible, and most effects are less than one standard error in magnitude. High church attendance seems to be related to lower Democratic preference prior to 1968 and to higher Democratic preference in 1968 and 1972. Similarly, high attendance is related to decreased Independent preference after 1960, but the pattern of effects on Republican identification is more erratic. These findings illustrate that while log-linear analysis can detect significant *statistical* interactions in a set of data, these relationships may not always have straightforward substantive interpretations.

The final interaction in model twelve involves the four-way relationship in which the association between attendance and party identification depends upon the joint level of religion and year of election. The effects shown in Table 2.6 apply to combinations of high attendance Protestants and low attendance Catholics, while the opposite values attach to categories of low attendance Protestants and high attendance Catholics. No linear or even monotonic trend is observed over time for any category of party preference. The largest standardized values occur in the Independent and Republican categories, and they are generally of the opposite sign in any year. The absence of a meaningful pattern to this last interaction suggests that perhaps model twelve provides "too good a fit." Despite its statistical improvement over model nine, it does not readily lend itself to improving our understanding of how church attendance relates to party identification over time. Thus model nine, which does provide an acceptable fit to the data, may well be the best model to account for the data. This model asserts that church attendance is significantly related to party identification, and that this association is contingent upon the level of religion, region, and time of election, in the manner revealed by the parameter values for these relations in Table 2.6, as discussed above.

The main question of the present inquiry—whether church attendance further specifies the relationship of religion and political orientation—has been answered tentatively in the affirmative. But the analysis did not probe a variety of plausible mechanisms by which involvement in religious institutions translates into secular political consequences. Distinctive political differences between Catholics and Protestants in America might be maintained through a variety of hypothesized factors. (1) Theological or value factors (Lipset, 1968a) include explicit doctrinal injunctions as well as the indirect predisposition of members to accept certain political ideologies. (2) Social group factors include religious-group-identified interests, for example, public support of religious educational institutions and the alliances between political parties and ethno-religious groups. (3) Under the socialization heading are included not only the passing of values and norms about religion and politics across generations but also adult learning and communication in primary and secondary associations with co-religionists.

These factors are not necessarily mutually exclusive hypotheses about how the religious influence on politics is maintained in the absence of specifically religious polarization in the national political arena. None of these factors can be rejected as causal mechanisms by the demonstration that church attendance has a significant impact on political preferences and voting. High rates of church attendance may expose one to greater theological instruction, to greater insight into the interests of one's religious group, and to greater interaction with one's fellow attenders. Which set of factors has the most important influence, if any, on reinforcing and preserving the distinctive political patterns of the religious groups is a matter not resolvable by an investigation focused primarily on determining the impact of church attendance on political orientation.

Summary

The preceding analyses uncovered four major relationships between religion and party identification in recent American history. First, a fundamental political cleavage has persisted between the major religious groups. Protestants are distinctly more Republican and Catholics and Jews more Democratic. With the exception of southern Protestants in recent years, there is no evidence of any trend towards convergence in partisanship. The possibility exists, of course, that party identification has become a less strong guide to voting choice, but the evidence here on party affiliation does not indicate an emerging Republican majority among either of the two main minority groups.

Second, important stable political cleavages within the large Protestant group were found. The high-status Protestant denominations exhibit strikingly higher degrees of Republicanism than do the lower-status denominations, and this difference remains even when differential stratification positions are taken into account. Like the cleavages between the major religious categories, the political differentiation of Protestants undoubtedly has historic roots, perhaps in the pietist-liturgical struggles that raged in the last century.

Third, the impact of religion on party identification is substantially stronger than the effect of the three most important stratification variables. Later chapters will explore more fully the contributions of occupation, education, and income to party affiliation, but the indication here is that religious membership, an ascriptive social group, is more powerful than achieved stratification position in determining party preferences.

Fourth, church attendance was found to have a significant association with party identification. Increases in attendance raise the level of Democratic support among Catholics and Republican support among Protestants. This church attendance-party identification association was also conditional upon time of election and region of residence.

Still unexplored are the specific roles of issues versus group interactions in socializing individuals to the norms of their religious groups. The data available did not permit an investigation of the explicit or latent effect of religious issues such as school prayer decisions, aid to religious schools, morality legislation, and the role of the church as an agent of social change. Evidence on the impact of such issues in swaying identifications with one of the major political parties is still fragmentary. The relationships are undoubtedly too complex to be reduced to a simple association of Democrats as the party of secular change and religious tolerance and Republicans as the party of special religious interests and government regulation of personal morality. The church attendance results are supportive of either a primary-group reinforcement hypothesis or of a doctrinal communication hypothesis. The face-to-face interaction arising from involvement in the formal religious organization may reinforce traditional partisan loyalties, but at the same time, it exposes the religious adherent to messages from the pulpit which may carry overt or indirect instructions for the rational translation of the denomination's religious interests into secular policy. Much further work remains to be done in explicating the ties between religion and the polity which have been unveiled in this chapter. If the preceding work has shown anything, it is how important religion has been, and will continue to be, for the political structure of the nation.

Chapter III

Region, Race, and Residence

"When will the South's politics conform to the national pattern?" Students of southern politics have speculated on the answer to this question since the first cracks in the solid Democratic composition of the region appeared decades ago. In the 1972 presidential election the South was solid once again—but solid Republican, for the first time in history. The meaning of this vote is unclear. It may signal the eclipse of the one-party system which has been the distinction of the region since the Civil War. Or it may be another instance of protest against the national Democratic party, similar to various third-party movements which have swept the South, beginning with Populism in the 1890's and continuing through the Wallace candidacy of 1968. Voting patterns in national elections have not yet effectively filtered down to the state and local level to bring about a competitive Republican party organization in the South.

To understand transformation and persistence in this unique region during the past twenty years, one must place the South in the context of a century of social, economic, and political development. The politics of the mass electorate in the region are intimately intertwined with the racial cleavages which are the legacy of the South's defeat in the War Between the States. More exhaustive studies of southern political history are available (Key, 1949; Havard, 1972), so only a brief review is attempted, in order to lay the groundwork for investigating recent changes in party identification.

Brief History

The victorious Radical Republican party imposed Negro enfranchisement upon the South under the Reconstruction Act of 1867. Led by white politicians, black voters rallied to the Republican party in state and local elections. But the compromise of 1877, which threw the disputed presidential election to Hayes in return for withdrawal of Federal troops from the South, spelled the end of black participation in the electorate. Between 1890 and

1908 a "Bourbon coup d'etat" in the southern legislatures disenfranchised nearly all blacks—and large numbers of whites—through a variety of schemes effectively circumventing the Fifteenth Amendment prohibition against denial of the vote on the basis of race. Mississippi, whose population was more than half Negro in 1890, led the way with a constitutional amendment requiring a poll tax, a literacy test (including "understanding" of the Constitution, a provision which allowed illiterate whites to be passed by election officials), and an extended period of residence for registration. By 1908 all the states of the former Confederacy had adopted some form of legal or extralegal restriction on black voting. Most effective was the "white primary": with the virtual liquidation of the Republican party organization in the South and confinement of the real contest among candidates to the Democratic party primaries not covered by the Fifteenth Amendment, participation was easily limited to whites only (see Lewinson, 1965).

V. O. Key pointed out (1949, pp. 539–50) that southern whites were bitterly divided over the drive to disenfranchise blacks. Impetus for the movement came largely from whites living in counties with black majorities, where interracial contest for power would be most acute. The currents of agrarian Populism sweeping through the South at the end of the century further accelerated efforts of conservative southern Democrats to close off any challenges to established power. The coalition of prosperous white plantation and industrial interests ultimately imposed a political hegemony founded on a monolithic party organization and backed by savage social and economic sanctions. The system dominated the region and congressional politics for more than half a century.

Through historical circumstances that placed a Republican in the White House during the Civil War, the South became and remained Democratic in party allegiance. The Roosevelt New Deal coalition which brought the Democratic party to national dominance included the southern electorate and congressional delegations as one of its key elements. Looking upon the scene at the end of this era, V. O. Key commented, at the end of his classic *Southern Politics in State and Nation*:

Moreover, the strength of the Democratic loyalties of most southern voters is not to be underestimated. In fact, partisan loyalties of Americans wherever they live have an extraordinary persistence. Southerners are no exception to the rule and Republicans have no easy task in making converts among the mass of southern voters. . . . The development of an opposition party in the South will probably depend more on events outside the South than on the exertions of native Republicans (1949, p. 674).

These prophetic words appeared just five years before a unanimous Supreme Court ruling overthrew the doctrine of "separate but equal" education, a cornerstone of the southern structure of racial inequality. The ensuing twenty years of social and political change are too familiar to require recounting in detail here. Pent-up forces found outlet in the civil rights movement, which eradicated the last vestiges of legal segregation and disenfranchisement. Action and reaction by southern blacks and whites set in motion the greatest changes in political party mass bases seen in the country in the last twenty years. The process is not yet finished, nor is the end result clearly in sight.

Racial Change in Party Identifications

Two trends have emerged in recent southern mass party identifications. (1) As blacks became enfranchised and developed political consciousness, they overwhelmingly supported the Democratic party in national elections. (2) Concomitantly, white southerners' support of the Democratic party steadily eroded, both in presidential voting and in party identification, although the latter appeared more resistant to change than the former. The changes of party identification among southern whites and blacks have been analyzed by Philip Converse, using several of the surveys in the present study (1963, 1971, 1972). This section recapitulates the main points of those analyses, but also contrasts the southern racial changes with those in the non-South, and extends the series to 1972.

When the Supreme Court in 1944 outlawed the "white primary," all but a handful of southern blacks had been effectively shut out from political participation for more than two generations. As a consequence of their exclusion from the electorate, many had not acquired the psychological attachments to parties which characterized whites and blacks outside the South. Insofar as any southern blacks had partisan inclinations, these were as likely to be Republican as Democratic prior to the Roosevelt realignment. Vestiges of southern black Republicanism after World War II were most likely to be found in older cohorts who still looked to the party of Lincoln.

The effects of isolation from meaningful political participation were still evident in the 1950's in the weakness and ambiguity of southern black party identifications. Data from the national panel conducted by the SRC between 1956 and 1960 revealed marked swings in black party preferences between the pre- and post-election reinterview (Converse, 1963). This lability of party preference, most concentrated among older, less educated blacks, probably reflected their ignorance and confusion about politics in general. But another subset of black party defectors during this period seemed to be more attuned to rational choice on the basis of the civil rights positions of the parties, which were sufficiently ambiguous during the Eisenhower years to lead to differing perceptions about which party was likely to offer most. This latter group's lability in party identification Converse considered a form of "watchful waiting" rather than apathetic instability (Converse, 1971). However, such political sophistication probably characterized only a handful of

TABLE 3.1.   PARTY IDENTIFICATION BY REGION, FOR BLACKS, 1952-1972

REGION AND PARTY	YEAR					
	1952	1956	1960	1964	1968	1972
Northern						
Democrat	58.9	55.5	42.9	67.2	76.1	70.6
Independent	25.0	22.2	40.3	18.1	18.3	17.5
Republican	10.7	20.7	11.7	13.1	2.8	9.2
Other	5.4	1.6	5.2	1.6	2.8	2.8
(N)	(56)	(63)	(77)	(61)	(71)	(109)
Southern						
Democrat	48.2	45.8	43.6	77.9	92.3	65.1
Independent	11.8	6.0	15.9	12.7	2.6	26.6
Republican	14.6	16.8	19.2	3.2	1.3	6.4
Other	25.4	31.3	21.3	6.3	3.8	1.9
(N)	(110)	(83)	(94)	(85)	(78)	(158)

southern blacks at the time. The black populace during the 1950's was bifurcated into a large apolitical mass and a small articulate activist group (Matthews and Prothro, 1966, p. 55).

In addition to the extreme lability of black southern party identification, a large minority of respondents during the 1950's did not identify with any party. About a third were classified as "apoliticals," but by the late sixties partisan mobilization had reduced this figure to about 2 percent, comparable to the apolitical rate among whites in the nation. This change was "perhaps the sharpest trend of a clearly secular nature" in party identification exhibited by that variable over the twenty years under study (Converse, 1972, p. 306). The magnitude of change in the southern black electorate can be grasped most readily in comparison with the distribution of party preference among its northern counterpart. Blacks outside the South, many of whom migrated North beginning in the 1930's, found the legal barriers to political participation much reduced. Thus they had opportunities over the years to build up psychological ties to the parties, reinforced by habitual voting. The Democratic response to the Depression and the structure of Negro political organizations in the major metropolitan areas of the North firmly wedded most northern blacks to the Democratic party decades before the electoral process was opened up in the South (see Wilson, 1960).

The distributions of party identifications of northern and southern blacks from 1952 to 1972 are displayed in Table 3.1. The South is the census South, including both the states of the old Confederacy (Deep South) and the border states. These two areas differ politically, as Key (1949) pointed out, but the small sample sizes prevent further subdivision of southern blacks.

Restrictions on blacks were much stronger in the "black belt" states than in the upper South and border states, so one can assume that treating the South as one undifferentiated political region obscures the larger differences between Deep South blacks and those in the North.

Through 1960 southern blacks have the highest rate of apolitical responses to the party identification question of any social group in the SRC surveys. The one-fifth to one-third apolitical rate is in sharp contrast to the 2 to 5 percent rate for northern blacks and the 1 percent rate of nonpartisanship for all whites. In a special survey of the Deep South in the spring of 1961, Matthews and Prothro (1966, p. 281) also found 22 percent of blacks, as compared with 6 percent of whites, were apolitical. At some point before the 1964 election, however, party affiliations were rapidly mobilized among this hard core of apolitical southern blacks. The change was compressed into less than two years (Converse, 1972, p. 312), probably under the impact of national events associated with the civil rights movement, Kennedy's assassination, Johnson's championing of the voting rights act, and the capture of the Republican party by Goldwater partisans. Whatever the specific causes, southern black apoliticals shrank in 1964 to only 6 percent, while the proportion of blacks in both regions identifying with the Democratic party increased by 25 percent or more.

In the three elections at the beginning of the series, modest levels of black Republicanism are maintained, but the Goldwater candidacy appears to have effectively repelled most southern blacks from the party. The percentage of black Independents in 1964 is noticeably smaller than in the previous election, when the Democratic candidacy of a Catholic seems to have led many northern Protestant blacks to temporarily disaffiliate with the Democratic party. Clearly the rapid diminution of the apolitical group in 1964 was not an artifact of southern blacks now labeling themselves Independents but represents genuine recruitment of new adherents to the Democratic party.

The Goldwater candidacy provided the electorate, particularly blacks, with a valuable political education which is reflected in party realignments conforming more closely to latent group interests. The presidential contest pitted an avowed states' rights, anti-welfare Republican against a southern Democratic incumbent who had delivered legislation, as promised, on voting rights, civil rights, and public accommodations. Goldwater pursued a "southern strategy" later successfully used by Nixon in seeking a coalition of Republicans and conservative southern white voters. While his notable electoral college successes came in the Deep South black belt states, Goldwater did less well in the region than had Eisenhower and Nixon (Converse, Clausen, and Miller, 1965; Cosman, 1966). The reason, of course, is that massive pro-Democratic voting among newly registered blacks offset the Republican presidential balloting among white voters attracted to Goldwater's promise to turn back the clock on civil rights.

Later elections reinforced the swing of blacks toward the Democrats in both regions. An incredible 92 percent of southern blacks in 1968 called themselves Democrats, more than double the rate of only eight years before. The percentages identifying with the Democratic party are lower in 1972, but this is primarily because of increases in Independents rather than in Republican identification. Blacks of both regions remain the most Democratic of all social groups, however; black leaders and voters alike made clear in recent years that Nixon Republicanism was not responsive to their political needs, and the Republican party virtually abandoned attempts to win black support.

The partisan changes in the black community, particularly in the South, grew out of the social and political events convulsing the nation during the 1960's. The sit-ins, riots, wars on poverty, and Vietnam all contributed to increased black consciousness of the need for political action on racial problems. The deliberate appeal of the national Democratic leadership for black support through promotion of favorable legislation produced virtually unanimous black Democratic voting from 1964 through 1972. Like a political Newton's law, the action in the black community was not without its reaction in the white community. The effects are most clearly shown in Figure 3.1, which plots the means on the five-point party identification scale for each of four race-region groups. (These means are based on partisans only, excluding the apoliticals in each year; "northern" in the present context means "non-southern" states of residence.) A sharp break in black partisanship in both regions occurs between 1960 and 1964. From 1952 to 1960, the two black and the white southern party means were almost indistinguishable and moved in tandem with the trend toward the Republican direction across the three elections.

The rising black means, especially among northern blacks in 1960, mainly represent increased Independent identification rather than Republicanism, as Table 3.1 points out. Oppenheim (1970, pp. 36–40) noted that 1956 produced larger race differences in presidential voting than did 1960, despite the greater importance of race issues in the latter election. She attributed the declining magnitude of the race-party linkage in 1960 to black wariness of a Catholic president. Apparently the political consequence of black Protestant uncertainty was for increased Independent party preference in 1960 relative to other elections.

The watershed election of 1964 finds all four racial-region group means moving in the Democratic direction, but at unequal rates. White southerners move least, while both black groups plummet toward the Democratic pole of the party continuum. While blacks and southern whites moved in parallel lines from 1952 to 1960, the next two periods see them drawing farther and farther apart while the mean party preferences of whites in both regions slowly converge. Such means, of course, disguise the distribution of identifications within a group, but they suggest the relative balance of

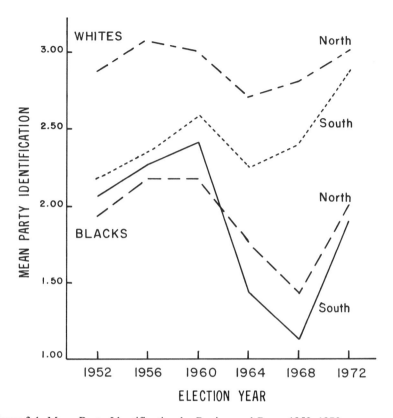

Figure 3.1. Mean Party Identification by Region and Race, 1952–1972

preferences between Democrats and Republicans. The mean difference between northern and southern whites in 1952 was .80, or more than half a standard deviation (1.35 points), but the gap had narrowed twenty years later to about .10.

The slow upward drift of southern white partisanship toward a pattern closely resembling that of northern whites is not the result of a conversion of southern Democrats into Republicans. The data on major party identifications among the four race and region categories appear in Table 3.2. The distribution of Republicanism among southern whites remains fairly stable across the two decades. The major source of aggregate change responsible for the trend in Figure 3.1 lies in the shifting balance between Democratic and Independent preferences. From a fairly steady 15 to 18 percent Independent from 1952 to 1964, southern whites doubled their Independent preference in 1968 to 35 percent. The increase may indicate a tendency for supporters of Wallace in 1968 to call themselves "Independents" after his

TABLE 3.2. PARTY IDENTIFICATION BY REGION AND RACE, 1952-1972

REGION (S), RACE (R) AND PARTY (P)	YEAR (T)					
	1952	1956	1960	1964	1968	1972
Non-South White:						
Democrat	39.5	36.3	39.1	44.3	39.0	34.3
Independent	27.2	28.0	25.1	25.9	29.5	38.7
Republican	33.4	35.7	35.8	29.8	31.5	27.0
(N)	(1209)	(1159)	(1175)	(1011)	(992)	(1667)
South White:						
Democrat	71.0	65.5	61.3	63.5	48.6	46.3
Independent	14.8	17.0	17.7	18.1	36.1	31.3
Republican	14.2	17.5	21.0	18.4	15.3	22.4
(N)	(373)	(412)	(542)	(376)	(395)	(728)
Non-South Black:						
Democrat	62.3	56.5	45.2	68.3	78.3	72.6
Independent	26.4	22.6	42.5	18.3	18.8	17.9
Republican	11.3	21.0	12.3	13.3	2.9	9.4
(N)	(53)	(62)	(73)	(60)	(69)	(106)
South Black:						
Democrat	64.6	66.7	55.4	83.1	96.0	66.5
Independent	15.9	8.8	20.3	13.5	2.7	27.1
Republican	19.5	24.6	24.3	3.4	1.3	6.5
(N)	(82)	(57)	(74)	(89)	(75)	(155)

American Independent Party, rather than indicating growing nonallegiance to any political party. However, the southern white party identification remains above 30 percent in 1972.

The surveys from two decades point to two major realignments in the American electorate. First, southern blacks have become more politically conscious and strongly attached to the Democratic party as their vehicle for social and political change. Second, in apparent reaction, the white southern electorate has weakened its ties to the national Democratic party, although at a somewhat less abrupt and dramatic rate. These trends provide an answer to the question raised at the beginning of the chapter. Southern political party distributions by race have come increasingly to resemble those of the rest of the nation. The simplest way to show this convergence is by the log-linear analysis of a four-way breakdown race by region by party by year (RSPT) in Table 3.2.

A "baseline" model allowing all variables except party identification to be related (RST) (P) obtains a very poor fit (chi-square equal to 917.9, d.f. = 46). Successive models incorporating two- and three-way interactions markedly reduce the discrepancies but fail to provide a significant fit. For example, the model positing all sets of three-variable interactions,

(RST) (RSP) (SPT) (RPT), yields a chi-square equal to 37.0 for ten degrees of freedom. While this model accounts for over 95 percent of the unexplained variation in the baseline model chi-square, it also indicates that a significant four-way interaction is present; that is, the interaction of race and region with party identification changes over time.

The meaning of this complex interaction is best grasped through separate models fitted to the data in each survey. The three-variable breakdown of race by region by party (RSP) requires a saturated model to account satisfactorily for the relationships from 1952 to 1960. In other words, the association between race and party identification differs in the South and the non-South during these years. But for each of the 1964–72 surveys, the loglinear models (RS)(RP)(SP) provide acceptable fits. The absence in these years of the three-way interaction between race, region, and party indicates that the association between race and party is now essentially the same in both regions. While the percentages in each party identification category still differ slightly in each region (and even this difference is diminishing over time), the racial alignments are essentially the same, with blacks more Democratic and whites more Republican in both regions. By any meaningful empirical criterion, then, one may conclude that the long-awaited partisan realignment of the South has finally occurred.

Change in Partisan Attitudes

An important component of regional and racial change in political behavior is the image that people hold of the two major parties. Individuals may remain nominal adherents of a party while their affective and cognitive orientations undergo considerable erosion as the party itself changes position on various issues. The net balance of Democratic and Republican images among the four regional race groups yields valuable insight into the process of partisan change in the past two decades.

The concept of "partisan attitude" was developed by Stokes to indicate the party direction and intensity of a person's attitude towards political objects (Stokes et al., 1958; Campbell et al., 1960, pp. 41-88; Stokes, 1966). Ultimately a model was developed which sorted the responses to open-ended questions on respondents' likes and dislikes about the parties and presidential candidates into six categories. These six components were found to have a high predictive relationship to the presidential vote in a linear regression (Campbell et al., 1960, p. 72; also Goldberg, 1966). Analyzing the net partisan advantage from each of the components from 1952 to 1964, Stokes (1966) found that considerable change had occurred, unlike the relatively stable party identifications. In particular, the initial Republican advantage in foreign policy and government management eroded, while the strongly favorable image of Eisenhower as a candidate was reduced under Nixon and destroyed under Goldwater. While the magnitude of change was much greater for candidates, "attitudes towards the parties are not inert." The net effect in the electorate as a whole was a switch of the party component from net Republican advantage in 1952 to net Democratic in 1956, an advantage which was maintained over the next two elections.

While Stokes' analysis dealt with the change in party perceptions in the nation as a whole, a similar analysis of change in "party image" in the South from 1961 to 1964 broke down the perceptions by race (Matthews and Prothro, 1966, pp. 378-88). Southern blacks showed a strong increase in pro-Democratic responses, while whites exhibited a slight increase in favorable Republican images. The most frequent negative responses among whites towards the Democratic party were that it was "too liberal" and "too good to Negroes." This analysis revealed increases in negative perceptions from 1961 to 1964, leading to decreased preference for Democrats at all levels of party identification.

This section investigates changes in partisan attitudes toward the Democratic and Republican parties within race, region, and party classifications from 1952 to 1968. (In 1972 the SRC used a different approach to assessing partisan attitudes, recording only three responses instead of the previous five, thus making comparison impossible.) The measure of net partisan attitudes is simple: add the number of favorable Republican and unfavorable Democratic responses and subtract the number of unfavorable Republican and favorable Democratic responses to the four open-ended questions about likes and dislikes towards the two major parties. The resulting score indicates both the direction and intensity of party-related attitudes, a positive score indicating pro-Republican disposition, a negative score pro-Democratic.

If we combine all responses regardless of content, we cannot distinguish among bases for political disposition. Clearly an ideological persuasion does not guide the responses of most persons, as Converse has demonstrated (1964; also Campbell et al., 1960, pp.216-65). Many of the answers recorded involve issueless criteria such as the politicians and groups supported by the parties or traditional bases of liking or disliking the parties. In keeping with the distinction in Chapter I that any bases for party preferences are admissible for rational choice, all responses are counted as valid. Since there was no informed basis for weighting responses, all were given equal weight in the tabulation. Although up to five answers to each of four queries were recorded, few individuals gave more than one or two; in fact, as much as one-fifth of the adherents of either party could not give even one reason for liking their party. More educated respondents tend to give slightly more responses, but the impact of education is relatively small and can be disregarded in the following analyses.

The first analysis compares the net partisan attitudes of the four regional race groups over the sixteen years. The results are displayed in Figure 3.2, similar to that for party identification in Figure 3.1. The balance of party

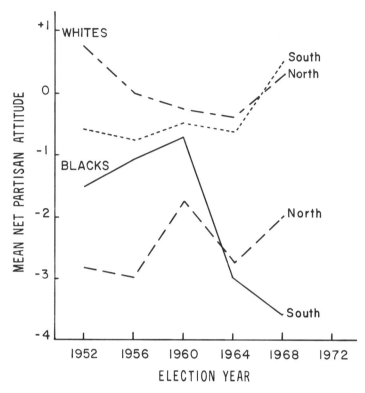

Figure 3.2. Mean Net Partisan Attitude by Region and Race, 1952–1968

sentiments clearly lies with the Democrats through most of the period: only non-southern whites in 1952 and 1968 and southern whites in 1968 have a net pro-Republican score. However, southern whites display a generally increasing trend towards pro-Republican responses from 1952 to 1968. In the last year, in fact, southern whites have a higher pro-Republican image than do non-southern whites. While this trend is more heavily centered among the small but increasing group of southern Republicans, it is not confined to these party identifiers, as will be seen shortly. The two black groups hold strongly pro-Democratic party images. Southern blacks are less Democratic than non-southern blacks from 1952 to 1960—just as they are less Democratic in party identification—but during the watershed election of 1964, their pro-Democratic and anti-Republican responses increase dramatically, eclipsing the means for non-southern blacks.

Changes in the partisan attitudes of the electorate are in part a function of changing party identification. Party adherents give more favorable responses to their own party and unfavorable ones to the opposing party.

TABLE 3.3.   MEAN NET PARTISAN ATTITUDE BY REGION, RACE, AND PARTY
             IDENTIFICATION, 1952-1968

| REGION, RACE, | YEAR | | | | |
AND PARTY	1952	1956	1960	1964	1968
Northern White					
Democrat	-2.27	-2.68	-2.69	-2.37	-1.34
Independent	0.22	0.11	-0.36	-0.22	0.46
Republican	3.38	2.29	2.25	1.86	2.58
Southern White					
Democrat	-1.17	-1.51	-1.52	-1.28	-0.45
Independent	0.44	0.44	0.15	0.82	1.16
Republican	1.94	1.83	2.51	2.17	2.60
Northern Black					
Democrat	-3.70	-3.50	-3.18	-3.13	-2.61
Independent	-1.30	-1.43	-0.16	-1.35	-0.31
Republican	0.33*	0.14	-0.55*	-1.98*	-1.00*
Southern Black					
Democrat	-2.73	-1.80	-1.80	-2.95	-3.63
Independent	-0.90	-1.20*	0.93	-1.16	-1.50*
Republican	1.20	0.46	1.16	-0.67*	0.00*
Total	-0.06	-0.36	-0.40	-0.69	0.16

*Based on fewer than 10 cases

When the party composition of the electorate shifts, as shown in Figure 3.1, the net balance of party images may be altered as a consequence. One way to eliminate the possible causal impact of party identification on net aggregate partisan attitudes is to hold party identification constant and observe the change over time in net partisan attitude. Table 3.3 shows the mean net partisan attitude of each race, region, and party identification group by year. The entries disclose that substantial erosion of Democratic disposition occurs among white Democrats of both regions. The mean net pro-Democratic responses among northern white Democrats falls by nearly half from 1952 to 1968, while the 1968 mean for southern white Democrats is only 40 percent of the 1952 value. In fact, the positive score for southern white Democrats in 1968 derives entirely from dislike of the Republican party, since the net balance of positive and negative attitudes towards the Democratic party is exactly zero. Massive discontent with their own party apparently allowed many southern white Democrats to cast their presidential votes for Wallace or Nixon despite their nominal partisanship.

Northern black Democrats display a monotonic decline in pro-Democratic responses from 1952 to 1968, while southern black Democrats increase their net Democratic images from 1956 on. These differentials are less important than the greater difference between whites and blacks in both regions within the same political party. Black Democrats find little to like in the Republican party and much to dislike. As a consequence, they are strongly confirmed in their dispostiion toward the Democratic party, while many whites who still call themselves Democrats steadily loosen their ties to the party.

The net balance of partisan attitudes among most Independents is very close to the equilibrium point throughout the period. Independents tend to give fewer responses of any type than do partisans, and they tend to counterbalance favorable with unfavorable comments. Yet small rises in pro-Republican responses can be detected among white Independents in both regions. With the exception of southern blacks in 1960, the net balance among Independent blacks of both regions lies with the Democrats, particularly in 1964, which helps to explain Goldwater's inability to win the votes of any black respondents in that sample.

Finally, Republican party identifiers do not reveal evidence of erosion in party attitudes comparable to that among Democrats. Black Republicans are too few in either region for us to draw any conclusions. Among northern white Republicans, pro-Republican images are highest during the first Eisenhower campaign, abetted by negative reactions to twenty years of Democratic control of the White House and Congress. But, while pro-Republican images dip slightly during the 1964 Goldwater candidacy, the average pro-Republican scores hover around slightly more than two for the period, and among southern Republicans, the favorable attitude toward the Republican party steadily increases throughout the sixteen years. This trend in net partisan attitudes, combined with the erosion of Democratic images among southern Democrats, is responsible for the eventual shift to a pro-Republican disposition by the southern white electorate by 1968. The net shift in partisan attitudes of the white South across all levels of party identification explains the ability of a Republican presidential candidate to obtain his largest majority in that region in 1972.

A more detailed breakdown of the reasons for liking and disliking the major parties might pinpoint specific issue areas which led to changes in partisan attitudes during this period. Here we can only look briefly at the impact of one attitude—civil rights— in the South. Prior to 1964, net references by white Democrats to party stands on civil rights, Negro support, or state's rights issues were favorable to the Democrats but occurred among fewer than three out of a hundred respondents. Similarly, southern black Democrats cited explicitly racial issues favoring the Democratic party on balance fewer than eleven times per hundred respondents. But during the 1964 campaign, with a Republican presidential candidate making covertly racist appeals to the southern white electorate, a dramatic shift took place. In that year references to racial issues favor the Republicans (an average of one-fifth among white Democratic respondents), while among southern black respondents nine of ten on balance favor the Democratic position. Stronger data on the racial polarization within the southern Democratic party could hardly be found. If anything, these estimates are conservative, for they do not take into consideration racially motivated dispositions which are not explicit, such as "law and order" or "poverty."

The analysis of partisan attitudes from 1952 to 1968 illuminates the character of party identification among the four main race and regional segments of the electorate. The exact causal relationship between partisan attitudes and party identification remains ambiguous. The erosion of attitudes disposing respondents to support a party may be a prelude to abandoning one's psychological identification with that party. The fact that party identifiers generally have more polarized partisan attitudes than do Independents lends support to this causal sequence. If so, the evident weakening of partisan attitudes among nominally Democratic southern whites in recent years foretells a continuing erosion of Democratic support in years to come.

Migration Effects on Party Identification

In his discussion of racial changes in party affiliations of the South, Converse (1963, 1972) proposed that different mechanisms produced the observed trends for blacks and whites. Most of the aggregate realignment of southern blacks to the Democratic party came from mobilization and shrinkage of the pool of apoliticals, rather than from conversion of Independents or Republicans. But the white southern population lacked such a pool of apoliticals, so aggregate change had to come from two other sources. The first source is individual conversion of party loyalties, from the Democratic party toward an Independent stance and Republicanism. The second are two processes that Converse labels "compositional changes": (1) the replacement of old cohorts by new ones entering the electorate in successive four-year periods, and (2) the interchange of populations between regions. Basing his conclusion on data prior to 1968, he suggested that cohort replacement appeared to contribute nothing toward long-term partisan change among southern whites (Converse, 1963). Migration, both out of and into the South, has been sufficiently large and selective by party preference to account for most of the aggregate change in southern party affiliations, about four-fifths of Converse's estimate of a 1 percent decrease in net Democratic "expected vote" every four years. In addition, the outward migration of southerners into other regions of the nation "contributed in a major way to the slow evolution of the non-Southern white electorate

TABLE 3.4. MEAN PARTY IDENTIFICATION BY REGION OF ORIGIN AND
            REGION OF CURRENT RESIDENCE, FOR WHITES, 1952-1972

REGION OF CURRENT RESIDENCE	REGION OF ORIGIN				TOTAL (N)
	Northeast	Midwest	South	Far West	
Mean Party Identification					
Northeast	2.97	2.96	2.52	3.12*	2.95
Midwest	3.13	2.94	2.49	3.36*	2.91
South	3.15	3.09	2.30	2.47*	2.38
Far West	2.39	3.03	2.29	2.74	2.71
Total	2.97	2.96	2.32	2.75	2.72
Percentage Distributions					
Northeast	91.4	2.1	5.8	0.7	100.0 (2417)
Midwest	2.9	87.5	8.9	0.7	100.0 (3227)
South	4.2	6.1	88.8	0.9	100.0 (3270)
Far West	6.3	23.0	15.3	56.4	100.0 (1483)
Total	23.3	31.0	31.4	14.3	100.0 (10,397)

*Based on less than 1/2% of total sample

toward the Democrats" (Converse, 1972, p. 315), a trend depicted in Figure
3.1. Oppenheim, however, disaggregated regional differences by eight-year
age cohorts and in a multiple regression analysis found that slopes for region
of origin were smaller among the younger cohorts than the older cohorts,
indicating greater regional convergence in party identification among newer
voters (Oppenheim, 1970, pp. 62-65). This section investigates the effects
of origin and destination regions on party identifications among white
respondents for the entire six elections combined. Rather than the usual
South–non-South dichotomy of region, four regions corresponding to the

census definitions are employed. Although one American in five changes residence every year, most of these moves occur within state or regional boundaries. Thus a majority of Americans reside in their regions of birth, although the range is considerable, from 91.4 percent in the Northeast to 56.4 percent in the Far West (Mountain and Pacific states). In Table 3.4 the origin region is taken as the region in which the respondent grew up rather than the region in which he was born. Even after aggregating over ten thousand cases, at least four cells had fewer than fifty cases (under ½ percent of the total sample), primarily reflecting the small rate of out-migration from the Far West. The party means of white respondents in these cells should be interpreted cautiously.

Comparing the row means for the four regions of current residence in the top panel of Table 3.4, the Northeast is found to be the most Republican and the South the most Democratic, with the Far West below the Midwest on the partisanship scale. If these row total means are compared to the means for the nonmigrants in the main diagonal of the table, only in the South do migrants exert a sizable impact on the partisanship of any region. Although in the Northeast migrants from the South are more Democratic than the natives, they counterbalance the in-migrants from the Midwest and the Far West, so that the overall partisanship of the region does not substantially differ from that of the natives.

In the Midwest, a similar equality of means for the region as a whole and for the natives results from offsetting contributions from the different migrant streams. Southern migrants to the Midwest arrive with substantially more Democratic orientations than the natives, but are counterbalanced by higher Republican preferences among migrants from the Northeast and the Far West. A similar pattern of partisan contributions from different migrant streams occurs in the Far West, 44 percent of whose population was not born in the region. Again, southern migrants to the Far West contribute a substantially more Democratic orientation than the native population. The two non-southern migrant groups are not identical in their party identifications: northeastern in-migrants have a substantially Democratic preference close to that of southern migrants to the Far West. But the midwestern migrants to the Far West are more Republican-leaning than those staying in the Midwest. Thus the midwestern migrants to the Far West exactly offset the tendency for southern and northeastern migrants to produce a more Democratic orientation in that region. The *American Voter* study of the political effects of migration into the Far West failed to separate northeastern from midwestern origins and thus did not discover that the two migrant streams are not identical, but rather counterbalancing, in their partisan impact on the region (Campbell et al., 1960, pp. 446–49). Non-southern migrants to the Far West on the whole appear more Republican than the native far westerners since 75 percent of them are from the Midwest. The explanation of why the northeastern migrants to the Far West are radically different in partisanship than northeastern migrants to other regions is not readily apparent, but the difference is too large to be attributable solely to sampling error.

The South, as mentioned before, is the only region in which the aggregate impact of migration noticeably alters the mean party identifications of the region from that of the non-moving native population. All three in-migrant streams are substantially less Democratic in party preferences than are the native whites. Comprising 11.2 percent of the sample of southern residents during this period, the migrants raise the mean party identification from the 2.30 of the natives to 2.38. The aggregation of samples over time obscures the fact that the non-southern contribution to the lessening Democratic orientation of the South has been growing over the past twenty years. Thus a substantial part of the trend in southern white partisanship away from monolithic Democratic preference shown in Figure 3.1 is due to the increasing proportion of non-southern-raised migrants now residing in the South.

As Converse's careful analysis of this major compositional change in the southern electorate points out, not only do these migrants exert a noticeable impact on the aggregate partisanship of the South, but because of their greater concentration in the urban and more industrial areas of the region, the non-southern migrants have a disproportionate effect on local politics (Converse, 1972, p. 314). Converse also states that the migration of southerners away from the South "has contributed in a major way to the slow evolution of the non-Southern white electorate towards the Democrats." By not differentiating among the three non-Southern regions, Converse obscures the fact that the southern contribution in each region is offset by the non-southern migrant party identifications, so that the net change from the native means is essentially zero in each region. Although Table 3.4 ignores the time dimension, the aggregate means for northern whites in Figure 3.1 show little secular trend over the twenty years.

Size-of-Place Hypothesis

Parallel to the regional analysis of political cleavages are studies of the political effects of the local community of residence. Centuries of demographic change have produced wide variations in population size and density of American settlement patterns, which now range from isolated rural homesteads to huge metropolitan sprawls. Long before the advent of the sample survey, politicians and historians were aware of divergent political interests and consequent voting patterns between the cities and the small-town–rural sectors, a cleavage exacerbated with the acceleration of large-scale urbanization at the turn of the century (see, for example, Diamond, 1941). The major cities eventually became strongholds of Democratic machines, while rural communities and small towns consistently returned Republican majorities for state and national legislatures.

Careful quantitative analyses of aggregate voting returns in recent years suggest that the urban sector is highly differentiated politically along the size dimension, with Democratic preferences increasing with population size. Epstein (1956) found a positive gradient of city size and Democratic voting in Wisconsin gubernatorial races from 1948 to 1954, and Adamany (1964) replicated the relationship for 1958 to 1962. However, a study of voting in Michigan in cities of over five thousand population concluded that size of place was an unreliable correlate of voting due to great within-class variation; occupational composition of the city was a much better predictor of the two-party vote (Masters and Wright, 1958). Two studies using some of the SRC surveys likewise pointed to associations between city size and party identification, although the magnitudes of the relationships are not as strong as for many other sociodemographic variables (Campbell et al., 1960, pp. 453–72; Hamilton, 1972, pp. 239–82).

The size-of-place findings have produced a proliferation of theoretical interpretations, ranging from the supposed "isolated alienated mass" of the metropolis to the hide-bound traditional political conformity of the small-town rural areas. Other theorists argue that the size-of-place correlation is a spurious consequence of differential racial, religious and occupational concentrations in central cities, suburbs, small towns, and rural areas (Hamilton, 1972, p. 253). Among the many size-of-place hypotheses is one offered in *The American Voter* concerning the impact of differential migration of individuals between metropolitan and other areas. Although white migrants to the metropolis have somewhat lower socioeconomic status than those leaving the large cities for suburbs and small towns, "the former big city dwellers and the onetime country folk are remarkably similar in the nature of their underlying partisan allegiances"—that is, both groups are predominantly Republican (Campbell et al., 1960, pp. 460–61). The long-time metropolitan dwellers tend to be more heavily Democratic. Converse (1968, p. 13) argued that United States data shows that "a surprising portion of the partisan variability within our large urban centers, and particularly within the working-class cores of those centers, derives from the continuing admixture of migrants from rural areas who frequently fail to take on at any rapid rate (if at all) the political coloring of their new milieu."

These observations on the political consequences of migration between the metropolis and the hinterland may be extended to encompass migration between other places of differing population size. To the extent that migrants have different party identifications than nonmigrants, variation in the partisanship of communities of various sizes may arise from differential migration. Geographically mobile individuals may reconcile the contradictory political influences of their origin and destination communities by arriving, in the aggregate, at a party identification intermediate to that of the communities in which they were raised and that in which they now reside. Statistically, this is an additive model in which origin and destination size-of-place effects combine to produce the party identifications of both migrants and nonmigrants.

The SRC surveys uniformly coded the size of place of the interview in a ten-category classification. These were collapsed into five categories of size of place of current residence: (1) the central cities of the twelve largest SMSA's; (2) SMSA's other than the twelve largest; (3) the suburban and fringe areas of the twelve largest SMSA's; (4) other urban places from 2,500 to 50,000 population; and (5) rural areas (size under 2,500). Respondents were asked the size of the place in which they were raised, and although some surveys distinguished as many as seven categories of origin size of place, to maintain comparability across all surveys only three categories were retained: (1) farm; (2) town or small city (up to 100,000); and (3) large city or metropolis (over 100,000).

In the following analyses, the data were restricted to white respondents residing outside the South and border states. In each year only a handful of cases occur in the twelve largest SMSA's from the census South, too few to permit a comparable analysis of size-of-place mobility in both regions of the country. The distribution of party identifications (P) across the three major categories for combinations of origin (O) and destination (D) size of place may be found in Table 3.5. A baseline model in which party preference is independent of both size-of-place variables (OD)(P) fails to fit the data adequately (chi-square equal to 118.2, d.f. = 28). Permitting party to associate with both size variables but not to interact jointly, (OD)(OP)(DP), produces a chi-square which, relative to degrees of freedom, has a probability just greater than .05 of occurring by chance (chi-square equal to 25.6, d.f. = 16). The data may be essentially described by an additive model in which both origin and destination size of place separately contribute to variation in party identification. The effects of destination are somewhat stronger than those of origin, as an inspection of the row and column marginals in Table 3.5 will confirm.

The observed origin totals imply that persons from large cities are less Republican than those from farm backgrounds, but the difference is less than 7 percent. The marginals for destination size of place have somewhat greater variation, descending on monotonic order from a high of 48.7 percent Democratic in the largest central cities to only 35.3 percent Democratic in rural areas. The effect parameters from the additive log-linear model show that Republican preference is greatest in rural and suburban areas, while Independent preference hits its peak in the small urban places. The small range in party identification variation for the size-of-place

TABLE 3.5. PARTY IDENTIFICATION BY SIZES OF CHILDHOOD RESIDENCE
            AND CURRENT RESIDENCE FOR WHITE NON-SOUTHERNERS,
            1952-1972

SIZE OF PLACE OF CHILDHOOD (O) AND PARTY (P)	SIZE OF PLACE OF CURRENT RESIDENCE (D)					
	Central City	Other SMSA	Suburb	Other Urban	Rural	Total
Farm:						
Democrat	55.7	36.8	40.6	36.2	37.5	38.2
Independent	19.8	27.1	27.5	30.0	26.3	27.2
Republican	24.5	36.1	31.9	33.8	36.2	34.6
(N)	(106)	(269)	(160)	(583)	(959)	(2077)
Small Town, City:						
Democrat	47.4	37.8	35.9	37.3	33.8	37.1
Independent	27.9	30.0	25.9	31.7	32.3	30.2
Republican	24.7	32.2	38.2	31.0	33.9	32.7
(N)	(247)	(447)	(579)	(1029)	(758)	(3060)
Large City:						
Democrat	48.1	43.6	37.8	27.6	31.8	40.2
Independent	28.9	31.2	32.3	36.2	34.9	31.8
Republican	23.0	25.2	29.8	36.2	33.3	28.0
(N)	(669)	(365)	(439)	(257)	(261)	(1191)
Total:						
Democrat	48.7	39.5	37.3	35.6	35.3	38.3
Independent	27.7	29.7	28.5	31.8	29.7	29.8
Republican	23.6	30.8	34.2	32.6	34.9	31.9
(N)	(1022)	(1081)	(1178)	(1869)	(1978)	(7128)

analysis, when contrasted to that obtained for race and region, lends support to Hamilton's (1972, p. 241) conclusion that, while the size-of-place hypothesis cannot be flatly rejected, "its importance has been somewhat exaggerated." An additive dummy variable regression analysis of the five-point party identification variable found that the additive effects of origin and destination size of place account for less than 2 percent of the variance, even when other factors have not been partialed out. The minor importance of community size for party preferences justifies ignoring this variable in subsequent analyses.

Summary

The analysis of racial and regional changes in party identification in the last twenty years disclosed dramatic changes in the distribution of this variable. Racial polarization occurred both between and within party groupings. The mobilization of the southern black electorate during the early 1960's saw a sharp drop in apolitical behavior and a rapid increase in the Democratic affiliation of blacks in both regions. In apparent reaction, Democratic affiliations among southern whites plummeted while Independent affiliations doubled. After 1960, the race-party alignments were similar in both regions, with blacks substantially more Democratic than whites.

The analysis of changes in party identification is supported by the changes which occurred in party images held by the four racial region groups. Net support for the Democratic party decreased sharply among whites in both regions, especially in the South. This change took place across the board, among nominal Democrats as well as non-Democrats. But the net advantage of the Democrats remained high among blacks, increasing strongly among southern blacks. Racial issues seem to be strongly implicated in attracting blacks to the Democratic party and repelling whites.

The effect of migration between regions was explored. Only in the South did mean party identification change noticeably under the influx of migrants. Migrants to the South brought markedly less Democratic orientation than found among native southerners. In the three regions outside the South, the differential effects of migrants from other areas of the country tended to offset each other, resulting in a mean party identification substantially the same as that prevailing among the natives.

Finally, the size-of-place hypothesis was shown to have little importance. The central cities of the twelve largest SMSA's were more Democratic than smaller places, and persons with origins in larger communities were slightly more Democratic than those from farms and small towns. However, the total variance in party identification accounted for by size-of-place variables was less than 2 percent, most of it due to the effect of destinations.

Chapter IV

Socioeconomic Status

Scientific study of the relationship between social class and political power largely originated in the work of Karl Marx. Formulated during the Industrial Revolution in England, the Marxist model of stratification and conflict in industrial society focused upon the relationships of men to the economic production system. Marx's work influenced social science both in the support and the reaction these ideas provoked. Max Weber's debate with the ghost of Marx resulted in elaboration and modification of concepts and principles of stratification. The Marxist and Weberian theories of stratification developed in the context of European social structural development and political systems. Attempts to apply them unaltered to the American situation can produce ludicrous distortions, yet a significant body of analysis of American politics manifests a strong Marxist or neo-Marxist flavor. A brief review of the basic components of Marx's and Weber's theories of stratification precedes the empirical analysis of the impact of contemporary stratification on American politics. Insight into the effect of the socioeconomic status attainment process on party identification grows out of recent research on stratification by American sociologists. This status-attainment model will be considered later in the chapter.

Class and Status

Marx's theory of class relationships in industrial society emphasized control of the means of material production. (In addition to works by Marx (1962, 1956), interpretations and modifications are found in Dahrendorf, 1959; Zeitlin, 1967; Lipset, 1968b; and Anderson, 1974.) Under the impact of expanding commerce and the rise of manufacturing, the medieval European feudal economic system broke down. In its place Marx saw evolving a two-class system in which a small number of families owned the productive capital and a large number of propertyless workers were forced to sell their labor for wages at less than the value of the goods they produced. The capitalists thus reaped disproportionate material benefits through exploitation of the rest of society. The economic interests of the two classes were opposed and irreconcilable. The political power of the capitalists grew out of their control of the means of production. Indeed, the modern state was but a means to administer society in the interests of the capitalist class.

Other classes—landowners, small businessmen, craftsmen—would be slowly eliminated by the rise of giant industry, which concentrated large, unskilled masses of workers into the factory system. Workers would begin to combine to fight against exploitation by the bourgeoisie. In the process of defending its interests, the proletariat would be transformed from an objective "class in itself" to a "class for itself"—that is, from a mere aggregate of individuals facing a common situation with regard to the means of production to an organization for achieving collective goals. For Marx these ends were not just the economic goals of better wages and working conditions but the achievement of political power. The vehicle of the class struggle would vary from country to country depending upon the nature of the political alternatives available. In autocratic nations like Germany, the ascendancy of the proletariat would probably require a violent revolution, but in England, where channels of democratic representation might be opened up, a workers' political party could contest elections for control of the state.

Marx's theory of class stratification placed economic relationships at the foundation of politics. As workers became increasingly conscious of their disadvantaged position in industrial society and demanded a redistribution of wealth and power, the party system would come to reflect opposing class interests. Political parties would be distinct in their class composition and their policy positions. Parties would draw voting support from one class to the exclusion of the other, so that class and party would be virtual synonyms.

Marx's influence on political sociology was profound. Lipset echoed his perspective when he wrote: "More than anything else the party struggle is a conflict among classes, and the most impressive single fact about political party support is that in virtually every economically developed country the lower income groups vote mainly for parties of the left, while the higher income groups vote mainly for parties of the right" (1960, p. 234). Alford (1963, p. 38) wrote in a similar vein, "In the modern democratic state, the political parties have developed largely as instruments of various class interests" but are not unitary representatives of economic interests because of cleavages which cut across social classes. The association of class and vote is "natural and expected" in Western democracies because of the existence of class interests; representation of these interests by political parties; regular association of certain parties with certain interests; and the "tendency of voters to choose the party historically associated with the social groups to which they belong—groups with a class and non-class character" (Alford, 1963, p. 12). Butler and Stokes (1969, ch. 4) further distinguished three types of class and party relationships: (1) politics as a conflict of opposed class interests; (2) politics as a simple representation of one's own class interest; and (3) politics as a class norm or tradition without perceptions of class interests being involved.

The core of the Marxist theory is its emphasis on the paramount importance of relationships in the labor market between employers and employees. Max Weber (1966) felt that this concern with conflict generated in one sphere of social interaction was too narrow to do justice to the complexity of stratification. Hierarchical inequalities could arise in economic markets other than the labor market and in noneconomic relationships as well. Each had the potential for political conflict. Whereas Marx believed that objective inequality and exploitation would inevitably lead to political consciousness, Weber felt that the development of class action was problematic. Differences in individual life chances within the labor, commodity, and credit markets may or may not result in collective action. Complicating matters is an autonomous dimension of stratification based on social *status*.

In contrast to the class dimension based on property position in the economic markets, the status dimension refers to positive and negative estimations of honor, or prestige, and deference due to persons and positions. Status is thus a subjective evaluation which may influence how groups and persons interact. Weber noted that although class and status could be correlated, status could and often did cut across class lines. Persons with different economic life chances may belong to the same status group, treating each other as equals and those outside the status group with deference or disdain. Since status is a limited quantity, groups with high prestige will attempt to deny outsiders access to the group. Especially in pre-industrial societies, status tends to be ascriptive and particularistic. As industrialization erodes the ascribed barriers of land and blood and replaces them with an achieved status hierarchy of occupational attainments, the amount of political conflict from structural inequalities diminishes. When status membership becomes more important and salient in a society, the political antagonism growing out of economic class conflicts will be pushed into the background.

Status stratification produces a much more complex politics than does classical Marxist class stratification. Occupations may form distinct status groups, such as professions or skilled crafts, which seek to monopolize prestige by refusing to cooperate politically with other occupations with whom they share similar economic class situations. The enormous division of labor in industrial society produces a proliferation of organized interest groups seeking social and economic advantages for their members. Occupational groups at similar economic class levels may differ sharply in prestige and consequently in political coloration.

Although class and status are analytically distinct concepts, difficulties are encountered in using them in the analysis of occupational effects on party identification. Virtually no survey analysts have been able to use class in Marx's sense of ownership and nonownership of productive capital. Generally, only a fraction of sampled respondents will be owners of major economic units. Anderson (1974, p. 134), for example, estimated that 2 percent or less of the United States population could be classified as "capitalists with decisive or total stakes in corporate property." Instead, empirical social scientists have introduced another definition of class which differentiates functional subclasses within Marx's proletariat. A "middle class" of white-collar workers is economically advantaged over "working-class" blue-collar workers in terms of income, job stability, and employer contact (Alford, 1963; but see reservations voiced by Hamilton, 1972, ch. 5). The most widely used criterion is occupation—nonmanual and manual. The contrasts in life styles, education, and values between these two aggregates have led many researchers to term the manual-nonmanual division a "class" boundary, despite the internal diversity of occupations within each class. Nevertheless, the division of the occupational structure into "middle" and "working" classes is consistent with the basic notion of class stratification as a labor market hierarchy.

Weber recognized that while the labor market was one source of class cleavage, occupations could also be considered status groups. If the occupations in manual and nonmanual classes are broken into finer classifications, income overlap occurs. "Middle-class" clerical and sales workers have lower earnings than "working class" craftsmen and foremen (Blau and Duncan, 1967, p. 27). However, despite the lower monetary rewards of white-collar work at the lower levels, these occupations are more highly esteemed than are blue-collar jobs. One major study of intergenerational mobility implied that downwardly mobile men reared in high-status nonmanual homes show little interest in moving into higher paying but lower prestige manual occupations, preferring instead to work in lower-level white-collar occupations which preserve their status of origin (Blau and Duncan, 1967, pp. 58–67). The occupational status hierarchy thus parallels the class division but further differentiates within the manual and nonmanual occupations. A description of the measurement of occupational status is deferred until a later section.

Brief History

Social class seems to have been generally unrelated to political party affiliation in the first third of the present century. The "System of 1896" which brought the Republican party to national and state dominance for a generation followed a major economic depression in 1893 under a

Democratic administration. Democratic losses occurred among all social and geographic groups as voters reacted against the "party of hard times" (Kleppner, 1972). But the presidential contest between Bryan and McKinley did not polarize the electorate along class lines, despite the rhetoric of class conflict employed by Bryan in his attempt to build a coalition of urban workers and farmers against the metropolitan centers. Party identifications of the period were deeply rooted in ethnic and religious cultural issues. McKinley's appeal among Democrats disaffected by Bryan's pietism and populism forged a coalition that was to endure until the next major economic catastrophe (Kleppner, 1972; McSeveney, 1972; Burnham, 1970, pp. 34–90; see also Wiley, 1967, who argued from a Weberian perspective that Bryan's inability to wed urban workers with agrarian interests stemmed from inconsistent class positions of these groups on the labor, credit, and commodity markets).

Unlike the relatively brief depression of 1893, which left little visible imprint upon class political alignments, the Great Depression, beginning in 1929 and lasting more than a decade, produced an immediate and enduring reorganization of the party system along class lines. The candidacy of an urban Catholic Democrat for president in 1928 drew substantial numbers of working-class immigrant-stock voters into the electorate, and the New Deal triumph of 1932–1936 solidified major class cleavages along party lines which had previously been structured mainly around sectional interests. The New Deal's appeal to the working class was, of course, its creation of a managerial government on the ruins of a bankrupt entrepreneurial rule of the national economy. Organized labor laid claim to an increasing share of power under Franklin D. Roosevelt (Ladd, 1970, pp. 190–93). Deprived blacks moved wholesale from Republican to Democratic party identification, setting the stage for their eventual political participation under Democratic sponsorship. Republican support diminished in the electorate to a hard core of big-business and small-town supporters. Initial Republican hostility to such Democratic ameliorative measures as social security, work relief, and deficit financing eventually gave way to acceptance of the new programs in general, if not to each of their specific features.

By stigmatizing the Republican party as responsible for the collapse and by championing legislation on behalf of the socioeconomic have-nots, the Democratic party sharpened the class differences in the mass bases of the two parties. The Democratic transition to the majority party was apparently the result of mobilizing previously nonparticipating segments of the population, rather than conversion of Republicans en masse:

There is reason to believe, however, that a good many of these Republicans who defected into the Democratic ranks during the early years of the Roosevelt period were soon disenchanted. Some erstwhile Republicans never returned to their party, but these party changers do not appear to have made up a very large part of the long-term Democratic increase. . . . a larger component of the gain came from young voters entering the electorate and older people who had previously failed to vote (Campbell et al., 1960, p. 153).

The Democratic hold on the Depression "generation" never disappeared. Even within this generation, Democratic party identification came disproportionately from lower socioeconomic groups in every region except the South. Adequate survey data are not available from the early 1930's, so much of the evidence on social class cleavage is based upon comparisons from the 1940's and 1950's, when rising prosperity may have blunted the full impact of the Depression experience upon partisan orientations.

The social and economic system emerging after World War II differed markedly from its predecessor. The affluent technological society posed special problems for the attainment of working-class consciousness which were not present during hard times. Ollman (1972), for example, argued that the progression from workers' perception of their objective class interests to class-conscious action is a complex process "achievement of which very few workers at any time have shown themselves capable, and there is little reason to believe this will change." Among the important barriers to development to class political action in contemporary Europe and America were greater interclass mobility, increased stratification within the working class, and absolute (but not relative) improvement in the workers' share of the material benefits of industrial society. Political radicalization of the working class is also thwarted by the imposition of normative values by the dominant class and the "pragmatic acceptance" by the subordinate class of a limited role in society (Mann, 1970; also Parkin, 1971). While many of the objective conditions for class conflict remain latent within the economic system, the question of their impact on party alignments within the occupational system is an empirical one, addressed in the following sections.

Index of Class Polarization

The Marxist theory of class conflict predicts that political parties will tend to draw support exclusively from one social class. Any support of bourgeois parties by working-class persons results from false consciousness of one's economic class interests. The major political parties of industrial democracies, however, draw significant voting strength from all class levels. Empirical research thus focuses upon variations in the class-party correlation across nations and over time.

The Survey Research Center developed a "status-polarization" index to measure the intensity of class identification in voting behavior. The association between occupational class (manual-nonmanual) or subjective class identification and the presidential vote (Democrat-Republican) declined steadily from 1948 to 1956 (Converse, 1958; Campbell et al., 1960, pp. 338–50). But Alford (1963, pp. 225–27), in a comparative study of four Anglo-American nations, found no evidence of a consistent decline in class voting in the United States from 1936 to 1960. Although the South had a lower level of class polarization than the rest of the country, he found "no evidence that the South, at least, is becoming more like other regions in its level of class voting" (p. 239). He found that the mean national difference in white-collar–blue-collar voting for Democratic candidates was 16 percent, as compared to mean differences of 40 percent in Great Britain, 33 percent in Australia, and only 8 percent in Canada, with voting for the "Left" party as the criterion. Alford attributed the lower level of class voting in the United States relative to Britain and Australia to the absence of class-based organizations to link the parties to specific class concerns and to the diversity of other social cleavages.

In a recent analysis of Gallup poll data from the 1940's to the late 1960's, Glenn (1973) analyzed occupational class differences in presidential voting and party preference of white respondents aged twenty-one to fifty-nine. He found a marked downward trend in class voting for the nation as a whole from 1936 to 1968. Broken down by region, the data revealed opposite trends. The percentage differences in the non-southern region generally declined, while manual-nonmanual differences within the South grew sharply, although not enough to offset the overall decline. But in an analysis of data from 1972, Glenn (1975) discovered that no significant class differences in presidential voting existed in either region.

When the major party identifiers were compared, class differences in Republican preference decreased from 16.2 percent in 1949 to 12.7 percent in 1957 but rose to 18 percent in 1961 and stayed at that level through the end of the decade. Even when Independents were included in the base on which class partisanship was calculated, the differences in 1969 were only slightly smaller than in the earlier five periods and exhibited no marked downward trend (Glenn, 1973, pp. 13–14). Glenn also broke the process down by age cohorts, finding generally greater class differences among older persons than among younger. In the 1972 election, a sharp drop in class partisanship among southern whites was observed, with differences in Republican preference dropping from 15.1 percent in 1969 to only 5 percent in 1972. The non-southern class differences in party identification remained unchanged at about 18 percent (Glenn, 1975).

Several measures of class-party association have been proposed, but for a 2×2 table in which class and party are both dichotomies, only three independent pieces of information are available (Korpi, 1972). The most frequently used index is one Alford called the "index of class voting," in which the percentage of nonmanual respondents supporting the Left party is subtracted from the percentage of manual workers supporting the Left. Alford (1963, p. 80) pointed out that the index of class voting is one of a family of such summary measures generally called "indices of dissimilarity" used by sociologists to compare two percentage distributions. In a completely class-polarized society where the entire working class supports the workers' party but none of the bourgeoisie does, the index would be 100 percent, the theoretical maximum. Of course, should such a state of affairs be approached, the distinction between class and party would be meaningless and civil war would probably have already broken out. On the other hand, if both the working and middle classes had equal rates of support for the Left party, the index would be 0, indicating that the classes were not politically distinct.

The convention is followed here of treating manual and nonmanual occupations as the yardstick for dividing the working and middle classes. The ambiguity of farming occupations in the class system (manual labor combined with capital ownership) makes their classification difficult (see Knoke and Long, 1975). Fortunately, they form such a small percentage of the labor force (under 5 percent) that they may be omitted without great impact on the index values. Classification of female respondents is more problematic. About 45 percent have occupations of their own, and a substantial portion of these are in a different class from those of their husbands. Fulltime housewives, however, can only be classified by their husbands' occupations. Since they lack personal involvement in the occupational structure, the impact of class on political preferences may be less strong on housewives than on women holding jobs. Therefore, the data to be presented on class and status effects on party identification will be based only upon white men of working age (twenty-one to sixty-five years) in nonfarm occupations. The larger sample, including women and blacks, would alter the exact percentages and regression coefficients, but not by such substantial margins as to negate or reverse the findings reported below.

Table 4.1 reports the indices of class partisanship for both the South and the non-South from 1952 to 1972. Following custom, the Democratic party is taken as the "Left" party, although comparable patterns might have been obtained using the Republican percentages. Independents are included in the base figures. The indices of class partisanship reveal no strong trend in either region. Among non-southern men the highest class polarization is in 1952, with a 25 percent difference between nonmanuals and manuals, but the second highest value is in 1964. The percentage of manual workers identifying with the Democrats is about 50 percent in both these years but in the other years averages 10 percent less. The nonmanuals are more stable, varying between 27 and 29 percent Democrat over the first five periods but falling to 22 percent in 1972, reflecting increased Independent identification during that election. The index value declines from 1952 to 1956 and 1960, as noted by Glenn and by Campbell et al. in their analyses based on both sexes.

TABLE 4.1.   CLASS PARTISANSHIP BY REGION, FOR WHITE MEN, 21 TO
             65 YEARS, 1952-1972

REGION, CLASS, AND PARTISANSHIP INDEX	YEAR					
	1952	1956	1960	1964	1968	1972
	Percent Democrat					
NON-SOUTH						
Nonmanual	27	28	29	28	29	22
Manual	52	40	42	49	40	38
Class Partisanship	25	12	13	21	11	16
(N)	(423)	(410)	(356)	(346)	(309)	(616)
SOUTH						
Nonmanual	73	69	62	54	38	37
Manual	70	71	74	70	48	48
Class Partisanship	-3	2	12	16	10	11
(N)	(108)	(132)	(155)	(118)	(116)	(274)

But the following three elections outside the South show neither trends of decrease nor of increase.

Class partisanship is not as strong in the South during the 1950's as it is elsewhere in the nation. In the two Eisenhower elections the percentages of southern Democratic men in both classes do not differ appreciably. The Democratic identification of manual workers remains stable at about 70 percent from 1952 through 1964, but that of nonmanual workers falls off steadily after 1956. As the gap between the classes widens, the index of partisanship in the South approaches that of the non-South by 1960. The election of 1968 is a watershed for party alignments in the South. Both classes experience a sharp dropoff in Democratic preferences from the previous election and a substantial increase in political Independents, as the previous chapter demonstrated. The change is greater among manual workers, according to the sample values for 1968, largely because they had not relinquished Democratic loyalty as early as nonmanual workers. Although southern manual preferences fall 22 percent between 1964 and

1968, nonmanual support also falls 16 percent, yielding a class partisanship of 10 percent, indistinguishable from the 11 percent index value for non-southern men in 1968. Southern class partisanship remains unchanged in 1972, although it rises five points outside the South. While the absolute level of Democratic preferences in the South is 10 to 15 percent higher than elsewhere, class polarization in the South changes over the twenty years until the region resembles the rest of the nation.

These findings on class partisanship parallel those of Alford on voting for the earlier period in American electoral history. The index fluctuates within the range of 10 to 20 percent, without evident direction. Except for the changes noted in the South, bringing that region into line with the rest of the country, class associations with party preferences did not undergo any substantial change over the two decades. A 10 to 20 percent difference in Democratic preference between nonmanual and manual workers may represent a persistent if minimal difference during the present political alignment. Some elections appear to provoke class cleavages more than others, especially that of 1952 in the non-South and 1964 in both regions. Whether these index values are chance sampling errors or real effects is hard to say. However, Glenn's figures from Gallup poll data for class voting in 1964 and class partisanship in 1965 were not higher than the preceding and following periods. As the Goldwater-Johnson campaign did not involve explicit class issues, and economic problems were no greater then than in other election years, the higher index value for 1964 did not appear to result from any important heightening of class tensions.

Economic Partisan Attitudes

Paralleling the analysis of party identifications of manual and nonmanual occupational classes are the changing party images with respect to economic issues. Respondents were asked their likes and dislikes about each party, and up to five open-ended responses to each question were recorded. In the present analysis only responses with specific economic or class content are scored. In general these responses fall into two categories. The first are specific policies felt to be advocated by the parties: for example, support of the Taft-Hartley amendment, wage or price controls, subsidies to farmers, or public works programs. Also included under the first category are "general conditions" associated with the party when in power, especially conditions of prosperity, depression, or inflation. A second general category of economic images has to do with economic groups felt to be favored by the party or likely to be kept in check by the party when in power—either specific referents such as farmers, big business, or labor unions or more general groups like "the common people."

The index of net economic partisan attitudes was formed, as in Chapter III, by summing the number of favorable Republican and unfavorable Democratic responses and subtracting the sum of pro-Democratic and anti-Republican responses. Although the theoretical maximum value is a score of plus or minus ten, most respondents seldom mentioned more than two or three economically related reasons for liking or disliking the two parties. For reasons mentioned previously, data from 1972 are not included.

Analyses of the partisan attitudes from the 1952 election (Campbell et al., 1954, 1960) disclosed an overwhelming net advantage to the Democrats on the basis of domestic issues of all types. The Democratic party benefited from the legacy of the New Deal and the Fair Deal, while many voters associated the Republican party with the economic distress of the Depression. Democrats were also thought to favor lower status groups and Republicans to support higher status groups (Campbell et al., 1960, p. 45). From 1952 to 1956, however, the Democratic net advantage deteriorated as a Republican took over the White House without a serious setback to the economy. References to prosperity and depression in the sample declined by half, and the margin of benefit to the Democrats declined to almost nothing. But other group references continued to be overwhelmingly in favor of the Democrats in both elections.

In the following analyses, distinctions are not made between the type of economic references, whether to policies or group-based, in calculating partisan attitudes toward economics. The average values for the sample and for both occupational classes are found in Table 4.2. Among white men in both regions, the net economic attitudes lie in the pro-Democratic direction for the entire sixteen years, yet more significant than the net advantage to the Democratic party is the dramatic decline across the series. During the Eisenhower years, the average score exceeds one response, but by 1968 the

TABLE 4.2. NET ECONOMIC PARTISAN ATTITUDES BY CLASS, FOR WHITE MEN, 21 TO 65 YEARS, 1952-1968

| CLASS | YEAR | | | | |
	1952	1956	1960	1964	1968
Nonmanual	-.33	-1.00	-.37	-.43	-.12
Manual	-1.66	-1.25	-1.11	-.96	-.57
Difference	1.33	.25	.74	.53	.45
Total	-1.09	-1.12	-.73	-.71	-.28

mean falls to only a quarter of a response in the Democrats' favor. In addition, the proportion of respondents with zero net economic partisan attitudes—either from pro-Republican responses canceling pro-Democratic responses, or from no reference at all to economic issues—increases from 27 percent in 1952 to 43 percent in 1964 and 1968. This 16 percent rise in neutral attitude occurs primarily at the expense of net favorable Democratic responses, which fall by 19 percent. The proportion of men with net responses favorable to the Republican party increases only 3 percent from 1952 to 1968.

Not only does mean net economic partisan attitude decline for the sample as a whole, but class differences also shrink dramatically. From a manual-nonmanual difference of one and a third responses in 1952, the series exhibits a nearly monotonic decline to less than half a response difference by 1968. The one exception occurs in 1956, when class differences were only .25. As manual workers show an uninterrupted decrease in net pro-Democratic economic attitudes, the main reason for the 1956 anomaly is the high pro-Democratic mean among nonmanual workers. A further breakdown reveals the source of this unusual value as an extremely high rate (–3.5 responses) among lower-level white-collar Democrats. The cause of this outburst of pro-Democratic fervor on economic issues is not apparent, however, and may be the result of sampling error. With the exception of 1956, the evidence for decline in the net balance of economic partisan attitudes favorable to the Democratic party is incontrovertible. This decline was concentrated in the manual class, thus producing a diminished class difference on economic partisan attitudes between 1952 and 1968.

Figure 4.1 further elaborates the sources of changing economic images of the parties by displaying the net partisan attitudes on economic issues by class and party identification. For clarity the Independents have not been graphed. As would be expected, Independents exhibit less polarized values than do partisans, with a tendency for both manual and nonmanual Independents to converge around the neutral point over time. There are three main facts to be observed in the figure. First, Republicans in either occupational class exhibit little temporal change in net economic attitudes. Nonmanual Republicans are the only group of the four whose net partisan attitude on economic issues always favors the Republican party, although the mean levels are also less extreme than either Democratic group. The manual Republicans are too close to the neutral point to argue that on economic issues they favor one party over the other during this period.

Second, the Democrats in both classes exhibit a marked secular decline in net economic attitudes favoring the Democrats. Clearly the pattern of class convergence found in Table 4.2 is mostly a consequence of shifts of economic perceptions of the Democratic party by the members of that party (a small part of the total change involves shifts among Independents). The

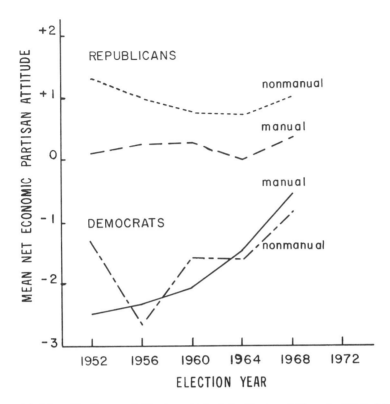

Figure 4.1. Mean Net Economic Partisan Attitude by Party and Class, for White Men, 21 to 65 Years, 1952–1968

decline is monotonic for manual Democrats, the numerically larger group, but more erratic for nonmanual Democrats in the first two elections.

Finally, the role of political party identification is much greater than occupational class in structuring net attitudes toward the parties on economic issues. The difference between the two parties is much greater than the difference between classes within a given party. Although manual Republicans are notably less pro-Republican on economic issues than their nonmanual counterparts, no class differential is evident within the Democratic party. Party identification overrides objective position in the occupational class structure in shaping net perceptions of the parties' economic policies and group benefits. This finding tends to support a traditional model of party identification. Under a rational process, if manual economic interests were perceived as better represented by the Democrats and nonmanual interests by the Republicans, one would expect to find nonmanual respondents on the pro-Republican side of the scale and manual respondents on the pro-Democratic side, regardless of personal party preference. While there is some slight evidence of this pattern among the Republicans, its absence among Democrats argues in favor of a traditional model in which perceptions of partisan positions derive from personal partisan predispositions.

The decreasing Democratic advantage on economic issues within the party's natural constituency, the Democratic working class, arises from several events of the past twenty years. As the Depression faded into history and the generations personally involved slowly disappeared from the electorate, this experience ceased to be a compelling source of Democratic support. The presence of a Republican president in the White House for eight years at the beginning of this period without a major setback to the economy helped diffuse the negative image the Republican party had inherited from Hoover. The unprecedented period of economic growth and high employment of the 1960's, while occurring under two Democratic administrations, had the unintended effect of driving concern with bread-and-butter issues into the political background as issues of race and life style emerged. The diminution of class and party differentials in the perception of the parties is undoubtedly an important factor in the persistent low indices of class voting and class partisanship during the period under study.

Occupational Status

While the manual-nonmanual division used in the preceding class analysis isolates a major economic division in the American occupational structure, it ignores crucial distinctions among occupations within each class. White- and blue-collar and farm occupations differ not only in incomes but in authority, skill, creativity, autonomy, and a host of other attributes. But perhaps the most important dimension on which students of stratification have focused is the prestige of occupations. The prestige of an occupation, the esteem in which it is held by the society, can be determined by asking a representative sample of the public the "general standing" of the occupation—excellent, good, average, fair, or poor. Two major studies by the National Opinion Research Center in 1947 and 1963 resulted in two widely used scales of occupational prestige (see Reiss, 1961; Hodge et al., 1964; Siegel, 1971). The first scale, used in this section, is the Socioeconomic Index (SEI), in which a metric from 0 to 96 is used to classify more than four hundred detailed occupational titles (for details, see Duncan, 1961; Blau and Duncan, 1967, pp. 117–28). For a sample of men in the labor force in 1962, the mean SEI was 36.3 with a standard deviation of about 25 points. The SEI correlates .86 with the prestige scale developed by Hodge et al. (Duncan et al., 1972, p. 48). Thus about three-fourths of the prestige variation in detailed occupations is accounted for by the SEI scores. We have decided to employ the SEI rather than the prestige scale because much of the recent work in stratification has also employed the first scale.

If the occupational status scores are treated as an interval measure, the linear relationship of party identification to status can be determined by a regression. Unfortunately, the quality of occupational information is highly uneven in the six surveys. Only the 1968 and 1972 surveys coded the respondents' occupations on the SEI for detailed occupations. Prior surveys recorded less information, often combining many occupations into a single broad category such as "operative." To make comparisons over time, consistency of measurement is necessary. Since detailed codes could not be used, ten major occupational groups were created and the average status scores of these categories assigned to the respondents in them.

The occupational categories and their average SEI scores are: professional, technical, and kindred workers (75); managers, officials, and proprietors, except farm (57); sales, clerical, and kindred workers (47); craftsmen, foremen, and kindred workers (31); operatives and kindred workers (18); service workers (17); farmers and farm managers (14); farm laborers and foremen (9); and laborers, except farm and mine (7). Although Duncan (1961) gives the SEI of sales workers as 49 and of clerical and kindred workers as 45, the average of these two numbers (47) was assigned to both groups because one survey originally coded these occupations in the same category. The correlation between the broad category means and the SEI scores of the detailed occupations for the men in the 1972 survey was +.87, indicating that 75 percent of the variance in prestige of the detailed occupations lies between the ten major occupational groups. More important, the zero-order correlation of the five-point party identification scale with the detailed scores was .164 and the correlation with the mean scores was .171, indicating that little explanatory power with respect to party identification is lost by grouping the occupations.

The five-point party identification scale was regressed upon the SEI scores and region of residence for white men aged twenty-one to sixty-five. The parameters estimated for the regression equation in each year are presented in Table 4.3. In effect there are two equations, since the variable for southern residence is a dummy variable, coded 1 if the respondent lives in the South and 0 if he resides elsewhere. For example, in 1952, the estimated party identification of non-southern residents is

$$\hat{Y} = 2.417 + .011 \text{ X}$$

and for southerners,

$$\hat{Y} = 1.696 + .011 \text{ X},$$

TABLE 4.3.   REGRESSION EQUATIONS FOR PARTY IDENTIFICATION BY
             OCCUPATIONAL STATUS AND REGION, FOR WHITE MEN, 21
             TO 65 YEARS, 1952-1972

REGRESSION	YEAR					
PARAMETERS	1952	1956	1960	1964	1968	1972
Constant	2.417	2.747	2.625	2.247	2.549	2.600
b Occupation	.011	.006	.008	.010	.010	.009
b South	-.721	-.834	-.494	-.300	-.369	-.217
Multiple R^2	.074	.086	.041	.034	.044	.034

where $\hat{Y}$ is the expected party identification and X is the respondent's occupational status. The constant in the equation for southerners includes the b parameter for southern residence.

The form of the equation implies an additive model of occupational and regional effects on party, i.e., that the effect of occupation on party preferences is the same in both regions. That the slopes for occupation are positive and essentially parallel in the South and in the non-South can be seen by the regression coefficients estimated by a separate analysis for non-southern men only. The values, from 1952 through 1972, respectively, are .015, .007, .012, .009, .010, and .010.

Inspection of the unstandardized regression parameters for the occupational variable across years reveals that the effect of prestige on party net of region has been relatively constant over the two decades. With the exception of the 1956 value, all the b's lie within .003 of each other. Typically, a change of one unit on the Duncan SEI scale results in an increment of .010 points on the five-point party identification scale. Since the effective range of the occupational scale is 68 SEI points, from laborer to professional and kindred workers, the expected difference between the means of these two occupational groups, when region is held constant, is about two-thirds of a point on the party scale. By comparison, the political party difference between South and non-South in 1952 and 1956 was larger than this occupational difference, although from 1960 on the regional parameter is less than the expected difference in party preference between the two most extreme occupational groups on the status scale.

Another way to assess the magnitude of the occupational status effect is to transform the difference between expected means for laborers and professionals into a standardized measure. Since the standard deviation in party identification from 1952 to 1964 is 1.35 units, the expected difference in occupational extremes varies from .30 to .55 standard deviations in party preference. The variance in party was smaller in 1968 (1.25) and in 1972 (1.20), indicating that the expected difference in extremes was from .50 to .60 standard deviations on the party scale.

As with the class analysis, the status analysis shows that more persons higher in prestige tend to be Republican than Democrat or Independent. Although we can be very confident that this is the form of the linear relationship of occupational status and party identification and that it has been highly stable over recent decades, the prediction of individuals' partisanship from prestige and region contains a great deal of error. The multiple R^2's reported in Table 4.3 show that the additive effects of prestige and region generally account for less than 5 percent of the total variation in party identification. Only in 1952 and 1956 are the R^2's above 5 percent and the larger part of that increase is the result of the strong effects of region, as shown in Chapter III. Clearly, then, while the prestige ordering of the ten occupational groups picks up some of the variation in party preferences, most of the variation lies off the multiple regression line.

Perhaps the true relationship between occupations and party identification is not linear, as the preceding regression analysis requires. A curvilinearity may exist between status and partisanship and may account for the failure of the linear regression to pick up much of the variation in the dependent variable. To test this proposition, the zero-order correlation between the occupational status scale and party identification is compared with the explanatory power of the ten occupational groups when the requirement of linearity is removed. The correlation ratio (eta) is calculated simply as the ratio of the between-category sum of squares for the ten groups to the total sum of squares. If the mean party identification of the groups is a linear, additive function of the occupational status, the eta should be no larger than the correlation coefficient (r) of the linear regression (in this case without the region variable). But if nonlinearities exist in the relationship of the two variables, then the correlation ratio should exceed the correlation coefficient. The larger the deviations of the category means from the regression line, the larger the discrepancy between eta and r. The values for these two statistics are reported in Table 4.4 for each sample year.

In every year the correlation ratio exceeds the correlation coefficient. The discrepancy is smallest in the last three years. In 1952 and 1956 eta is about half again as large as r, and in 1960 it is nearly three times as large. Thus occupational prestige does a fairly good job in predicting the observed party means for the occupational groups in 1964, 1968, and 1972, but does a poorer job in the three preceding periods. For example, Figure 4.2 graphs the 1960 least-squares regression line and the observed occupational group means. Three groups fall below the regression line, each with a score in the middle of the status hierarchy; operatives (18), craftsmen and foremen (31),

TABLE 4.4.   ZERO-ORDER CORRELATION (r) AND CORRELATION RATIO (η)
             BETWEEN OCCUPATIONAL STATUS AND PARTY IDENTIFICATION,
             FOR WHITE MEN, 21 TO 65 YEARS, 1952-1972

STATISTICS	YEAR					
	1952	1956	1960	1964	1968	1972
Correlation (r)	.163	.105	.117	.156	.161	.164
Correlation ratio (η)	.242	.162	.314	.176	.202	.202

and clerical and kindred workers (47). The other occupational groups with higher and lower status are all above the line, indicating that they are more Republican than would be expected on the basis of occupational prestige alone.

(Figure 4.2, like Table 4.5, omits the display of observed and expected means for farm laborers [SEI = 9] because very few respondents in any sample were classified in these categories. Of twenty-one farm laborers in all six samples, ten are found in 1972 and none in 1952 and 1956. With so few cases, the mean party identifications are highly unreliable.)

Such deviations may be chance fluctuations due to sampling error or may represent the vagaries of a particular election. On the other hand, departures from linearity in the relationship of party identification to occupational status may be stable, enduring aspects of the occupational structure. To determine the consistency of relationships between occupational groups and their expected partisanship, similar comparisons of observed and expected party means were performed on each sample. But where Figure 4.2 and Table 4.4 are based on the zero-order relationship of party identification and occupational status, without controls for other independent variables, the calculation of expected party means for occupational groups in Table 4.5 is based upon the multiple regression equations in Table 4.3, which include an additive effect for southern and non-southern residence. Thus the expected party identification of respondents in a given occupational category depends not only upon the SEI score of that category but also upon the relative proportions of southerners and non-southerners. Since the regional distributions of occupational groups differ, the expected group party means do not conform to a simple regression line as depicted in Figure 4.2. The tabular display of observed and expected means in Table 4.5 is thus the most efficient way to exhibit the relationships.

The detail of occupational codes in the 1952 study was insufficient to allocate respondents among the ten status groups. Four categories are approximations to the classifications used in the other five surveys. Clerical and sales workers were coded together in the same category; this combination poses no problem for the regression analysis since both groups were scored with an SEI of 47. The original category "skilled workers" was equated with craftsmen and foremen (SEI = 31), "semiskilled workers" with operatives and service workers (SEI = 18), and "unskilled workers" with laborers (SEI = 7). As can readily be seen by the frequency distributions in the last panel of Table 4.5, the craftsmen-foremen category was disproportionately large relative to the operative-service workers when compared to the following years. Obviously, different criteria were used by the original coders to separate skilled and semiskilled workers. These differences in classification of occupations in 1952 caution against direct comparison with findings for the following years and are presented here largely for the sake of completeness.

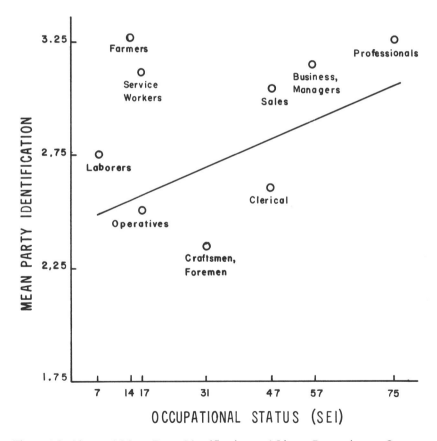

Figure 4.2. Observed Mean Party Identification and Linear Regression on Occupational Status, for White Men, 21 to 65 Years, 1960

TABLE 4.5. OBSERVED AND EXPECTED PARTY IDENTIFICATION MEANS FOR
OCCUPATIONAL STATUS GROUPS, FOR WHITE MEN, 21 TO 65
YEARS, 1952-1972

OCCUPATIONAL STATUS GROUP	YEAR					
	1952	1956	1960	1964	1968	1972

Observed Means

	1952	1956	1960	1964	1968	1972
Professionals	3.15	3.22	3.26	2.81	3.18	3.05
Business, Managers	2.87	2.75	3.16	2.79	2.93	3.25
Clerical	2.99*	2.65	2.61	2.82	2.75	2.89
Sales		2.83	2.98	2.68	3.11	3.15
Craftsmen, Foremen	2.35*	2.65	2.34	2.38	2.63	2.82
Operatives	3.25*	2.66	2.51	2.39	2.63	2.52
Service Workers		2.71	3.12	2.33	2.73	2.72
Farmers	2.76	2.86	3.27	2.38	3.04	2.67
Laborers	2.18*	2.46	2.74	2.06	2.09	2.57
Total	2.63	2.77	2.81	2.54	2.83	2.90

Expected Means

	1952	1956	1960	1964	1968	1972
Professionals	3.09	3.08	3.12	2.94	3.14	3.20
Business, Managers	2.90	2.83	2.91	2.73	2.98	3.03
Clerical	2.78*	2.86	2.86	2.60	2.96	2.95
Sales		2.76	2.94	2.60	2.88	2.93
Craftsmen, Foremen	2.62*	2.73	2.72	2.49	2.75	2.80
Operatives	2.42*	2.73	2.69	2.37	2.62	2.68
Service Workers		2.62	2.72	2.35	2.61	2.65
Farmers	2.38	2.52	2.54	2.26	2.53	2.66
Laborers	2.31*	2.57	2.61	2.25	2.49	2.59

Observed Minus Expected Means

	1952	1956	1960	1964	1968	1972
Professionals	.06	.15	.14	-.13	.04	-.15
Business, Managers	-.03	-.08	.25	.06	-.05	.22
Clerical	.20*	-.21	-.25	.21	-.21	-.06
Sales		.07	.04	.08	.23	.22
Craftsmen, Foremen	-.27*	-.08	-.38	-.11	-.12	.02
Operatives	.83*	-.07	-.18	.02	.00	-.16
Service Workers		.10	.41	-.01	.12	.12
Farmers	.38	.34	.74	.12	.51	.01
Laborers	-.13*	-.11	.13	-.18	-.40	-.02

Because of the small number of cases involved in some occupational groups, great confidence should not be placed in any given value for party identification. The consistency of observed and of expected party identification over time is the most important consideration. These patterns are found in the third panel of Table 4.5. For example, farmers are consistently above

TABLE 4.5. Continued

OCCUPATIONAL	YEAR					
GROUP	1952	1956	1960	1964	1968	1972
			Frequencies			
Professionals	52	76	70	67	88	159
Business, Managers	106	99	93	103	83	148
Clerical	67*	23	18	22	32	53
Sales		35	48	47	19	41
Craftsmen, Foremen	234*	147	161	110	117	199
Operatives	12*	87	116	96	64	146
Service Workers		35	33	30	11	39
Farmers	74	51	59	29	25	21
Laborers	60*	41	19	16	11	28
Total	605	594	617	520	450	834

*Matching to occupations in 1952 is approximate

the regression line in each sample, as are sales workers, indicating that these two groups are always more Republican in their actual preferences than would be expected on the basis of status and region of residence. The magnitudes of these deviations vary greatly, at times being very close to the regression line. Yet the fact that these occupations bear a consistent relationship to their expected values suggests that certain structural aspects besides status and region affect the political orientation of their members.

In the case of farmers, the SEI score may not adequately reflect the true prestige of this occupational group. Farmers are low on the SEI scale (14) primarily because of the low monetary incomes and low educational attainments of the group as a whole. However, direct estimates of their prestige by public polls generally place them much higher in the prestige hierarchy, towards the middle (see Siegel, 1971). Farmers have long been noted for their Republican support, especially outside the South (Knoke and Long, 1975), so that high Republicanism coupled with mismeasurement of their status may well explain the consistent underestimation of their party identification in the linear regression analysis.

The tendency of sales workers to be more Republican than expected is not so readily explained. Individuals in these occupations are in the lowest prestige category of the nonmanual occupations. They may anticipate subsequent upward mobility and adopt party preferences more in line with persons of higher status. However, if anticipatory politicization (or a "status panic") accounts for Republicanism of salesmen, it does not explain why clerical and kindred workers generally exhibit an opposite pattern. Except for 1964, clerical workers are always more Democratic than the predicted partisanship, and non-southern clerical workers are always below the regression line. Men in these occupations are more likely to experience upward mobility than are sales workers (Blau and Duncan, 1967, p. 31). Yet the two groups with equivalent occupational prestige have very different political patterns. The causes of this political differentiation are not apparent and call for further research not possible with the present data. These findings underscore the danger of combining clerical and sales workers into a single "lower white-collar" classification for purposes of political research.

Two manual occupations, craftsmen-foremen and laborers, show deviations below the regression line in all but one of the surveys. These occupations are more Democratic than expected on the basis of status and region. One possible explanation is unionization. Workers in these occupations who belong to major industrial or craft unions may be more disposed to support the Democratic party and may thus deflect the group as a whole from the expected value for party identification. The other occupational groups—professionals, business-managerial, and operatives—do not display a consistent pattern to explain the discrepancies between observed and expected party identification. Sometimes above and sometimes below the multiple regression line, these deviations are probably best interpreted as random fluctuations around the prediction of party from status and region.

The picture emerging from the status analysis of occupational relationship to party identification is more complex than the class analysis of the preceding sections. The positive slopes to the regression analysis indicate that as prestige rises, Republicanism increases, on the average. But important discrepancies exist, some of which can be interpreted on the basis of occupational group characteristics, while others await further clarification from future research. Each economic class is internally differentiated politically. Some groups at the same prestige levels, such as clerical and sales workers, have distinctly different political profiles. Sharp breaks do not exist between the manual and nonmanual occupations. In some years craftsmen, operatives, or service workers are as Republican or more Republican than clerical and sales personnel. The existence of a status continuum with gradated political effects and the diversity of occupational interests within each economic class may contribute to the blurring of a distinctive class politics in the United States. Another factor which may cut across the economic interests of occupational groups is the subjective class identifications of manual and nonmanual workers.

Subjective Social Class

Class identification must be distinguished from class-consciousness when dealing with the political consequences of subjective class stratification in the United States. Class identification refers to subjective perception of one's location in a stratification system, while class-consciousness refers to a series of effects growing out of class identification, such as hostility toward other classes and organization for political action on behalf of one's own class. The research tradition in the United States, beginning with Centers' pioneering study (1949), emphasizes class identification while generally failing to find much evidence of class-consciousness.

Centers conceptualized class as a "psychological phenomenon in the fullest sence of the word. That is, a man's class is part of his ego, a feeling on his part of his belongingness to something: an identification with something larger than himself." He premised his inquiry into the nature of class identification on an "interest group theory" of social classes:

This theory implies that a person's status and role with respect to the economic processes of society imposes upon him certain attitudes, values, and interests relating to his role and status in the political and economic sphere. It holds, further, that the status and role of the individual in relation to the means of production and exchange of goods and service gives rise in him to a consciousness of membership in some social class which shares those attitudes, values and interests (p. 28).

Centers demonstrated that respondents in his samples believed that each class had distinctive occupational strata as members and that a respondent's present occupation was systematically related to self-identification with one of the classes (primarily "middle" and "working"). Manual occupations predominated in the working-class and nonmanual jobs in the middle-class identifications. Centers' findings—an insignificant nonresponse rate to a force-choice question, a majority claiming working-class membership, and the covariation of subjective class and occupation—have proved stable and replicable over the past two decades.

Wilensky (1966), in a review of the literature, suggested that the objective conditions of social stratification have converged greatly between classes, while internal differentiation of major strata has proceeded apace. As a result, the Marxist concept of class-consciousness, with its notions of class militancy and political action, would be inapplicable to the American context. An empirical analysis by Hodge and Treiman (1968) found that while occupation was more important than income and education in explaining respondents' subjective class identifications, the three stratification measures together accounted for only a fifth of the variation in their measure. They concluded: "Education, income and occupation do not cumulate in a manner conducive to the formation of well-defined, objective class structure around which class identifications can be unambiguously formed. . . . The failure of class consciousness to crystalize *uniquely* around objective measure of socioeconomic status is, therefore, partially engendered by the loose associations between such objective measures." With the addition of a variable for status of social contacts, the proportion of explained variance increased somewhat. Hodge and Treiman suggested that the interest group theory of classes is defective in its neglect of the "great range of between-class contacts" which prevent consolidation of class identities around political issues (see also Jackman and Jackman, 1973).

Since subjective class identification bears only a moderate relation to so-called objective stratification measures, it is likely to have some independent impact upon political party preferences. The higher one's subjective class placement, the more likely one is to be a Republican in partisanship and voting behavior. The more interesting relationships concern the joint effect of subjective class and occupational group membership. If manual-nonmanual occupation is taken as a measure of "true" class interests, then a small but significant proportion of each class "mis-identifies" its subjective location. Centers (1949, p. 126) hypothesized that such persons "should differ in attitudes or politico-economic orientation, i.e., in conservatism-radicalism, from the 'members' of their own occupational stratum and differ in the direction characteristic of the classes with which they identify themselves." Subsequent research has tended to support Centers' hypothesis. With "objective" stratification variables held constant, middle-class identifiers have tended to be more Republican than working-class identifiers (Cooper, 1959; Eulau, 1962).

The questions to be investigated in this section are the extent to which "objective" class (manual-nonmanual occupation) and subjective class identification jointly and separately account for variation in party preferences. The Survey Research Center has asked a standard question in each presidential survey since 1952: "There's quite a bit of talk these days about different social classes. Most people say they belong either to the middle class or working class. Do you think of yourself as being in one of these classes?" Those answering yes are asked which one. Those answering no, about a quarter to a third of the sample, are asked to pick one of the classes anyway. Altogether, more than 95 percent of the respondents designate a subjective class. The handful of persons insisting on calling themselves upper or lower class were incorporated into the middle- and working-class categories, respectively.

Table 4.6 shows the breakdown of three-category party identification by subjective class identification (K), occupational class (C), region (S), and year (T) for white men twenty-one to sixty-five years old. In general, at any given level of occupation and region, the subjectively middle-class men are less likely to be Democratic and more likely to be Republican than are those who identified themselves as working class. The percentage Democratic is higher among middle-class manual workers than among middle-class non-manuals in each year outside the South, but the pattern is less clear-cut in the South, where in half the years the nonmanual middle-class men were equally or more Democratic than their manual counterparts. Among working-class identifiers, consistent political differences do not occur in either region. Farmers are too few in some years to discern a reliable pattern.

A log-linear analysis of the data in Table 4.6 cuts through the minor fluctuations to organize the data in a relatively simple model. The baseline model hypothesizes that party identification is related to region and time but not to occupational class or subjective class. This model, (CKST)(SPT), has 120 degrees of freedom but gives an unacceptable chi-square of 269.1, as the tests in Table 4.7 show. Models 2 through 5 test for the additive and interactive effects of occupational class and subjective class on party. Both additive effects are significant, but a comparison of chi-square differences between models four and five shows that the interaction (CKP) is not significant. Hence, both occupational class and subjective class exerted independent net effects on party identification of approximately equal magnitude.

Models six through ten assess whether either stratification variable interacts with region or time in its effect upon party identification. Both region marginals, (KSP) and (CSP), significantly reduce the chi-square in model five relative to the degrees of freedom, but neither interaction involving year (T) offers an improvement. Thus model ten, which includes both terms involving interactions with region, provides the most parsimonious fit to the data (Chi-square = 100.6, d.f. = 108). The association between occupational class and party identification and between subjective class and party varies between regions but is constant over time. To conserve space the effect parameters are not presented. They show that the subjectively middle class tend to be more Republican in the non-South than in the South (KSP). Nonmanual workers are more Republican and less Democratic outside the South, while manual workers are somewhat less Independent in the non-South than in the South (CSP).

Stratification and Party

Occupational and subjective class membership are not the only measures of stratification position in industrial society. The achievement process should also take into account educational attainments and income earnings. Many researchers previously constructed composite measures of "socioeconomic status" (SES) by summing values across a number of objective and subjective indicators of social stratification. More recently, however, some researchers pointed out that variables such as education, occupation, income, and subjective class are not merely imperfect indicators of an underlying unitary SES but are important causal factors in the achievement process (Duncan et al., 1972). When a composite SES index is used as an

TABLE 4.6.   PARTY IDENTIFICATION BY CLASS, SUBJECTIVE CLASS, AND
             REGION, FOR WHITE MEN, 21 TO 65 YEARS, 1952-1972

REGION (S), CLASS (C) SUBJECTIVE CLASS (K)	YEAR					
	1952	1956	1960	1964	1968	1972
NON-SOUTH						
Nonmanual Middle						
Democrat	21.9	21.4	17.0	34.8	24.1	23.1
Independent	30.7	36.6	34.9	29.6	36.6	42.2
Republican	47.4	42.0	48.1	35.7	39.3	34.7
(N)	(114)	(112)	(106)	(115)	(112)	(199)
Nonmanual Working						
Democrat	39.3	42.0	27.5	50.9	42.9	27.8
Independent	37.3	38.0	37.3	30.2	26.2	45.6
Republican	23.0	20.0	35.3	18.9	31.0	26.7
(N)	(61)	(50)	(51)	(53)	(42)	(90)
Manual Middle						
Democrat	45.0	32.7	28.6	44.7	43.2	31.6
Independent	20.0	38.8	28.6	34.0	37.8	53.2
Republican	35.0	28.6	42.9	21.3	18.9	15.2
(N)	(40)	(49)	(28)	(47)	(37)	(79)
Manual Working						
Democrat	54.1	41.6	46.5	53.8	41.0	35.7
Independent	28.6	32.4	34.1	30.3	34.2	46.4
Republican	17.3	25.9	19.4	15.9	24.8	17.9
(N)	(196)	(185)	(217)	(145)	(117)	(196)
Farm Middle						
Democrat	35.0	25.0	23.1	0	28.6	0
Independent	30.0	33.3	15.4	33.3	14.3	33.3
Republican	35.0	41.7	61.5	66.7	57.1	66.7
(N)	(20)	(12)	(13)	(3)	(7)	(3)
Farm Working						
Democrat	31.4	31.8	33.3	75.0	36.4	43.8
Independent	42.9	36.4	42.9	8.3	27.3	25.0
Republican	25.7	31.8	23.8	16.7	36.4	31.3
(N)	(35)	(22)	(21)	(12)	(11)	(16)

independent variable, it frequently has different relationships among its
components to various dependent variables (Hodge and Siegel, 1968;
Hodge, 1970). The relationship of the four stratification measures to party
identification may vary considerably over the twenty years. Thus rather than
construct a single index value to correlate with party preferences, the
separate variables are entered into a multiple regression equation, and the
linear additive effects are estimated from the resulting coefficients. The
analysis in this section does not control for all additional independent
variables known to influence party choice. In effect, the present analysis

TABLE 4.6.   Continued

REGION (S), CLASS (C)	YEAR					
SUBJECTIVE CLASS (K)	1952	1956	1960	1964	1968	1972
SOUTH						
Nonmanual Middle						
Democrat	63.6	63.6	51.1	51.3	37.8	41.7
Independent	27.3	25.0	26.7	25.6	43.2	33.3
Republican	9.1	11.4	22.2	23.1	18.9	25.0
(N)	(22)	(44)	(45)	(39)	(37)	(72)
Nonmanual Working						
Democrat	78.3	87.5	80.8	62.5	45.5	34.2
Independent	21.7	6.3	11.5	16.7	45.5	36.8
Republican	0	6.3	7.7	20.8	9.1	28.9
(N)	(23)	(16)	(26)	(24)	(22)	(38)
Manual Middle						
Democrat	53.3	64.7	71.4	64.7	28.6	41.2
Independent	20.0	11.8	14.3	29.4	71.4	47.1
Republican	26.7	23.5	14.3	5.9	0	11.8
(N)	(15)	(17)	(14)	(17)	(7)	(34)
Manual Working						
Democrat	73.5	72.0	73.9	73.0	51.1	48.6
Independent	16.3	20.0	15.9	13.5	35.6	39.3
Republican	10.2	8.0	10.1	13.5	13.3	12.1
(N)	(49)	(50)	(69)	(37)	(45)	(107)
Farm Middle						
Democrat	83.3	75.0	0	50.0	0	100.0
Independent	16.7	25.0	0	25.0	100.0	0
Republican	0	0	100.0	25.0	0	0
(N)	(6)	(4)	(4)	(4)	(2)	(1)
Farm Working						
Democrat	66.7	69.2	32.0	80.0	62.5	55.6
Independent	0	0	16.0	0	12.5	22.2
Republican	33.3	30.8	52.0	20.0	25.0	22.2
(N)	(12)	(13)	(25)	(10)	(8)	(9)

estimates the "zero-order" effect of stratification on party identification and the partials among the four stratification variables controlling for each other's effects. Occupation was measured as the average SEI for the ten occupational groups. Subjective class was a four-point scale with "lower class" scored as 1, "working class" as 2, "middle class" as 3, and "upper class" as 4. Education was the number of years of formal schooling of the respondent. Income was the reported or expected total annual income of the family unit, coded to the nearest $1,000, using the midpoint of the income intervals supplied in the original codes.

TABLE 4.7.   LOG-LINEAR MODELS FOR PARTY IDENTIFICATION, OCCUPA-
             TIONAL CLASS, SUBJECTIVE CLASS, AND REGION, FOR
             WHITE MEN, 21 TO 65 YEARS, 1952-1972

MODEL	FITTED MARGINALS			df	χ^2
1.	(CKST) (SPT)			120	269.1
2.	(CKST) (SPT) (CP)			116	163.6
3.	(CKST) (SPT) (KP)			118	171.7
4.	(CKST) (SPT) (CKP)			110	116.5
5.	(CKST) (SPT) (CP)	(KP)		114	119.1
6.	(CKST) (SPT) (CP)	(KSP)		112	112.2
7.	(CKST) (SPT) (KP)	(CSP)		110	104.1
8.	(CKST) (SPT) (KP)	(CPT)		94	94.3
9.	(CKST) (SPT) (CP)	(KPT)		104	107.3
10.	(CKST) (SPT) (CSP)	(KSP)		108	100.6

Table 4.8 contains both the standardized and unstandardized regression coefficients, as well as the multiple R^2. Although each of the four stratification variables correlates positively on the zero order with party identification in each year, once the effects of the other three variables are held constant, a few of the coefficients are shown to have negative signs. However, none of these parameters exceeds twice its standard error, indicating that the confidence interval for these coefficients includes the zero slope. All of the stratification variables are significant only in 1952, using the criterion that the b exceed twice its standard error. However, income and subjective class are significant in five surveys. In each case, the higher the family income and the higher the respondent's subjective class, net of the other variables, the more likely the respondent is to be a Republican.

If we accept Converse's (1958) conclusion that class polarization was higher in the years immediately after World War II than in the 1950's, it appears that the impact of occupational status on party preferences hit a low point in the late 1950's and early 1960's but resurged in 1968 and 1972. The high value of the class partisanship index for 1964 found in Table 4.1 seems to have been a spurious consequence of subjective class, income, and education. As the coefficients for the regression analysis in Table 4.8 show, once these three stratification variables are controlled, the effect of occupation in 1964 is essentially nil.

Respondent's education does not appear to have much of an independent effect upon party identification. Only in 1952 and 1964 do its regression coefficients exceed twice their standard errors. In these instances, the higher the respondent's formal education, the more likely he is to be Republican. As will be elaborated in the next chapter, education is the most temporally antecedent of the four stratification variables, and most of its impact upon partisanship is likely to be indirect, through its causal effects upon the other status attainment variables.

The multiple R^2's indicate the proportion of variance in men's party identifications which can be attributed to the additive effects of the four stratification variables. In no year does the total of explained variance approach 10 percent, and in four of the six periods it is below 5 percent. Judged by this criterion, objective and subjective social stratification do not have the importance that is frequently attributed to them by class conflict

TABLE 4.8. STANDARDIZED AND UNSTANDARDIZED REGRESSION COEFFICIENTS FOR PREDICTION OF PARTY IDENTIFICATION FROM OCCUPATION, INCOME, EDUCATION, AND SUBJECTIVE CLASS, FOR WHITE MEN, 21 TO 65 YEARS, 1952-1972

INDEPENDENT VARIABLES	YEAR					
	1952	1956	1960	1964	1968	1972
Unstandardized b's						
Occupation	.003*	.002	-.002	-.0001	.007*	.006*
Income	.03*	.05*	.03*	.02*	-.005	.02*
Education	.032*	-.006	.014	.064*	.024	.014
Subjective Class	.449*	.205*	.426*	.358*	.223*	.011
Standardized β's						
Occupation	.049	.037	-.028	-.002	.119	.111
Income	.055	.107	.091	.074	-.001	.104
Education	.075	-.015	.036	.166	.063	.037
Subjective Class	.175	.074	.149	.134	.090	.004
Multiple R^2	.0748	.0285	.0435	.0881	.0496	.0399

*Coefficients at least twice their standard errors

theory. The comparison of religion and stratification in Chapter II pointed
out that the denominational memberships of individuals was generally more
important for party preferences than the three objective SES measures
considered jointly. The relationship of occupation, education, income, and
subjective class to party identification is not permanently fixed, however.
The period under consideration in the present study was not characterized
by any great economic crises, although at least three recessions intervened
for several months. Given the secular trend of growing GNP and rising
consumer prosperity, the low correlations of occupation and other SES
indicators with party identification is understandable. The real test of the
economic self-interest thesis must await the occurrence of a major economic
upheaval which would bring class and economic relationships to the
forefront of the political agenda. The present chapter establishes a baseline
against which such future change may be measured.

Summary

Socioeconomic differences play a relatively minor role in structuring
political party affiliations in postwar America. Among white men in the
labor force, manual-nonmanual differentials in support of the Democratic
party fluctuated between 10 and 20 percent throughout most of the period.
In the South, some evidence exists that class polarization was not present
during the Eisenhower period but emerged from 1960 on, with levels
approaching that of men outside the South. The economic welfare component of partisan attitudes has been clearly diminishing since 1952, with the
gap between manual and nonmanual workers likewise shrinking. Much of
the decline in the Democratic party advantage has occurred among the
party's main constituency, manual workers. The impact of "good times" and
the abating stigmatization of the Republican party during the Great
Depression are important factors in the erosion of class differentials in
economic partisan attitudes.

The analysis of occupational status effects on party identification revealed
several interesting departures from a linear relationship. Sales workers and
clerical workers have the same occupational prestige, yet the former tend to
be more Republican in preference and the latter more Democratic than
would be predicted on the basis of prestige alone. Farmers tend to be more
Republican and craftsmen-foremen more Democratic than the linear regression predicts. These relationships suggest more complicated effects of social
status of occupational groups upon political preference than the simple
manual-nonmanual classification.

Subjective class identification and occupational class both have independent effects on party affiliation, conditional upon region of residence but
constant over time. When four measures of socioeconomic stratification

were considered simultaneously, all were important predictors of party identification only in 1952. Subjective class and income had significant net effects more often than occupational status or education. The total additive effect of stratification variables rarely exceeded 5 percent of the variance in party identification during the two decades. These findings taken together suggest that stratification position is not a major determinant of the political party affiliations of white men of prime working age. Whatever latent potential for class conflict may exist in the United States, it seems to require the stimulus of economic upheaval in order to be mobilized.

Chapter V

A Causal Model of Party Identification

The analysis of party identification to this point has taken the form of separate investigations of the major ascribed and achieved social groups, controlling at most for one or two other variables, to determine the effect of membership in these groups on party identification. This chapter integrates the findings from the previous chapters into a coherent causal model. The crucial assumption that party preferences are largely socialized in the family of origin is investigated. A multivariate causal technique, path analysis, is used to construct and estimate parameters of a causal model which is replicated for each survey in the twenty-year series. The analysis includes adjustments of the data for measurement error.

Previous Causal Research

Despite the recent proliferation of path analysis and other multivariate causal techniques in other substantive areas of sociology, particularly stratification, political sociologists were slow to apply these methods to their own work. Previous causal analysis of party identification, in fact, is largely the work of two authors. The present analysis undertakes clarification and elaboration of these earlier efforts and will replicate them across all six surveys.

Goldberg's (1966) series of models of voting behavior used the so-called Simon-Blalock method of partial correlation to deduce the direct and indirect effects of social characteristics, party identification, and partisan attitudes on the 1956 presidential vote. After fitting several models to the data, he selected a final one that he felt best fit the data (his model IV). The portion of the model which most concerns the present research is the causal effect of respondents' and fathers' social characteristics and fathers' party identifications upon the party preferences of the respondent. Except for a small effect of social background on partisan attitudes (which Goldberg tentatively attributed to transmission of parental status aspirations to the offspring), the effects of these variables on the vote are all indirect, operating through their effects on respondents' party identifications. Party preference is thus the "pivotal encapsulator" of social background and political socialization. Social origins have no direct impact on party preferences, but have an impact primarily through fathers' party identification. The strong partial coefficient of the path from fathers' to respondents' party identification reveals the great importance of political socialization in the adolescent home, a point developed later in the present research.

Recently, Schulman and Pomper (1975), replicated Goldberg's study with the 1956, 1964, and 1972 SRC surveys. While their main focus was also upon the causes of presidential voting, their models all show that the impact of father's party identification is larger than that of respondent's social characteristics on the respondent's party identification. As in the original study, social origins have no direct effect on a respondent's party preferences.

Goldberg's pioneering study had a number of shortcomings as a plausible model of party identification formation. He restricted his estimation of parameters to a subsample of respondents on whom he had complete data on all variables and who held either a Republican or Democratic identification. Since Independent identification has increased in recent years, such restriction would omit a large proportion of the electorate. His measures of respondents' and fathers' social characteristics were single-valued indices built from five original variables: religion, class, community size, region, and race. Index scores were derived from a regression of fathers' or respondents' party identifications against the appropriate social characteristics and calculating the expected value of being a Republican. This procedure obscures the relationships among the social characteristics as well as preventing estimation of their separate contributions to party preferences. On the latter point Sewell Wright (1960) has cautioned for regression analysis: "If one part of a composite variable (such as a total or average) is more significant in one relation and another part in another, the treatment of the variable as if it were a unit may lead to grossly erroneous results."

An extension of Goldberg's model, as well as of several noncausal multivariate analyses of party identification, was undertaken by Knoke (1972) using the 1968 SRC survey for male respondents. Social characteristics were disaggregated into separate variables and entered into a path analysis. Since the analyses to be presented below are similar to earlier work, the results from Knoke's study are not presented here in detail. The basic finding was that father's and mother's party identifications had the strongest direct path to respondent's partisanship. As in the Goldberg model, none of the social origin characteristics, such as father's occupation or the family's social class, had direct paths to the party preference of the son. The respondent's own social class and occupation and his ethnoreligious group all had direct causal paths to party, but region of residence and size of community did not. Apparently, regional effects disappeared once the direct socialization of a party choice was taken into account through the party identifications of the parents. The measure of "ethnoreligion" was a set of dummy variables which combined religion and race, thus precluding a separate estimation of the contribution of these two ascriptive variables. Also, while all party preferences were included in the dependent variable, the restriction of the sample to males limited the generalizability of findings. These shortcomings will be rectified in the following analyses. More recent extensions of Knoke's basic model can be found in Knoke (1974c) and Knoke and Hout (1974).

Political Socialization

Chapter I drew attention to the centrality of childhood and adolescent political socialization in the traditional model of party identification. This section spells out that relationship in greater detail. In a major inventory of the literature, Hyman (1959, p. 69) wrote, "Foremost among agencies of socialization into politics is the family." Independent measurements and comparisons of children's and parent's political views implied that the family was more important than school, peers, and community in establishing early and lasting political orientations. Party identification seems to be socialized in its most complete form before adulthood. Hyman reviewed empirical studies in which parent-child agreements on party choice, whether measured directly on both or by children's reports on parents, are all positive and mostly in the 50 to 80 percent range. Subsequent researchers have established the acquisition of a definite party choice in children by the late elementary school years (Hess and Torney, 1967; Greenstein, 1965b). The authors of *The American Voter* stand in general agreement with this perspective on early familial transmission of party identification. They presented data to support the further contention that early strong party attachment, "once established, is an attachment which is not easily changed" (Campbell et al., 1960, p. 149). But a recent panel study found sizable change in party identification over six months in a sample of San Francisco Bay Area grade school children, indicating some instability at this age (Vaillancourt and Niemi, 1974).

Childhood party affiliation, like the adult variety, appears to be relatively innocent of ideological connotations: "The logically congruent area of ideology is less differentiated, suggesting that party loyalty, because of the greater simplicity of symbols involved or because of greater direct indoctrination or the lesser range of alternatives available, is more readily transmitted in the course of socialization" (Hyman, 1959, p. 49).

Explanations of the transmission process tend to stress psychological concepts such as emotional and affective bonds between parent and child. As mentioned in Chapter I, Hess and Torney (1965, pp. 23, 110) call this the "Identification Model," in which emulation of adult role models occurs without requiring a conscious attempt by adults to persuade the child to adopt a point of view. Children presumably acquire their party affiliation from their parents without having prior ability to differentiate between the parties on ideological grounds. Initial associations of the parties are with candidates' personalities. Only near the end of elementary school do issue-specific differences between the parties begin to be salient. Even then, party choice is not accompanied by consistency of beliefs about what positions the party will take on given issues—findings similar to those on adults (Converse, 1964, 1970).

If the party label and attachments tend to precede cognitive understanding of the party system, party identifications must serve principally to order the child's political world while he acquires greater sophistication. With the initial socialization of a party preference occuring mainly on a symbolic, affective level, the psychological costs of later changing affiliations are much greater than those of continuing to process and filter political information to fit the preconceived framework. Thus intergenerational transmission of party affiliation is a case of new ideological wine in old party-label bottles: party preferences are established early and tend to persist despite wide subsequent diversity of partisans' positions on issues, many of which may go unrepresented in the councils of the party. Childhood and adolescent party socialization are in part responsible for the widely noted heterogeneity of political attitudes among adherents of each of the major parties.

Though the foregoing might give an impression of lockstep partisan indoctrination of children by parents with no possibility of political deviation, recent work has demonstrated structural sources of partisan disagreement within the nuclear family. The degree to which children take on the party identifications of the family of orientation varies with the degree of agreement between parents. The greater the disagreement between mother and father on party preferences, the more likely the children are to differ among themselves and to be Independents rather than partisans of one of the major parties. When parents are split between the parties, the mother seems to have slightly greater influence on the party choices of her children (see Jennings and Niemi, 1968, 1974; Langton and Jennings, 1969; and Goldberg, 1969).

Influence of Father's Party

The SRC surveys do not contain independent evidence on the partisan composition of the respondent's home while growing up, but all surveys except those of 1956 and 1960 contain retrospective reports by respondents. Individuals were asked whether their fathers and mothers had any interest in politics and, if so, the party with which they identified. The correlation of reported father's and mother's party identifications exceeds .80, indicating either substantial agreement within the family of origin or, at least, respondents' recollection of such political harmony. This multicollinearity, however, renders estimates of the net contribution of each variable in a regression analysis highly unstable (see Gordon, 1968). Since high multicollinearity between the two parental party measures prevents effective separation of the effects of mother and father on offspring's party identification, the following analyses use only the father's reported party preference. (The question of reliability of retrospective reports of fathers' party identifications will be taken up in the following sections).

Correlations of father's with respondent's party in each of the four samples in which the question was asked showed no systematic variation. The average correlation was about .48 between the three major categories, and the individual correlations differed by less than ±.02 around the average r. In Table 5.1, therefore, the responses have been aggregated across all four samples. About one-fifth of respondents were excluded for not knowing their father's party preference, but these missing cases were not related to respondent's own partisanship.

The distribution of fathers' party preferences in the row totals of Table 5.1 does not represent the identifications of any real population or cohort of fathers at some specific time in the past. The fathers represented by these reports of their offspring are a heterogeneous lot. Fathers who had many

TABLE 5.1. RESPONDENT'S PARTY IDENTIFICATIONS BY RECALLED FATHER'S
            PARTY IDENTIFICATIONS, 1952, 1964, 1968, AND 1972
            SURVEYS COMBINED

FATHER'S PARTY	RESPONDENT'S PARTY			Total (N)
	Democrat	Independent	Republican	
Democrat	64.4	23.7	11.9	100.0% (3626)
Independent	25.1	57.3	17.6	100.0% (431)
Republican	18.6	25.4	55.9	100.0% (1969)
Total	46.6 (2810)	26.7 (1608)	26.7 (1608)	100.0% (6026)

offspring are over-represented in the data, while men who had no surviving children are not represented at all. Several generations are potentially present as both parents and offspring. Men who died while their children were young or who concealed their political preferences from their offspring would have been placed in the "don't know" response category and omitted from the cross-tabulation. This inability to represent the distribution of fathers' party identifications faithfully with data of this nature prevents treatment of the estimates in Table 5.1 as a transition matrix of intergenerational party change, for use in a Markov process model. (However, this logical difficulty does not apply to intragenerational change, which is treated in Chapter VI.) For a fuller discussion of the problem as it applies to intergenerational mobility, see Duncan (1966).

A majority of persons in Table 5.1 reported retaining the broad party preference of their father or father-substitute, although the rates of defection differ across paternal partisan persuasion. Democratic fathers were apparently slightly more successful in socializing a partisanship which is retained into adulthood than were Republicans, who had 10 percent fewer children retain the family political tradition. The most likely destination of defectors was not the opposition party but political independence. About a quarter of the children from Democratic and Republican households became Independents, leading to the substantial increase in this category from about 7 percent among the recalled fathers to 26.7 percent of all respondents. When complete conversion from the father's party to the opposite party is considered, the net rates of defection clearly favor the Democrats (gaining 18.6 percent of Republican offspring) over the Republicans (gaining only 11.9 percent of Democratic sons and daughters).

The gross rates of defection are somewhat misleading. According to the column marginals in Table 5.1, there are substantially more respondents from Democratic than from Republican backgrounds. When these differences in partisan origins of the population are taken into account, the differential rates of conversion of loyalties translate into an opposite pattern of gains and losses in actual *numbers* of partisans. In the data for these four samples, 432 respondents with Democratic fathers became Republicans, but only 366 respondents with Republican fathers converted to the Democratic party. Thus, despite the higher rate of retention and lower defection among Democratic households, the net balance of exchange between parties slightly favors the Republican party. This pattern of differential rates and frequencies was also found in Jennings and Niemi's (1974, p. 41) study of adolescents and their parents.

Conversions across the party spectrum are relatively rare. Democrat-to-Republican and Republican-to-Democrat switches account for only a third of all intergenerational party differences. The bulk of party changes are from partisanship to an Independent preference, and vice versa. As noted above, the net change has been an increase in Independent party preference. Of course, many of those who proclaim themselves Independent on the first question in the party identification measure are persuaded on the probe to say that they are closer to one of the major parties than to the other. When Independents close to the Democratic party or to the Republican party are included in the measure of intergenerational party inheritance, the rate of retention for Democrats rises to about 75 percent, and for Republicans, to about 67 percent. Among those with Independent fathers, only 25 percent prefer an Independent position unbiased by leanings towards either major party. When broken down by individual surveys, the rates of defection appear the same among those from partisan backgrounds, but among those with Independent fathers, the percentage holding a strict Independent preference rises from 14 percent in 1952 to 30 percent in 1968 and 1972. The rise in this preference thus appears to be due in part to more successful socialization of that preference among children from nonpartisan families.

Although intergenerational transmission of party identification is an important process in the expressed loyalties of Americans, sufficient change occurs between generations to implicate other factors in the formation of party affiliations. Many of these social group factors were investigated individually in preceding chapters. These variables now will be brought together with the retrospective paternal party in a multivariate causal analysis. The next section explores these variables and presents a method to correct for measurement error.

Measurement Error

Variables which will be used in the causal models estimated below are characteristics of both the respondents and their fathers. That errors are likely to be made when proxy reports of fathers' occupations or party preferences are obtained would seem self-evident, but errors may also occur in the respondent's reports of his or her own characteristics and attitudes. Such errors of measurement are usually ignored, as was the case in the analyses in previous chapters. Errors are often presumed to exist and to affect the standard deviations of the variables, and hence the estimates of significant relationships, but they are not presumed to have much effect on the estimates of regression slopes. In this chapter an alternative course is pursued with regard to measurement error.

Since the basis of multivariate causal analysis is the matrix of linear correlations between pairs of variables in the model, adjustments are made on these correlations to correct for the presence of random measurement error. One of the best short treatments of the measurement error problem is found in Appendix B of Jencks et al. (1972, pp. 330–36). Jencks pointed out that sources of error need not be random but can arise from systematic biases in the measurement process. His solution was to calculate values for path models based on both the uncorrected correlation matrices and the matrices adjusted for random error and to compare the results. For data on intergenerational occupational mobility, he found that "The differences do not seem large enough to warrant serious concern." A similar conclusion was reached in the present study.

To make such corrections for attenuation of the correlation coefficients due to random error, estimates of the reliability of each of the variables as measured in the SRC surveys must be obtained. A standard approach to reliabilities is the correlation of one measure of a variable with the same measure on the same set of respondents in an immediately subsequent point in time. This method is the familiar "test-retest" correlation used for the reliabilities of many psychological scales.

One difficulty encountered in using the zero-order correlation between two measures of the same variable over time is the possibility that real change in the values has occurred. Heise (1969a) showed how the problem of separating reliability from stability in the test-retest correlation could be resolved by using three serial measures. The formula for reliability is

$$r_{xx} = \frac{r_{12} \, r_{23}}{r_{13}}$$

where r_{xx} is the reliability coefficient and where the subscripts of the other correlations refer to the point in time at which measurements occurred.

One difficulty in making practical use of this method to obtain estimates of reliabilities is that relatively few bodies of data contain three-wave panels with repeated measurement of variables. In many instances the present study borrows reliabilities from other research which calculated simple test-retest correlations.

To adjust an observed correlation between two variables for attenuation due to random measurement error, it is divided by the geometric mean of the reliabilities of the two variables (i.e., the square root of the product of the two reliabilities). Unless both reliabilities are perfect ($r = 1.0$), the adjustment will increase the size of the observed bivariate correlations. The more error in the observed variable, the lower will be its estimated reliability and, hence, the larger will be the increase in the corrected correlation when compared to adjustments of correlations based on more reliable measures. For an illustration of the use of an adjusted correlation matrix in causal analysis, see Kelley (1973).

The sources of information on the reliabilities used in the present analysis are either published reports or, where it was possible to obtain them, estimates based directly on the SRC surveys. The following set of variables were used in the causal analysis, including a description of their measurement and a report on the reliability coefficient used in making adjustments.

Respondents' party identifications were measured in the standard five-point scale, from Democrat to Republican, with Independents in the middle. Two estimates of the reliability of this self-placement measure are available, although both draw upon the same SRC data used in the present analysis. In the 1960 survey, respondents were asked the party identification question in both the pre-election and the post-election interviews. These panels were separated by from six weeks to two months, although the intervention of the 1960 presidential election and its outcome may have generated some real changes in party preferences. However, the correlation of the two five-point scales is +.90, suggesting that both the stability of the item over this short span and its reliability are quite high, certainly much higher than the typical test-retest correlations of other political attitudes (Converse, 1970).

The second source for the estimated reliability of self-reported party identification is a national panel study of respondents in the 1956, 1958, and 1960 SRC political surveys. The correlations of the party scale between these three points in time permit a separation of stability from reliability, using the formula presented by Heise. The estimate is +.84, which is reasonably close to the value estimated from the 1960 survey mentioned above. Since the estimate from 1956 to 1960 covers a longer time period than the usual test-retest procedure, we have decided to use the higher of the two values as the reliability.

The reliability of respondents' recall of their fathers' party identification is less readily ascertained. Since the SRC measure asked only for the three broad designations and not for relative strengths within each party, only correct imputation with these categories is required for perfect reliability. Probably the best set of national survey data on parent-child party identification employing the SRC version of the question is the study of high-school seniors conducted in 1965 by the SRC (Jennings and Niemi, 1968). Although the sampled population is biased in favor of those 74 percent of students still in school by the 12th grade, the study did obtain direct reports of party affiliation from the parents, rather than simply rely upon children's reports. Goldberg (1969) reported that 78 percent of the students correctly identified their fathers as being within the three broad categories of Democrat, Independent, and Republican. The 22 percent incorrect ascriptions were split about evenly between incorrect assignment of the father to the Independent category and incorrect partisanship. The data reported in Niemi (1973) allow calculation of a correlation of +.66 between parents' and offspring's reports of the parents' party identification.

There are probably an equal number of good reasons for expecting the value of the correlation for adult children's reports of their father's partisanship to be higher or lower than this value. Adults are further removed in time and space from their parents than are high-school students, while those respondents whose parents are still alive may be inclined to report their father's *current* party identification, rather than the one held by the father while the respondent was growing up, as requested by the interviewer. The absence of high-school and grade-school dropouts in the Jennings study may have resulted in a higher parent-child agreement on the father's party, because the disproportionate dropout rate among lower SES students may remove a sizable part of the population having less awareness of the parents' political attitudes. In the absence of direct evidence on the agreement of adults' reports with the true values of paternal partisanship, the reliability used in the study was +.70. This is less than the reliability for respondents' reports of their own party but somewhat greater than the value from the study of adolescents.

To illustrate how the correction for attenuation of correlation due to random measurement affects the observed correlations, we take the typical observed correlation between respondent's and the reported father's party identification, $r = +.48$. With the two reliabilities of .90 and .70, respectively, the new correlation will be $r = (.48)/[(.90)(.70)]^{1/2} = +.60$. This is a substantial rise in the correlation coefficient, amounting to an increase in jointly shared variance from 23 percent to 36 percent. Yet, interestingly, the corrected value of the father-offspring correlation in party identifications is identical to that reported between the high-school students and their parents: +.59 (Jennings and Niemi, 1968). Thus the correction for attenuation does not lead, in the present instance, to an unreasonable estimate of the true correlation.

Reliability estimates for the "objective" measures of stratification—occupation, education, and income—do not require such tortuous derivations. Previous research by students of stratification has produced reliability estimates for these variables. The classic paper in this area, by Siegel and Hodge (1968), uses the reports of the Current Population Survey and Post Enumeration Survey of 1960 as the standard of accuracy against which reports to the 1960 census are to be judged. They find the following reliability coefficients: occupation scored on the Duncan SEI scale, .861; education in years of formal schooling, .933; and annual income, .852. A coefficient of .718 for adult sons' reports of fathers' occupations was reported in Featherman and Hauser (1973). These values were used in the present study.

Two measures of subjective social class identification, for the respondent and for the respondent's family while he or she was growing up, are used in the causal analyses below. No evidence yet exists on the reliabilities of these self-reported or retrospective items. In lieu of such evidence, the reliabilities for subjective class were surmised to be very similar to those for party identification; therefore, the study used a reliability of .90 for self-reported subjective class and of .70 for the report of family of orientation's subjective class. Since the typical unadjusted correlation of these two variables is about

.45, the effect of correction for error raises the correlation to about .58, or about as strong as the intergenerational party identification agreement.

The final three variables in the model—religion, race, and region of residence—would appear to involve little or no measurement error in self-report or the coding of interviewers. Reliabilities are likely to be so close to 1.00 that adjustment will not significantly affect the observed correlations. Therefore, lacking independent assessments of reliabilities of these variables, they were all assigned reliabilities of .99.

The Basic Model

The determination of direct and indirect effects of the causal variables upon party identification depends upon the temporal ordering among the ten independent variables. Figure 5.1 exhibits a basic causal model to be examined for each of the six surveys. The model draws heavily upon the previous work by Knoke (1972) and the sources cited therein. Six "exogenous" variables are considered to be prior in time to the others but not analyzable in terms of their causal sequence. Two are characteristics of the social stratification position of the family of origin: the father's occupation and the subjective social class of the family. Neither is expected to have any direct impact upon the party identification of the respondent. Rather, they are expected to have causal impact upon intervening social stratification variables of the respondent. Thus the effects of paternal occupation and social class are expected to be indirect. Three other exogenous variables refer to respondents' ascribed characteristics—race, religion, and region of current residence—but since these variables are largely determined at birth and are not subject to modification for most persons, they are conceptualized in the basic model as antecedent to other variables in the model. Obviously, some ascribed statuses, such as regional residence, are more readily modified than others, such as race. However, we do not have adequate variables to represent interregional movement and hence are forced to represent this variable as simply intercorrelated with the other exogenous variables in the model. The sixth predetermined variable is the father's party identification, which was dealt with extensively above.

Four other variables are considered to intervene between the exogenous variables and party identification. These four—education, occupation, income, and subjective social class—all pertain to the position of the respondent and his or her current family in the stratification system and are thus achievement variables. Some of the achievement variables are conceptualized as dependent upon others. The sources for this causal sequence are sociologists of the stratification process (Blau and Duncan, 1967; Duncan et al., 1972; Jencks, 1972). The temporal order of variables is

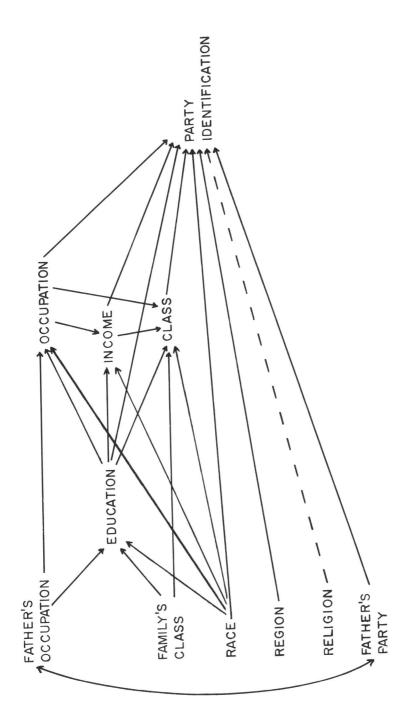

Figure 5.1. Basic Causal Model for Party Identification

helpful in determining the causal sequence. The respondent's education is shown as dependent upon the position of the family of origin as well as upon the ascribed variables of race and region. In turn, education is perhaps the most important factor in later occupational attainment. In the present analysis, the occupational measure is that of the head of the household, which is not the respondent's occupation if she is a currently married woman. In such instances, the causal path from education to occupation represents an assortative mating process by which highly educated women tend to marry high occupational achievers. Education and occupation are conceptualized as causes of family income. These three "objective" stratification indicators all affect the subjective class estimates. Each of the four stratification variables is shown to be influenced by the race of the respondent, indicating that whites will tend to have higher levels of achievement on all four variables than will blacks. Religion is not expected to have significant effects on stratification position once the other relevant causal processes are taken into account.

With the aforenoted exceptions (of father's occupation and class of family of origin), all independent variables are hypothesized to have significant direct effects on the party identification of the respondents in each sample year. These effects are net effects; that is, they are influences remaining after variation on the other independent variables is held constant. To test whether such a hypothesized basic model is realistic, the initial data analysis regressed the dependent variable simultaneously on all ten independent variables (including father's characteristics) and then eliminated those variables from the estimating equation, which did not have significant path coefficients in any year.

Parameter Estimates

A problem was encountered in attempts to estimate parameters for the full regression model, which included father's occupation and family of orientation's social class. The latter variable was so highly intercorrelated with respondent's own subjective social class ($r = .80$) that stable, meaningful coefficients could not be obtained. This problem of multicollinearity (Gordon, 1968) among the independent variables is best overcome by omitting one of the offending variables from the regression equation. Since family of origin's social class was hypothesized on theoretical grounds to have lesser impact than current social class identification, it was dropped from subsequent analysis. Father's occupation was removed from the causal model because it failed to have a significant impact upon the explained variance in respondent's party identification when the other variables were in the estimating equation. Thus, as hypothesized, neither measure of origin

TABLE 5.2.   UNSTANDARDIZED REGRESSION COEFFICIENTS (b's) FOR MULTI-
VARIATE CAUSAL MODEL OF PARTY IDENTIFICATION, 1952-1972

INDEPENDENT VARIABLES	YEAR					
	1952	1956	1960	1964	1968	1972
STRATIFICATION						
Income	.013	.021	.008	.007	.008	.017*
Education	.023*	-.035*	.009	.037*	.033*	.003
Occupation	.004*	.003*	-.002	-.001	.003*	.003*
Social Class	.226*	.329*	.358*	.316*	.040	.044
RELIGION**						
Protestant	.097	.086	.297	.059	.074	.059
Catholic	-.114	-.125	-.261	-.097	-.158	-.073
Jew	-.823	-.579	-.264	-.475	-.667	-.502
Other	-.182	-.637	.049	-.127	-.196	-.206
RACE	.365*	.134	.100	.587*	1.053*	.498*
REGION	-.247*	-.394*	-.244*	-.169*	-.080	.167*
FATHER'S PARTY	.892*	.849*	.846*	.808*	.701*	.855*
CONSTANT	-.323	.015	.431	-.600	-.300	.138
MULTIPLE R^2	.4728	.4199	.4122	.4234	.4161	.4688

*Regression coefficients at least twice their standard errors
**Structural coefficients

stratification position was permitted to have direct effects on party identification in the final causal model.

The unstandardized parameter estimates for the regression of the five-point party identification scale upon the remaining eight causal variables appear in Table 5.2. Not all parameters would be considered statistically significant by the usual criterion that the coefficient exceed twice its standard error (that is, the confidence interval not contain the zero slope). Those values which do exceed this criterion are indicated with asterisks. With unstandardized coefficients, direct comparison of values across the six elections is possible, to indicate trends over time.

The four intervening stratification, or achievement, variables may be considered as a set, as in the preceding chapter. In no year are income, education, occupation, and social class simultaneously statistically significant. Given the common underlying socioeconomic dimension which they measure, the variables must be retained in the model. Interesting comparisons may be made between the coefficients in Table 5.2 and those in Table 4.8, which reported the effect of these four achievement variables alone upon the party preferences of white men. The major difference between the models for white men and those based on samples of the full population is the insignificance of familial income in the latter. Income is an important predictor of white males' partisanship in every year except 1968, but it is significant only in 1972 for the total population. The difference in the importance of income may arise from the inclusion of other control variables in the models for the full population, but it may also have a substantive importance. In families where the male head of the household is the only income-producer, income may not be a relevant causal factor in the political orientations of other members, particularly housewives. Income may be a salient indicator to men of their position in the economy, thereby disposing them toward support of the Democratic party if they have low incomes and toward the Republican party if they are at the higher end of the income scale. But income may be a relatively less important cue to socioeconomic status among nonworking women, thus diminishing the net effect of income on party identification in the total population. The sex differential in the effect of income on party preference is borne out to some extent by inspection of zero-order correlations between income and party identification. In every sample year the correlation is lower among women than among men. While the salience-of-income hypothesis is a possible explanation for differences between Tables 4.8 and 5.2, the finding is clouded by the fact that the only available measure of income was annual income for the entire family unit, rather than for the respondent or principal wage-earner. Until a more careful measurement of the political consequences of personal versus familial income can be made, the implications of the present analysis will remain ambiguous.

The respondent's education and the head of household's occupation are significant causes of party identifications in four of the six election years. In general, the higher the education or socioeconomic status of the job, the more likely the respondent is to be Republican. Curiously, however, in 1956 education has a net negative impact. The observed zero-order correlation of education and party is close to zero in that year ($r = .07$); but when other causal variables are held constant, the direction of the relationship reversed. This finding is anomalous and is apparently without substantive importance. As is the case in the findings for white men in Chapter IV, head of household's occupation is insignificantly negative in 1960 and 1964 but significantly positive in the other years. Apparently both education and occupation are more politically potent indicators of socioeconomic position than is the first "objective" indicator, income.

Subjective social class identification has a strong impact on party preferences in the first four years but disappears in 1968 and 1972. Since most of the sample are self-declared middle- or working-class respondents, the difference in subjective class amounts to between a fifth and a third of a point in party identification on the five-point party identification scale from 1952 to 1968. An assessment of the relative importance of all four stratification variables in the causal models will be made after inspecting the other parameters.

The three measures of ascriptive social position—religion, race, and region—perform in the multivariate model much as they did in the detailed treatments of Chapters II and III. The regression coefficients for the four religious categories have been transformed in Table 5.2 into structural (MCA) coefficients, which express the effects as deviations from the grand mean of the sample, thus facilitating comparisons over years. The Protestants are always above the mean and Catholics and Jews below it, and the latter are always more Democratic in preference. Protestant-Catholic differences reach their peak in 1960, the Kennedy election year, with a net difference in coefficients of .558 points, while the smallest spread, less than an eighth of a point, occurs in 1972. The residual Other-None group fluctuates, generally on the Democratic side of the mean.

The effect of race of respondent contains few surprises, although the estimated effect was strong in 1952 but insignificant in 1956 and 1960. Racial effects assert themselves very strongly in the 1964–72 samples, again peaking during the 1968 election, when the net difference between whites and blacks exceeds one point on the five-point scale. The regional effects are more interesting and unexpected, given the analyses of Chapter III. The coefficients are negative from 1952 to 1968, reflecting the greater Democratic partisanship of the South. The magnitudes of the effects diminish steadily after 1956, becoming insignificant in 1968. However, in 1972 the coefficient for region not only became significant, but the sign reversed! When other causal variables were held constant, the South was seen to be *more* Republican than the rest of the nation. The zero-order correlation of region and party is still in the usual direction ($r = -.10$); that is, the South is still more Democratic than the non-South when other factors are not controlled. But when the South is made statistically equivalent to the non-South through multivariate analysis, the parameter for region shifts from insignificant to positive; that is, the South is less Democratic than the rest of the nation. This finding suggests that as the South continues to evolve in its social structure toward greater similarity with the rest of the nation, its political allegiances are likely to undergo the long-anticipated realignment toward the Republican party.

The last variable in the regression equation is the party identification of the respondent's father. For the two surveys in which this variable was not measured (1956 and 1960), the average intercorrelation with variables in the other four years was substituted in the matrix of zero-order correlations. Thus estimates of the net causal impact of father's party—in effect, the degree of political inheritance—could be estimated for all samples. In every year except 1968, the coefficient exceeds .80, and in 1968 it is .70. Thus, a difference of one point of the father's preference (on the three-point scale) results in a difference of more than three-quarters of a point for the son or daughter (on the five-point scale). To put it another way, two fathers with identical profiles on the achievement and ascription dimensions, but one a Republican and one a Democrat, would on the average have offspring differing in party preference by between 1.40 and 1.80 points on the five-point scale. (Since the difference between a Republican and Democratic father is two points on the three-point paternal party scale, multiply the regression coefficient (b) for that variable by two.) No greater difference between extremes was produced by any other independent variable in the multivariate analysis.

Just how strong the effect of paternal partisanship is, relative to the other independent variables in the model, can be seen in an analysis of the standardized regression coefficients in Table 5.3. When the unstandardized regression coefficients (b) in Table 5.2 are multiplied by the ratio of the standard deviations of the independent to the dependent variables, the result is a standardized regression or path coefficient. Path coefficients disclose the net direct effect of each independent variable on party identification in standard units. For example, a change of one standard deviation in income

TABLE 5.3. STANDARDIZED REGRESSION COEFFICIENTS (β's) FOR MULTI-
VARIATE CAUSAL MODEL OF PARTY IDENTIFICATION, 1952-1972

INDEPENDENT	YEAR					
VARIABLES	1952	1956	1960	1964	1968	1972
STRATIFICATION						
Income	.025	.044	.022	.022	.038	.106
Education	.052	-.077	.022	.091	.085	.008
Occupation	.064	.051	-.036	-.020	.045	.057
Social Class	.091	.113	.121	.118	.015	.018
RELIGION *						
Protestant	.033	.027	.097	.020	.026	.022
Catholic	-.033	-.036	-.073	-.030	-.050	-.025
Jew	-.103	-.072	-.033	-.059	-.083	-.060
Other	-.042	-.073	.010	-.020	-.033	-.036
RACE	.077	.026	.020	.130	.239	.118
REGION	-.079	-.127	-.082	-.057	-.029	.063
FATHER'S PARTY	.595	.559	.555	.546	.501	.625

*Standardized structural coefficients

in 1952 results in a .025 standard deviation change in party preference. Whereas the unstandardized b coefficients are useful for assessing changes over time, the value of the path coefficients is in comparing the relative importance of causal variables measured on different scales within a given year. Clearly, father's party identification is the most important determinant of the respondent's party in each year. A difference of one standard deviation in fathers' parties results in more than half a standard deviation difference in offsprings' parties. This relationship is the well-known regression towards the mean: two individuals from diverse social origins will, on average, be closer to one another than their respective parents are.

In any given year very few variables have a direct path coefficient which exceeds more than a tenth of a standard deviation. The only indirect paths from exogenous variables in the basic model hypothesized in Figure 5.1 run from race through the intervening socioeconomic stratification variables and from region through education. Since the path coefficients for these variables in Table 5.3 are relatively small, the indirect effects of race and region on party are, for all practical purposes, negligible. The square of the path coefficient indicates the proportion of variance in party identification caused by the independent variable. A more comprehensive indication of impact may be gained from a partitioning of explained variance.

The last row of Table 5.2 contains the coefficient of determination (Multiple R^2) for the regression equation of each year. The proportion of variance in the five-point party identification scale attributable to the eight causal variables ranges between .41 to .47, or nearly half. Only in 1952 and 1972 does the R^2 approach the latter figure, however. In Table 5.4 the total "explained" variance is allocated to different portions of the causal scheme. Three such portions can be identified in Figure 5.1. The four stratification variables form an achievement cluster intervening between the dependent variable and the exogenous factors. Among the exogenous variables, father's party, or political socialization, is distinguished from the three ascribed variables—race, region, and religion. Since the two stratification variables of family of origin have no direct impact on party, they are omitted.

The second line of Table 5.4 reports the "reduced" form of the causal model; that is, it omits the intervening variables and reports only the impact of the four exogenous variables. Each reduced model accounts for more than 39 percent of the total variance. The difference between line one (the full model) and line two indicates how much additional variance in party is *uniquely* contributed by all four stratification variables. This increment to variance explained ranges between 3 percent in 1964 and 1½ percent in 1960. This net increment to stratification may be compared with the variance explained by stratification alone in the last line of the table. In general, the unique contribution to explained variance is about half the total variance in

TABLE 5.4. PARTITION OF MULTIPLE R^2 AMONG INDEPENDENT VARIABLES IN
            MULTIVARIATE CAUSAL MODEL OF PARTY IDENTIFICATION,
            1952-1972

VARIABLES IN	YEAR					
THE MODEL	1952	1956	1960	1964	1968	1972
1. Full Model	.4728	.4199	.4122	.4234	.4161	.4688
2. Father's Party and Ascribed Variables	.4444	.4012	.3968	.3936	.3955	.4476
3. Father's Party Only	.4074	.3780	.3780	.3609	.3226	.4243
4. Stratification Only	.0616	.0387	.0387	.0783	.0667	.0365

party preferences attributable to stratification when other causal variables
are ignored.

The third line reports the Multiple R^2 from the regression of respondent's
party on father's party alone. From 32 to 42 percent of the variance in party
preferences is accounted for by political socialization. The difference
between line three and line one indicates how much additional variance the
other seven variables add to the ability of political inheritance to explain
party identifications. In 1968, the other independent variables add another 9
percent to the R^2 of father's party alone, but in the remaining years the range
is only between 3.4 and 6.5 percent. In effect, father's party contains the
overwhelming share of the explanatory power of the causal model,
contributing 80 to 90 percent of the total R^2 in the full model. By themselves,
the other seven independent variables do not account for even half of the
variance explained in the full model.

Summary

The multivariate causal analysis of party identification revealed net
effects of ascribed and achieved social group memberships similar to those
disclosed in the preceding chapters, in which fewer other variables had been
held constant. Some unexpected differences from the zero-order correlations
were found—most notably the positive effect of region in 1972. Differences
in the size and significance of the social group effects across the samples
underscore the importance of not aggregating these causes into a single
"social characteristics index," as some analysts have done.

While each independent variable has a significant impact in at least some years, the father's party clearly exerts the predominant influence on respondent's current party identification. The path coefficients decreased in size monotonically from 1952 to 1968, implying a gradual lessening in parental socialization of party preference. But the sharp rebound in 1972 cautions against facile conclusions that the intergenerational transmission of party loyalties is waning. This finding is based upon an adult sample; yet the correlation of respondents' own party with retrospective reports about the fathers' party identification, once corrected for reliability, equals that obtained in a national sample of contemporary high school students and their parents. For most Americans, the politics of the dinner table still provides the earliest and most enduring orientation to the polity.

The path models in this chapter do not account for all or even half of the variation in party identification. The influence of social group memberships and parental socialization is far from the complete story. Missing from the analysis is the influence of political events in shaking partisans and Independents alike loose from their moorings. No psychological law prohibits individuals from abandoning support of a party under the pressure of rational interests or traditional social forces. Accordingly, the next chapter will attempt to introduce a dynamic perspective by focusing on change and stability in party identification at the individual level.

Chapter VI

Change in Party Identification

The path analyses in Chapter V account for less than half the variation in party identification. By using data from cross-sectional surveys, path models may give the impression that party identification is relatively impervious to change. Similarly, the high correlation between party identifications of fathers and those of their offspring may imply a rigidity in the socialization of a party preference. Yet disagreement between parental and children's party identifications occurs with sufficient frequency to raise the question of party defection, both between and within generations.

Inquiry into this change will proceed along two lines. The first relies upon reports of respondents' previous affiliations with other political parties. The second uses a unique set of panel data which measured respondents several times over four years. By comparing responses, the rates of change and stability in party identification are readily calculated. Neither method is without pitfalls, however. Measurement error in the form of distorted recall plagues the reliability of retrospective reports (Weir, 1975). Even if one could assume the absence of memory lapse or of deliberate prevarication, the panel data span only a short time, which is inadequate to develop a picture of change of party in the long run. The relationships observed may be peculiar to the political circumstances of that time. The results, then, are inferences of somewhat questionable generalizability. Nevertheless, they will, I hope, serve as a bench mark for future comparison.

Retrospective Loyalties

In each SRC survey, immediately following the question on current party identifications, respondents were asked, "Was there ever a time when you thought of yourself as a Democrat (or Republican)?" Ideally, this information could be used to construct a 3-by-3 category turnover table of initial and current party preferences. Unfortunately, in the surveys from 1952 to 1968 the only information recorded was former Democratic or Republican preference. With the exception of 1972, one cannot tell how many current

Democrats or Republicans were once Independents. The proportion of current Independents who have switched from one of the major parties can be reconstructed, however.

Analyzing the first two surveys, the authors of *The American Voter* found that 20 percent of respondents said they had switched parties (Campbell et al., 1960, p. 148). Although the item was not analyzed in greater detail, a substantial number of the defections seemed to occur among older persons, and these defections seemed to be a consequence of the political realignments of the New Deal. If this hypothesis is correct, the aggregate rate of party defection should gradually decline as these older cohorts pass out of the electorate—unless their departure is offset by comparable rates of party defection among younger persons. An alternative hypothesis might be that the rate of party defection will increase as Independent preference grows at the expense of the two major parties. This theory presumes that a substantial portion of the Independents are former partisans rather than newly-enfranchised youths. One might also anticipate finding upsurges in party defection rates in the 1964 and 1972 elections, when the Republican and Democratic parties, respectively, fielded presidential candidates unpalatable to large numbers of their partisans.

Although respondents were asked the year in which they had changed party preference, the data are inadequate to determine the recency of defection. Not all respondents provided the time information, and the likelihood of inaccuracy increases along with distance from the attributed time of change. Of those persons who supplied their date of defection, between 30 and 40 percent cited the four-year span since the last election. Presumably, many persons who had converted in the distant past failed to mention having once considered themselves members of the other party. Undoubtedly, the data to be presented underreport the gross rate of lifetime defections, ignore the frequencies among persons who have changed more than once, and overrepresent changes which occurred more recently.

Since the samples' party identifications for any given year in the past cannot be reconstructed, the alternative is to present the percentage of current partisans and Independents who claim to have identified with one or the other of the two major parties in the past. Despite all the caveats, the retrospective data on party changing provide the only inferential evidence on long-term stability of party identifications in the electorate.

The pattern of reported party defections in each election year, illustrated in Table 6.1, follows neither a declining nor an increasing rate of change in aggregate party preferences. The average rate of recalled defection fluctuates between 20 and 26 percent. The high point, which was only 25.4 percent, came in 1968. Whether this peak resulted from the presence of George Wallace on the national ballot, some residual impact of Barry Goldwater's candidacy in the previous presidential election, or simply random sampling

TABLE 6.1.   RETROSPECTIVE PARTY STABILITY, 1952-1972

PARTY STABILITY	YEAR					
	1952	1956	1960	1964	1968	1972
Never Changed	79.4	78.8	76.7	77.7	74.6	77.3
Switched Parties	20.6	21.2	23.3	22.3	25.4	22.7
Total	100.0	100.0	100.0	100.0	100.0	100.0
(N)	(1681)	(1668)	(1836)	(1552)	(1513)	(2066)

error is impossible to discover from the aggregate analysis. Clearly, however, no trend in aggregate defection rates is detectable during this period.

A breakdown of the data by respondents' ages reveals that rates of reported defection are usually lowest among those under thirty years and over eighty years old, but the middle-aged report little systematic difference in party changes. These relationships are compatible with both a generational difference and an aging hypothesis. Table 6.1 does not distinguish the party from which defections occur in a given survey. Defections from Republicanism may increase in certain years while Democratic departures drop off, and the reverse may be true in other years, so that no net change in the aggregate rate of party defection rates occurs, despite differential change by partisan origin. Some rough indicators of differential rates of defection between parties appear in Table 6.2.

The first line of Table 6.2 indicates the percentage of Democrats who recall once having been Republicans. From 1952 through 1960, Republican defectors form an increasing proportion of the Democratic identifiers, with the proportion rising from 10 to almost 18 percent. This trend is partially matched in line two by a declining rate of Democratic defection among Republican supporters. Among Independents (in lines three and four) the proportion of former Democrats holds constant at about one quarter from 1952 to 1960, while the percentage of Republican defectors increases by a half, from 12.5 to 18.7 percent. Thus, the Republicans lost adherents to both the Democratic party and the Independent category, while attracting few members of either party. These figures for the Eisenhower-Kennedy elections hint at the dynamics by which Republican strength eroded and the two other party affiliations increased in number.

According to conventional wisdom, the 1964 election further aggravated Republican woes. Goldwater supposedly repelled his party's adherents and failed to attract support among other partisans and Independents. Yet the retrospective data provide scant evidence of this negative impact. The proportion of former Republicans among the current Democrats in 1964 actually falls by 2 percent, and the percentage of Republicans claiming to once have been Democrats *increases* to an all-time high! Only the Independent category upholds the popular impression of the Goldwater debacle's effect on party alignments. Former Republicans make up a quarter of 1964 Independents, and former Democrats fall to their lowest level in the six surveys, 16.4 percent. Obviously, not all these party changes can be attributed to the effects of the presidential campaign during the survey in which they are recorded. Many changes, in fact, predate the survey by a number of years. However, instead of suggesting that the Goldwater-Johnson contest produced an unusually high rate of Republican-to-Democratic conversion, the evidence indicates that the opposite was true. The main adverse effect of the presidential contest upon the Republican party appears in the increase of former Republicans and the decrease of former Democrats among the current Independents.

The 1960 and 1964 elections illustrate the way the apparent absence of aggregate party change found in Table 6.1 masks major differences in movement, which are revealed when the data are disaggregated by parties. In 1960, about 46 percent of all Independents had once belonged to another party, and in 1964 the figure was 42 percent. Yet the proportions of former Democrats and Republicans nearly reverse between the two periods, indicating different patterns of party defection in the two elections. National political campaigns undoubtedly play a role in this differential rate of change, although the full process cannot be depicted in these crude change rates.

TABLE 6.2. CURRENT PARTY IDENTIFIERS REPORTING PREVIOUS IDEN-
TIFICATION WITH ANOTHER PARTY, 1952-1972

CURRENT AND PREVIOUS PARTY	YEAR					
	1952	1956	1960	1964	1968	1972
Democrats formerly Republican	9.9	12.4	17.6	15.0	14.9	6.8*
(N)	(816)	(761)	(854)	(800)	(697)	(1084)
Republicans formerly Democrat	24.4	21.2	18.7	25.7	25.2	21.4**
(N)	(472)	(510)	(552)	(381)	(373)	(632)
Independents formerly Democrat	25.7	26.7	27.2	16.4	29.3	20.6
Independents formerly Republican	12.5	11.3	18.7	25.7	25.2	21.4
(N)	(393)	(397)	(430)	(341)	(443)	(350)

*In 1972, 7.8% of Democrats were former Independent
**In 1972, 9.7% of Republicans were former Independent

Following the 1964 election, defection rates in all categories except Democrat-to-Independent remain largely unchanged. The proportion of Independents who formerly were Democrats almost doubles from 1964 to 1968. Again, presidential politics may have played an important role in the increased defection from a major party. Wallace's candidacy on a party bearing the name "Independent," and his strong regional appeal among southern Democrats, may be responsible for much of the upsurge in such defections. The 1972 rate is almost 9 percent lower than the 1968 rate, demonstrating the impact Wallace had had on Democratic support four years earlier. The other rates of cross-party defection for 1972 are not strictly comparable with previous years, since a change in the alternative choices available may have affected responses. Still, the proportion of Democratic defectors among Republicans in 1972 is about the same as in years past, while Republican defectors among the Democrats are far fewer; this finding may demonstrate another effect of an unpopular presidential candidate who is unable to attract support from the opposition party.

The preceding analysis has unveiled some aspects of change and stability in party preferences, at least at the aggregate level of party composition. Unfortunately, incomplete information about past preferences before 1972 and the fallibility of memory render the retrospective data imprecise. The availability of a panel within a subset of the SRC surveys allows a more accurate analysis of party changes, at least over a four-year period.

Party Change as a Markov Process

Some of the respondents from the 1956 presidential survey were re-interviewed as part of the 1958 and 1960 SRC surveys. The standard party identification question was posed in each pre-election interview (only a post-election interview was held in 1958). Due to relocations, deaths, non-cooperation, and failures to re-interview for other reasons, the total sample size of the panel with completed interviews (N = 1514) was somewhat smaller than the original 1956 survey (N = 1762). In subsequent years, new respondents were selected to fill positions vacated by the panel mortality, thus preserving the representativeness of each cross-sectional survey. The population to which panel results can be generalized is thus a selective one: it is somewhat more highly educated, less geographically mobile, and more motivated to cooperate than the non-re-interviewed respondents. Nevertheless, substantial differences in party identification and party change would not be expected between the panel members and the complete sample.

When the five-category party preferences of 1045 respondents giving complete information were cross-classified at two points in time, the turnover matrices in Table 6.3 resulted. The three turnover tables bear a

TABLE 6.3.   PARTY IDENTIFICATION TURNOVER AMONG ALL RESPONDENTS,
             1956-1958-1960

PARTY AT FIRST PERIOD	PARTY AT SECOND PERIOD					Total	(N)
	Strong Dem.	Weak Dem.	Strict Ind.	Weak Rep.	Strong Rep.		
1956				1958			
Strong Dem.	77.6	20.6	0.4	0.0	1.3	100.0	(228)
Weak Dem.	29.7	63.9	3.2	2.9	0.3	100.0	(310)
Strict Ind.	3.4	27.0	41.6	24.7	3.4	100.0	(89)
Weak Rep.	2.4	13.9	8.7	59.5	15.5	100.0	(252)
Strong Rep.	3.6	2.4	0.6	34.9	59.0	100.0	(166)
Total	27.1	29.5	6.8	22.9	13.8	100.0	(1045)
1958				1960			
Strong Dem.	68.9	27.2	2.5	1.1	0.4	100.0	(283)
Weak Dem.	20.5	64.3	7.1	7.5	0.6	100.0	(308)
Strict Ind.	5.6	16.9	52.1	25.4	0.0	100.0	(71)
Weak Rep.	1.3	6.3	7.5	61.9	23.0	100.0	(239)
Strong Rep.	1.4	1.4	0.7	27.1	69.4	100.0	(144)
Total	25.6	29.1	8.1	22.1	15.1	100.0	(1045)
1956				1960			
Strong Dem.	71.5	26.8	0.4	0.4	0.9	100.0	(228)
Weak Dem.	28.7	58.1	7.7	4.8	0.7	100.0	(310)
Strict Ind.	4.5	28.1	38.2	27.0	2.2	100.0	(89)
Weak Rep.	2.8	13.9	9.5	55.6	18.3	100.0	(252)
Strong Rep.	2.4	1.8	1.2	30.7	63.9	100.0	(166)
Total	25.6	29.1	8.1	22.1	15.1	100.0	(1045)

strong similarity to the father-by-respondent turnover table in Chapter V. In each row, the largest percentage appears on the main diagonal, indicating that more respondents remain in their original preference than change. In general, persons who change move to a neighboring category, instead of making the leap to a more distant affiliation. This gradient in the turnover matrices is among the strongest pieces of evidence that the five-category party classification is an ordinal, if not an interval, measure. As with the intergenerational turnover table in the previous chapter, each matrix in Table 6.3 exhibits higher rates of defection from the Republican than from the Democratic categories. Such differential rates are consistent with the cross-sectional samples from these years, which show a net gain for Democrats and a net loss for Republicans in the aggregate party distributions.

Upon closer comparison of the three matrices, the estimated turnover rates (or transition probabilities) vary considerably. To focus only on the two strongly partisan groups, the first matrix—1956 to 1958—shows that stability of strong Democrats is 18.6 percent higher than that of strong Republicans. In the second period—1958 to 1960—the strong Republicans actually changed .5 percent less than the strong Democrats. The cause of the differential stability and change by time may lie in the nature of presidential politics of the period. The 1956 election was an Eisenhower landslide, in which many traditional Democrats voted for a Republican president. After this high point of Republican popularity, the erosion of support began. The 1958 election, in the midst of a major postwar recession, produced a large Democratic congressional majority. Thus, the 1956–58 period may be seen as a readjustment in which individuals who had called themselves Republicans during Eisenhower's campaign severed their ties to that party. The Democratic party, on the other hand, not having attracted "floating" partisans in 1956, did not experience the disengagement of marginally committed individuals to the same extent as did the Republicans. The 1958–60 matrix, on the other hand, may resemble a "normal" rate of transition among party positions more closely, with the rates of inflow and outflow between the major parties more evenly balanced.

If this interpretation of the observed differences in change at two-year intervals is correct, one would anticipate a similar pattern in the first matrix after any landslide election. Data from 1964 to 1966 would probably reveal greater defection by the Democrats than by the hard-core Republican partisans who remained loyal to Goldwater. Similarly, the 1972–74 turnover table for the post-Nixon landslide ought to look much like the 1956–58 matrix. Indeed, the evidence from cross-sectional surveys of these two-year periods indicates that the party whose candidate had won a landslide lost adherents by the next congressional election. Unfortunately, panel data comparable to those for the first period are not available, so hypotheses about turnover on the individual level must remain conjectures.

While one may make plausible substantive interpretations of the patterns observed in Table 6.3, an alternative interpretation has been argued by Philip Converse (1964, 1970, 1974a; see also Pierce and Rose, 1974). In investigating the changes in several political orientations across all three panel waves, Converse noted that only two processes could account for the observed patterns. One is "sufficiently nonsensical for us to reject . . . out of hand," since it assumes some respondents deliberately choose different responses from one point to the next. The second model posits the existence of two groups: one whose choices remain stable over time and another whose movement is statistically random. Thus the turnover table between two points in time is a function of the relative proportions of these two populations (Converse, 1964, p. 242). While Converse's argument was aimed primarily at "nonattitudes" about public issues in the late 1950's, some researchers have applied the random change model to the panel data for party identification.

Dreyer (1973) pointed out that the correlation between two-year waves of the panel was about the same as that between pre- and post-election interviews in 1960, suggesting to him that the rate of change was independent of time and political circumstance. Dreyer applied Converse's implication of random change of attitude among a portion of the population and perfect stability in the remainder to partition the turnover tables into these two groups. He reported that observed correlations among these samples are nearly identical to the expected proportions under the random change model. He concluded that "by and large the only change that occurred over this period was random change." Dobson and Meeter (1974) tested three alternative models for turnover in party identification, all of which are essentially decompositions of a Markov process into component processes. The model providing the best fit to the data posited that the process is not stationary and that all transition probabilities may vary with time.

Log-linear analysis may be used to test whether a Markov process produces the successive panel observations (Bishop et al., 1975, pp. 257–79). A first-order Markov chain model assumes (1) that an individual's preference at any time depends only upon his previous position, not upon his position at any prior time, and (2) that the transition probabilities remain unchanged (stationary). To test whether a first-order Markov chain operates from 1956 to 1958 and from 1958 to 1960, the following set of marginals are fitted to the first two matrices in Table 6.3:

$$(FS) (FT)$$

where F is the distribution at the beginning of the transition, S is the distribution at the end of the transition, and T is the period of observation. This model has a chi-square of 47.0 for twenty degrees of freedom, indicating it is reasonable to conclude that the transition probabilities are not stationary. Apparently, then, the process of change in party identification differs at different points in time. Although methods are available to test for higher order Markov processes, they will not be pursued here.

Another demonstration of the inadequacy of the Markovian hypothesis uses a path analysis of the inter-temporal correlation coefficients. The Pearsonian r's for each matrix are (1956–60): .66; (1956–58): .81; and (1958–60): .80. If one assumes a simple causal chain in which party identification at time one causes party identification at time two, which causes party identification at time three, i.e.,

PARTY1956 ⎯⎯⎯⎯⎯► PARTY1958 ⎯⎯⎯⎯⎯► PARTY1960

then, according to Blalock (1961, ch. 3), the correlation between 1956 and 1960 should be the product of the two intervening correlations (paths): $(.81)(.80) = .648$. But this expected value is substantially lower than the observed correlation, indicating that the simple chain model does not adequately represent the causal process. Presumably, other factors are responsible for the tendency of party identifications to maintain themselves over time. Working with aggregate time series data on the two-party division of the presidential and congressional vote, Stokes and Iversen (1962) found that an equilibrium-free model of random movements did not account for the observed tendency of the vote division to stay within a range of from 35 to 65 percent. They hypothesized the existence of "restoring forces," which would tend to return the balance toward a modal division. The above analysis of panel data points to the possibility of similar restoring forces on the individual level which stabilize the party distribution over time.

Presidential Voting and Party Change

A model of party identification, partisan attitudes, and voting behavior developed by Goldberg (1966) and elaborated by others conceptualized party identification as the outcome of social characteristics and, in turn, as a cause of partisan attitudes and voting. But the recursive structure of this model did not allow any feedback from political attitudes or voting behavior to party preferences. In Goldberg's words, "As this model stands, party identification is nearly immutable." Yet the preceding sections have demonstrated that sizable turnover in party preferences occurs even within a four-year span. Goldberg's proposed solution to apparent rigidity in party identification was to incorporate partisan attitudes and perceptions of political events as causes of party identification, in addition to the usual social antecedents. He suggested that cross-sectional data were inappropriate to the task (in 1966 most political scientists and sociologists were unfamiliar with nonrecursive modeling techniques for estimating simultaneous effects between variables), and that panel data could be effectively used to measure the impact of political variables on party identification.

An early use of panel survey data in studying changes in political intentions was the Erie County study by Lazarsfeld and his colleagues (1948). Re-interviews with respondents were held at short intervals throughout the 1940 presidential campaign; attitude for and against the Republican candidate and Republican or Democratic voting intention were assessed at each point. The result was a famous 16-fold turnover table of vote intention (X_1) and candidate opinion (X_2) for two points in time, a contingency table which has been subsequently analyzed by several persons. The data are an instance of the two-wave two-variable (2W2V) problem for discrete variables. One analysis of the Lazarsfeld data suggested a "harmonizing process" in which "basic political attitudes and attitudes toward the candidate tend to be consonant" (Boudon, 1968, p. 228). Changes in voting intention were seen as being influenced by earlier disposition toward the candidate, and vice versa. (This harmonization model is diagrammed in Figure 6.1.)

Later re-analysis of the same 16-fold data by Goodman (1973b), utilizing log-linear modeling techniques, found that the previous models had ignored the synchronous effects of the two variables in the second period. When the effects of candidate opinion and voting intention upon each other at the second point in time were taken into account, the "cross-lag" paths between variables over time were not necessary to account adequately for variation in the contingency table. A causal diagram of the latter process is also shown in Figure 6.1. Both the harmonizing model and the simple recursive model

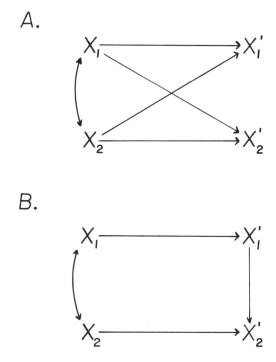

Figure 6.1. Causal Models for Lazarsfeld Panel Data: *A*, Harmonizing Model, after Boudon (1968); *B*, Recursive Model, after Goodman (1973)

TABLE 6.4.   OBSERVED FREQUENCIES FOR PARTY IDENTIFICATION, PRESI-
DENTIAL VOTE, AND RELIGION, 1956-1960 PANEL

FIRST WAVE (1956)		SECOND WAVE (1960)					
PARTY (P_1)	VOTE (V_1)	PARTY(P_2): Dem. VOTE(V_2) : Dem.	Dem. Rep.	Ind. Dem.	Ind. Rep.	Rep. Dem.	Rep. Rep.
CATHOLICS							
Democrat	Democrat	69	1	2	1	1	0
Democrat	Republican	26	4	1	0	0	0
Independent	Democrat	7	0	11	1	0	0
Independent	Republican	12	0	11	7	3	3
Republican	Democrat	1	0	0	0	1	0
Republican	Republican	8	2	6	3	6	15
NONCATHOLICS							
Democrat	Democrat	127	29	17	2	0	0
Democrat	Republican	15	24	4	4	0	3
Independent	Democrat	11	3	9	5	0	1
Independent	Republican	1	6	21	52	1	33
Republican	Democrat	1	0	3	0	1	1
Republican	Republican	2	0	2	16	9	181

without cross-lagged effects are reasonable hypotheses for 2W2V models of the causal relationship between party identification and presidential voting.

The following section will analyze the mutual effects of party identification and presidential voting choice within the 2W2V framework, using log-linear techniques. Of particular interest will be the extent to which presidential voting behavior at the first wave of the panel (1956) influences party identification at the second wave (1960). The initial choice may affect subsequent attitudes, either reinforcing a traditional party loyalty through the supporting of its candidate or weakening that loyalty by defecting to the other party's candidate. The process may be even further complicated by interaction effects; that is, deviation from voting support of one's party may have different implications for Republicans than it has for Democrats.

The data to be analyzed come from the 786 panel respondents who voted either Republican or Democratic in the 1956 and 1960 elections and who stated a party identification in both waves. Party preference was trichotomized at the three major categories (Democrat, Independent, and Republican) to avoid the excessive number of empty cells which would have resulted from a more detailed classification. Since religion is known to have played an important role in the 1960 election, a Catholic-non-Catholic dichotomy was included in the five-variable cross-tabulation. The observed frequencies in Table 6.4 nevertheless have nineteen empty cells out of 72. Following Goodman's advice (1972b: 1048), I added a value of one-half to each cell frequency before performing the log-linear analysis. For convenience in stating models, the following notation is used: (P_1) party identification in 1956; (P_2) party identification in 1960; (V_1) presidential vote in 1956; (V_2) presidential vote in 1960; and (R) religion.

Since P_1, V_1, and R were all measured at the first wave of the panel, they may be treated as causally prior to P_2 and V_2. The three-way relationship ($P_1 V_1 R$) will be taken as fixed when various log-linear models are fitted to the data in Table 6.4. If this three-way cross-tabulation is formed by the appropriate collapsing of the five-way table, one finds that the three-way interaction ($P_1 V_1 R$) is significant, since deleting this relationship yields a chi-square equal to 7.2 for d.f. = 2. The presence of the three-way relationship among the antecedent measures ensures that parameters from these varia-bles to the 1960 measures may be taken as one-way causal effects.

The initial model to be tested is a simple recursive structure, designated model 1 in Table 6.5. Each variable is causally linked with the others, but no relationship depends upon the levels of some third variable. Model one, which has a chi-square of 54.3, actually provides an acceptable fit to the data, since the probability is .12 of observing a chi-square this large with 43 degrees of freedom. However, an improved fit to the data might be possible from one of two perspectives. Perhaps this model omits some significant three-way interactions, or perhaps some of the two-way associations are not required for an adequate description of the data.

Since there are nine other three-way relationships among the five varia-bles besides ($P_1 V_1 R$), not all these models will be presented, in order to save space. Models two and three contain the only three-way marginals of the nine which produce sizable reductions in chi-square relative to the change in degrees of freedom over the completely recursive model 1. Both ($P_1 P_2 R$) and

TABLE 6.5. LOG-LINEAR MODELS FOR RELIGION, PARTY IDENTIFICATION, AND PRESIDENTIAL VOTE, 1956-1960 PANEL

MODEL	FITTED MARGINALS	df	LIKELIHOOD-RATIO χ^2
1	$(P_1 V_1 R) (P_1 P_2) (V_1 V_2) (P_1 V_2) (V_1 P_2) (P_2 V_2) (P_2 R) (V_2 R)$	43	54.3
2	$(P_1 V_1 R) (P_1 P_2 R) (V_1 V_2) (P_1 V_2) (V_1 P_2) (P_2 V_2) (V_2 R)$	39	43.3
3	$(P_1 V_1 R) (V_1 P_2 R) (V_1 V_2) (P_1 V_2) (P_2 V_2) (V_2 R)$	41	41.4
4	$(P_1 V_1 R) (P_1 P_2 R) (V_1 P_2 R) (V_1 V_2) (P_1 V_2) (P_2 V_2) (V_2 R)$	37	33.1
5	$(P_1 V_1 R) (P_1 P_2 R) (V_1 P_2 R) (V_1 V_2) (P_2 V_2) (V_2 R)$	39	36.2
6	$(P_1 V_1 R) (V_1 P_2 R) (V_1 V_2) (P_1 P_2) (P_2 V_2) (V_2 R)$	43	44.3

(V_1P_2R), indicating conditional associations involving religious group membership, are separately significant, while model four shows that together they provide a significantly improved fit to the data relative to model one (difference in chi-square = 21.3, difference in d.f. = 6). There are four two-way relationships not subsumed by the three-way interactions. These marginals were tested against model 4, and all except one of the cross-lag paths, (P_1V_2), is necessary in order to fit the data.

While model five provides a satisfactory explanation of the data and omits no associations or interactions of significance, it is not the most parsimonious model possible. As model six shows, by dropping one of the three-way interactions, (P_1P_2R), the rise in chi-square is not significant at $p = .05$ for four additional degrees of freedom. Hence, model six provides the best fit to the data, since it requires the fewest complex relationships and does not omit any significant relationships.

The substantive interpretation of model six is best understood by reference to Figure 6.2. This causal diagram blends some elements from both the harmonizing process and the simple recursive models in Figure 6.1 for a 2W2V problem, but it also contains unique elements. Two stability relationships, (P_1P_2) and (V_1V_2), indicate the propensity of individuals to continue in their original party identifications and voting choices over time. The cross-lag path, (V_1P_2), seems to represent some type of harmonizing process by

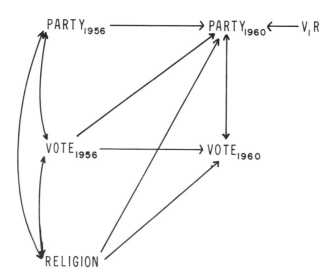

Figure 6.2. Causal Model for Party Identification, Presidential Vote, and Religion, 1956–1960 Panel

which voting choice in the first election brings about consistency in party identification by the second election—an effect independent of the persistence of party identification, (P_1P_2). Religion, in addition to correlating with the initial measures of vote and party, has effects upon these variables at the latter election, (V_2R) and (P_2R), as anticipated from previous analyses of the cross-sectional data. The double-headed arrow connecting the 1960 measures of party identification and presidential vote, (P_2V_2), denotes an inability to specify a causal priority between these contemporaneous measures. This simultaneous relationship represents a mutual reinforcement of attitude and behavior during a particular election and implies that causal processes associate party and vote independently of their persistence over time.

The only interaction in the model, (V_1P_2R), is diagrammed in Figure 6.2 as a conditional effect of V_1R on 1960 party identification. Although a statistical interaction may be interpreted in several ways, perhaps the most comprehensible way to interpret this one is to postulate that the association between a 1956 presidential vote and a party preference in the subsequent election differs between the religious groups. This conditional effect can be seen by forming the three-way table from the observed data in Table 6.4 and comparing the party-vote association for Catholics and non-Catholics. Among Eisenhower voters, the later party identification distributions are identical in both religious groups: 16 percent Democrat, 30 percent Independent and 54 percent Republican. But among persons voting for Stevenson, the party identifications in 1960 differ between religious groups. Only 57 percent of Catholics who voted for Stevenson were Democrats in 1960, while 73 percent of non-Catholics were. The difference is about evenly distributed among Independent and Republican preferences. This interaction suggests that non-Catholics had a slightly higher consistency between presidential vote and subsequent party identification than did Catholics. The differences are not great enough to imply substantially dissimilar harmonizing processes, but the interaction is nonetheless statistically significant.

Some idea of the relative importance of the relationships in model six and Figure 6.2 can be gained from inspecting the standardized effect parameters for the additive log-linear model in Table 6.6. In this table the parameters apply to the categories of a Democratic presidential vote and a Catholic religion. Parameters for a Republican vote and a non-Catholic religion have the same values but opposite signs. Since all parameters were standardized by dividing by their standard errors, only those of at least two or greater may be viewed as highly significant. For example, the (V_1R) value is only $-.12$, indicating that religion and vote were basically uncorrelated in 1956. The (V_2R) parameter, however, is 3.37, indicating a substantial association between Catholicism and a vote for Kennedy. This association is as strong as the stability coefficient for the vote from 1956 to 1960, (V_1V_2).

TABLE 6.6.   λ EFFECTS (STANDARDIZED) IN MODEL 6 FOR PRESIDENTIAL VOTE,
             PARTY IDENTIFICATION, AND RELIGION, 1956-1960 PANEL

VOTE	(V_1V_2)	(V_1R)	(V_2R)							
Democrat	3.39	-.12	3.37							

PARTY	(P_1P_2)									
	Dem	Ind	Rep	(P_1V_1)	(P_2V_2)	(P_2V_1)	(P_1R)	(P_2R)	(P_2V_1R)	(P_1V_1R)
Democrat	6.33	-1.12	-3.85	3.36	2.55	1.16	-.80	.86	-1.63	.16
Indepen.	-1.95	3.14	-.84	-.36	0.99	.11	.63	-1.06	-.31	.44
Republican	-3.18	-1.28	5.35	-2.75	-3.36	-1.23	.13	.13	1.85	-.48

Parameters involving party identification are slightly more complex, since party has three categories. Positive values mean that this category is associated with the second variable, and negative values mean that it is not. Thus the nine (P_1P_2) parameters have positive values on the main diagonal and negative values on the off-diagonal combinations, indicating that initial party identification positively predicts the same preference at the later date. The two contemporaneous associations of party and vote, which occur in 1956, (P_1V_1), and in 1960, (P_2V_2), are both about equal in magnitude, but the cross-lag effect, (P_2V_1) is substantially weaker. However, the three-way interaction which subsumes this relationship, (V_1P_2R), has standardized values approaching statistical significance. The conditional interaction among the three 1956 measures, (P_1V_1R), is not significant by the usual criterion and is only present to assure a recursivity to the model.

In all, the best-fitting log-linear model for the panel data is relatively simple. Except for the special role of religion in the 1960 election, Figure 6.2 may well represent the typical causal process of voting behavior and party affiliation across elections. All relationships between vote and party identification are additive, in the sense that the association between any two measures of vote and party do not depend upon the level of some third measure. The main processes involved are persistence of party and vote over time, and mutual relations at each election. Only one relatively weak cross-lag effect was found, but its presence is an important reminder that prior behavioral choices may compel a subsequent attitude congruent with that choice.

Summary

The evidence from both recall data and a panel covering four years testifies to the variation in individual party identifications over time. On the aggregate, the proportion of the electorate reporting never having changed party affiliations has been constant within a 75 to 80 percent range over the past two decades. But disaggregation of this retrospective data by current and previous party preferences reveals a responsiveness of party defection to political events, especially presidential campaigns. The proportions of former Democrats or Republicans within the opposite party or in the Independent voter category appear to grow or shrink with the popularity of the major party candidates; but this inference is somewhat clouded by the inability to pinpoint the exact date at which party defections occur.

A three-wave panel, from 1956, 1958, and 1960, produced turnover tables of party identification which show a gradient of defection. Most persons are still within their initial partisan categories two years later, but those who do change are more likely to be found in an adjacent category than in a distant one. A comparison of the turnover in the first two years with that in the last two years found that the process did not follow a first-order Markov chain with fixed probabilities. More change occurred between 1956 and 1958 than in the following two years, and this change was largely away from the Republican party. The evidence points to a realignment of party preferences in the aftermath of Eisenhower's attraction of marginal partisans to Republican affiliation. This falling-off pattern may typify all such landslide elections, although comparable data are not available.

Analysis of the presidential vote and party identification in the panel revealed a relatively simple model of stability and change. Initial party identification and voting choices strongly predict subsequent positions. The small, yet significant, effect of the 1956 vote on 1960 party identification implies a tendency for party affiliations to be brought into line with previous voting behavior. While the strength of this cross-lag effect differs between Catholics and non-Catholics, for the most part the relationship of voting and party identification over time is not conditional upon religious membership. Except for the unusual impact of religion on party and vote in 1960, which has already been well-documented, the causal model of intrapersonal change over time in the panel may reflect the general process of this period fairly accurately.

Chapter VII

Party and Voting Behavior

The analyses to this point have focused largely upon group and individual factors in party identifications. This chapter will consider the relationship between party identification and voting behavior among individual voters. The distribution of party support between the two major parties and the Independent grouping has slowly but noticeably changed over the 1952–72 period. Popular and scholarly journals continue to debate about whether such changes portend a realignment of relative power between the major parties and hence between the social groups which form the core of the parties' support. A predominant alternative view is that the party system, instead of undergoing a classic realignment of voting blocs, may be dissolving, as party identifications become irrelevant as guides to behavior in the political marketplace. This chapter will lay the foundation for an understanding of the aggregate changes in party and voting behavior to be analyzed in the next chapter.

Realignment or Disintegration?

At periodic intervals, as new surveys are conducted, the distributions of party identifications in the adult population become available for detailed inspection of partisan change. This scrutiny has a certain oracular fascination, and the slightest deviation in Democratic or Republican strength is examined for signs of things to come. Yet, of itself, party identification has no political significance. Only in the intimate association between psychological "belongingness" and behavior in the polling booth does the importance of party identification reveal itself.

The electorate's disposition by standing party preference was explicitly described nearly a decade ago in Converse's (1966b) seminal article on the concept of the normal vote. Prevailing party identifications within a population act as a baseline against which to measure voting deviations of a short-term or long-run nature. The frequency with which the party strength indicated by landslide presidential elections in the post–World War II era has evaporated in subsequent elections suggests both the importance of short-term forces and the stability of underlying party identifications in restoring the party system to an equilibrium. In some historical eras, however, short-term forces appear to be sufficiently powerful to disrupt the underlying distribution of party preferences, leading to a conversion of loyalties among individuals on such a grand scale that the normal vote of the electorate differs substantially from that of the preceding period (Campbell, 1966; Pomper, 1967). The analysis of major realigning periods in American history reveals the factors usually associated with such changes.

The term "critical election" was first used by Key (1955) to characterize a period of rapid change in the social base of party support in New England from 1928 to 1936. Subsequently, a number of authors (MacRae and Meldrum, 1959; Campbell et al., 1960; Pomper, 1967; Sellers, 1965; Burnham, 1970) have concluded that the realigning process covers a period of time, however compressed, rather than a single election. Perhaps the most succinct description of a national critical realignment is Burnham's (1970, p. 10) summary:

To recapitulate, then, eras of critical realignment are marked by short, sharp reorganizations of the mass coalitional bases of the major parties which occur at periodic intervals on the national level; are often preceded by major third-party revolts which reveal the incapacity of "politics as usual" to integrate, much less aggregate, emergent political demand; are closely associated with abnormal stress in the socioeconomic system; are marked by ideological polarizations and issue-distances between the major parties which are exceptionally large by normal standards; and have durable consequences as constituent acts which determine the outer boundaries of policy in general, though not necessarily of policies in detail.

Using these criteria, students of national realignment phenomena have generally agreed that three major realignments have occurred since the formation of the second party system in 1828: (1) the Civil War realignment with regional polarizations of the 1850's; (2) the agrarian-urban cleavages in the "system of 1896"; and (3) the socioeconomic realignment of the Depression-New Deal, 1928–36. The periodic recurrence of such national realignments (in a 35–40 year cycle), raises the question of whether the present party system, in which the Democratic party is in the ascendant among the electorate, is overdue for realignment. Such is the thesis of Kevin Phillips' book, *The Emerging Republican Majority* (1969), which appeared in the wake of Nixon's first election and predicted the successful use of a "Southern strategy" (see also Lubell, 1970). Several key elements cited by Burnham as necessary for critical realignment appeared in the late 1960's and early 1970's. The Goldwater and McGovern candidacies marked a greater ideological and issue-polarization than had been typical of presidential politics of the period (Pomper, 1972). The urban and racial situations, as well as the Vietnam War, were inadequately handled by both major parties. A major third-party movement, based initially on a regional issue, soon mushroomed to national prominence. The emergence of "stagflation" as an endemic condition of the national economy during the 1970's fulfilled the condition of abnormal stress in the socioeconomic system.

Burnham traced voting patterns in the late 1960's and speculated on the emergence of a "sixth party system." The social-group cleavages might be organized along lines differing from the New Deal coalition—black against white, peripheral regions against the center, blue-collar whites opposing blacks and affluent white liberals (Burnham, 1970, p. 169). A triggering event of great magnitude was missing, however. Burnham added that "the party system may have already moved beyond the possibility of critical realignment because of the dissolution of party-related identification and voting choice at the mass base" (173). Similarly, journalist David Broder (1972) argued that while realignment had long been overdue, a polarizing issue to "end the aimless drift of voters between the parties" was hard to discern.

Ladd and Lipset echoed the theme of "party disaggregation" in a pamphlet written after the 1972 election. They cited several indications that a large-scale restructuring of the party mass bases was not imminent, and that the parties were rapidly losing their ability to guide voters' choices. The weakening of party ties was alleged to be evident in (1) the rapid growth in self-identified Independents in the late 1960's; (2) the massive incidence of ticket-splitting (see also DeVries and Tarrance, 1972); and (3) the increased proportion of states and congressional districts with split outcomes in presidential, gubernatorial, senatorial, or House elections (Ladd and Lipset, 1973, pp. 33–65). The sources of disengagement of the electorate from the parties included increased higher education and electronic media usage and the breakup of traditional group alignments of the New Deal. The authors concluded: "It is a simple fact that Americans need parties much less now than in the past as intermediaries in shaping their electoral decisions. The electorate has become, for the long run, more issue oriented and more candidate oriented and, consequently, less party oriented" (Ladd and Lipset, 1973, p. 52).

Not all students of electoral behavior are convinced that major party disintegration has begun. In an article written after the 1968 election, Converse (1972) reported that recent SRC surveys did not show a steady decline in the ability of party identification to predict voting choice at various levels of office. Many of the so-called indicators of the erosion of party fidelity could be influenced by factors other than lowered relevance of party loyalties. For example, voting for different parties for president could be "strongly affected by particular sequences of candidate pairings and events that throw up third party intrusions" (Converse, 1972, p. 318). Increased ticket-splitting in recent state and local elections may reflect the greater partisan competition for office, especially in the South. Converse presented data on the rates of voluntary defection among party identifiers for presidential, gubernatorial, senatorial, and House elections. A significant decline (5 percent) in party fidelity was observed for the late 1960's, but Converse noted that the statistics "provide no proof whatever that party allegiance has been steadily declining in salience since the turn of the century."

Converse also cautioned against mistaking life-cycle effects—younger people entering the electorate with initially weaker partisan ties than habituated voters, for instance—for disaggregation. Since demographic change in the next decade will be very large, due to the maturation of the postwar baby crop and to lower voting age, "the evolution of the age table for the country will produce an electorate that shows higher partisan volatility" (Converse, 1972, p. 322). Despite evidence of weaker partisanship by 1968, Converse disagreed with the theory that party identification had become less important than issues or candidates: "party allegiance remained far and away the strongest determinant of most political cognitions and behavioral choices in the electorate." (The argument between Burnham and Converse over historical voting patterns has continued in their 1974 articles.)

In a similar vein, Rusk (1974) argued that not only was evidence of impending realignment scanty, but that the signs did not point to sufficient deterioration of voters' party ties to make an "end of parties" era possible. Studies of the key concerns in recent national elections have found little voter attention to economic issues, a crucial variable in any realignment. Instead, public concern with Vietnam, civil rights, and law and order contributed to voting volatility in 1968. But by 1970–72, the major parties had absorbed these "new issues" to the extent that their threat to the two-party system had been basically defused (Rusk, 1974, p. 1047).

The evidence presented in the following sections supports the contention that voter attachment to political parties has seriously eroded over the past twenty years; but to conclude that this fluidity foretells imminent realignment or disintegration may be to mistake short-term deflections for the trend line. James L. Sundquist's masterful *Dynamics of the Party System* (1973) developed a detailed model of the realignment process, drawn from the full history of American party systems. A key point to bear in mind in attempting to discern the direction of the current period is his contention that "if new issues arise that coincide with the existing line of party cleavage, they strengthen party cohesion, increase the distance between the parties, and reinforce the existing alignment" (1973, p. 297).

The issues prompting the party realignment/disintegration thesis were race, the Vietnam War, and the life-style conflicts that surfaced during the affluent late 1960's. These crises cut across existing party lines in the classic manner of realignment crises of the past. The major parties' ineptness in handling these issues within the framework of traditional party politics contributed to the disruption of the party coalitions built primarily upon the socioeconomic cleavages of the Great Depression. Had these crises continued to defy the parties' attempts to incorporate them onto the national agenda, and had they worsened steadily, they might very well have either forced a major realignment of the partisan loyalties in the electorate or completely fragmented the system. But to extrapolate along the direction in which the party system appeared to be heading through the early 1970's, as did several writers of the period, may lead to predictions ultimately falsified by an unforeseen turn of events.

Several years have passed since the promulgation of the realignment/disintegration theses, and the exacerbating issues have changed. The Vietnam War is over, the racial upheavals of the city have abated, and the cultural issues have given way to the economic concerns of unemployment and inflation. The economic crisis which festered throughout the Nixon administration and erupted in Ford's first months in office is exactly the type of "new issue" which coincides with the existing line of party cleavage. Instead of polarizing voters across party lines, as did the noneconomic issues of the 1960's, the economic crisis polarizes voters along those class lines which form the very backbone of the contemporary party system. The result may be a reidentification of traditional party bonds within the electorate. The voters' pocketbook interests may overwhelm their concern with a fading war, a dormant racial conflict, or crime, abortion, and marijuana. The potential revival of the existing party system under the impact of new economic issues must be kept in mind as the evidence for realignment and disintegration is examined.

Distribution of Party Identification

Considerable fluctuation in the aggregate distribution of party identifications for the six elections under study, grouped by the three major classifications, can be observed in the top panel of Table 7.1. From 1952 to 1972 the general pattern is one of decreasing identification with the two major parties and increasing Independent preference. However, the trends are not monotonic: Democratic preference is at a maximum in 1964, reflecting the impact of Goldwater, while Republican peaks occurred in 1956 and 1960, reflecting the legacy of the Eisenhower era. Independent preference is virtually constant over the first four elections of the series, showing marked increases only in 1968 and 1972, which suggests that disaggregation, if that is what the increased Independent preference truly represents, is a relatively recent phenomenon.

When respondents are assigned to one of the three main party groupings according to their responses to the first party identification question,

TABLE 7.1. PARTY IDENTIFICATION, 1952-1972

PARTY IDENTIFICATION	YEAR					
	1952	1956	1960	1964	1968	1972
Major Party Groups						
Democrats	48.1	45.3	46.4	52.2	46.0	41.0
Independents	24.0	24.4	23.4	23.0	29.5	35.2
Republicans	27.9	30.3	30.2	24.8	24.5	23.8
Total	100.0	100.0	100.0	100.0	100.0	100.0
Strength of Attachment						
Strong Democrat	22.8	21.5	20.9	27.1	20.3	14.9
Weak Democrat, Independent	35.0	30.4	32.0	34.4	35.7	37.3
Strict Independent	7.2	9.2	10.1	7.9	10.6	13.3
Weak Republican, Independent	21.0	23.4	21.0	19.4	23.6	24.0
Strong Republican	14.0	15.5	16.0	11.1	9.7	10.5
Total	100.0	100.0	100.0	100.0	100.0	100.0
(N)	(1718)	(1690)	(1864)	(1536)	(1531)	(2656)

Independents appear to increase 11 percent from 1952 to 1972, and there is a corresponding drop in party support. However, when the leaning tendencies among the Independents are allocated to the parties in the bottom panel of Table 7.1, the amount of change is less dramatic. Strong and weak Democrats and leaning Independents are 57.8 percent of the electorate in 1952 and 52.2 percent in 1972. Strong, weak, and leaning Republicans make up 35 percent in 1952 and 34.5 percent in 1972. Strict Independents without any partisan inclinations increase only 6.1 percent over the twenty years. And if the average across the first three surveys is taken as a baseline, strict Independents are only 1.8 percent more prevalent in 1968 than in 1952 and 4.5 percent more prevalent in 1972. The latter figures hardly suggest a stampede to abandon orientations towards either of the major parties.

Changes in party preference have occurred *within* the major parties, from strong commitment to a less strong attachment. The percentages of strong

Democrats and strong Republicans in 1972 are about two-thirds those of the 1950's. In this sense, party loyalties have noticeably weakened. However, Independents who lean toward one party are considerably more likely to support the candidates of that party than are strict Independents or those leaning towards the other party.

The detailed distributions in the lower panel of Table 7.1 indicate less dramatic shifts in party preference than do the top panel gross category percentages. Yet these distributions differ from one another in degree of similarity, as the paired measures of dissimilarity in Table 7.2 attest. These figures represent the percentage of respondents in one year who would have to shift their party identification in order to produce a distribution identical to another year. The lowest index values occur in the first three elections, indicating a high degree of stability in aggregate partisanship during the Eisenhower era. Much of this difference is probably sampling error and random fluctuations between elections. Higher values (between 6.8 and 8.7 percent) occur in the 1964 and 1968 elections than in the earlier elections, with the one exception of 1952-1964. But the highest level of disjuncture is for the 1972 election compared with all previous elections except 1968. The average dissimilarity is almost 12 percent. Most of this dissimilarity between 1972 and the four earliest periods arises from the previously noted differences in proportions of strong party supporters. The 1972 election does not break sharply with previous periods, as might have been expected of a critical election. Its index of dissimilarity with the 1968 election is only 5.5 percent, suggesting a stability in partisanship over this four-year period comparable to that which existed during the Eisenhower era. In fact, 1968 is less similar to any preceding election than it is to 1972. Thus, these latter two elections appear to cluster apart from the earlier 1952-60 period under surveillance, with 1964 occupying a position intermediate to both sets of

TABLE 7.2.   INDICES OF DISSIMILARITY IN PARTY IDENTIFICATION
             BETWEEN PAIRS OF ELECTIONS, 1952-1972

YEAR	YEAR				
	1956	1960	1964	1968	1972
1952	5.9	4.9	5.1	6.8	11.4
1956		3.5	8.7	7.0	11.6
1960			8.7	6.8	11.5
1964				8.2	12.9
1968					5.5

party identification distributions. Whether the 1972 figures lie exceptionally out of line due to unique circumstances of the specific national elections will only be determined by the results of the next election survey.

Growth of Independence

Our analysis indicates that changes in the distribution of party identifiers in the electorate occur at a glacial pace over the twenty years under study, particularly when the "hidden" identifiers among the Independents are allocated to the parties. The last two elections in the series appear to be substantially dissimilar to the earlier ones. These years are also associated with the largest upsurge in Independent preference as a first response to the partisanship question. This section inquires further into the processes underlying this increased Independent preference during the late 1960's and early 1970's. Of particular interest is whether the phenomenon of increasing detachment from parties is uniform throughout the population or concentrated within subpopulations. Since specific individuals were not followed across the two decades, direct evidence is not available on the rates of change of party identification. However, on the assumption that sample age groups represent the populations in those age categories at the given points in time, one can trace the changes in aggregate rates as birth cohorts age over the two decades.

The analysis of social change as a process of "demographic metabolism"—a succession of birth cohorts with unique experiences through the social system—has been widely accepted by demographers (Ryder, 1965). A growing number of studies apply the cohort-aging model to the analysis of political behavior (Oppenheim, 1970; Glenn and Grimes, 1968; Glenn, 1972; Abramson, 1974). Technical problems of separating effects due to aging, cohort succession, and period effects plagued efforts to isolate the unique contributions of demographic processes (Mason et al., 1973). The general findings on the Independent preference are that the most recent birth cohorts (after World War II) and the oldest cohorts (pre-1900's) are typically more independent than those born in between (Knoke and Hout, 1974). Thus, the conclusion that individuals become less Independent and more attached to major parties as they pass through the life cycle (Campbell et al., 1960, ch. 6; Merelman, 1970) may be an erroneous conclusion based upon cross-sectional analyses of samples drawn from several birth cohorts with different levels of Independent preference. Analysis of cohort rates of party identification over time may resolve the question of "generational" versus "life cycle" effects on Independent preference.

Table 7.3 presents the percentage of party preferences in each of four birth cohorts of approximately twenty years' separation. On the assumption that most individuals in a cohort are not eligible to enter the electorate until

TABLE 7.3.   PARTY IDENTIFICATION IN FOUR BIRTH COHORTS, 1952-1972

BIRTH COHORT (B) AND PARTY (P)	1952	1956	1960	YEAR (T) 1964	1968	1972	MEAN
1. Before 1905:							
Democrat	44.3	41.4	45.1	49.9	52.3	45.0	45.6
Independent	20.9	20.4	16.7	14.2	14.9	19.0	18.2
Republican	34.8	38.1	38.2	35.9	32.7	35.9	36.2
(N)	(661)	(499)	(539)	(337)	(281)	(315)	(2632)
2. 1905-1924:							
Democrat	50.4	48.4	46.6	54.9	46.1	46.7	48.7
Independent	26.1	23.1	25.8	21.6	27.2	25.1	24.8
Republican	23.5	28.5	27.6	23.5	26.7	28.3	26.5
(N)	(812)	(796)	(837)	(603)	(547)	(778)	(4373)
3. 1925-1944:							
Democrat	52.2	44.0	47.5	51.0	44.5	39.5	45.2
Independent	27.5	32.5	26.8	29.3	34.9	38.6	33.0
Republican	20.2	23.5	25.6	19.8	20.6	22.0	21.9
(N)	(222)	(375)	(488)	(590)	(611)	(952)	(3238)
4. 1945 & After:							
Democrat	-	-	-	-	36.8	33.3	33.8
Independent	-	-	-	-	51.7	51.9	51.9
Republican	-	-	-	-	11.5	14.7	14.3
(N)	-	-	-	-	(87)	(597)	(684)
Total:							
Democrat	48.3	45.3	46.4	52.3	46.1	40.9	46.0
Independent	24.2	24.4	23.4	22.9	29.4	35.3	27.3
Republican	27.5	30.3	30.2	24.8	24.5	23.8	26.7
(N)	(1695)	(1670)	(1864)	(1530)	(1526)	(2642)	(10927

twenty-one years of age (the exception was in 1972, when the voting age was lowered to eighteen), members of the oldest cohort (those born before 1905) had all entered the electorate before the Depression. By the time these individuals were first sampled in 1952, the youngest members were at least forty-seven years old. This cohort is 20.9 percent Independent in 1952, the least Independent and most Republican group in that year. This oldest cohort remains the least Independent and most Republican in each of the subsequently sampled years, when the cohort was a decreasing proportion of the electorate due to attrition of its members and the entry of younger cohorts. The mean level of Independent preference in the oldest cohort is not constant over the six observations, but generally declines about 5 percent through 1968, until it increases in 1972 to 19 percent. These changes may be due to sampling error but may also be due to genuine changes in the level of Independent preference due to period-specific short-term effects.

The second cohort, born between 1905 and 1924, entered the electorate in a period ranging from just prior to the Great Depression through the end of World War II. Their experiences during the politically formative years were largely shaped by the New Deal. As a result, they are the most Democratic of the four cohorts (averaged across the six sample values). The percentages of Independents and Republicans lie between the oldest and next youngest cohort.

The third birth cohort came to political maturity in the post–World War II era. The oldest members of this cold war cohort did not enter the electorate until 1946; hence, their proportion of the total population nearly triples from 1952 to 1968, when it begins to diminish. The Independent preference level is higher and the Republican level lower than it is in the two preceding cohorts. Some evidence that the Independent preference of this cohort increases over time is found in the highest levels at the last two years of the series. The third cohort is the only one in which the rate of Independent preference rises substantially over the period. However, this pattern contradicts the "life-cycle" hypothesis, which predicts a diminution of Independence as individuals age and establish ties to the major parties.

The life-cycle hypothesis was built upon cross-sectional studies in which inter-cohort comparisons had to be made. This pattern is equivalent to comparisons within the mean column in Table 7.3. The basic fallacy of the life-cycle hypothesis is its assumption that each successive cohort retraces the pattern of Independent preference traversed by previous cohorts. The present replication analysis finds no evidence that Independent preference *within* each cohort diminishes over time; in fact, this preference actually increases in one cohort. It is to be hoped that the present analysis will lay the life-cycle hypothesis to its well-deserved rest.

The fourth birth cohort's political record has barely begun. These persons were born during and after the last year of World War II, and hence could not enter the electorate until at least 1966 in most states. In 1972, the cohort was considerably expanded by the lowering of the voting age to 18; therefore, the cohort accounts for more than a fifth of the electorate. This cohort is sharply demarcated from the others, since a majority of its members are Independent in both 1968 and 1972. As additional members of this cohort continue to be added through the 1984 election, the mean level of Independent preference may undergo revision upward or downward. However, the evidence from the preceding three cohorts suggests that any substantial drop, i.e., to the levels of earlier cohorts, would be atypical.

The fundamental stability of party identification within cohorts over time is demonstrated by a log-linear analysis of Table 7.3. The baseline model which asserts an identical distribution of party identification in each cohort, (BT)(P), of course fails to fit the data (chi-square equal to 520.2, d.f. equal to 46). Allowing party to associate with time reduces this unexplained variation somewhat (chi-square equal to 369.5, d.f. equal to 36), but adding an association for party and cohort, (BT)(TP)(BP), yields a final model which accounts for the distributions in the table satisfactorily (chi-square equal to 34.2, d.f. equal to 30). Thus, one need not posit that the distributions of party preference within cohorts are changing over time, since the three-way interaction (BPT) is not required in the model.

The analysis establishes very clearly that the mean level of Independent preference in the electorate at any given historical period is primarily a consequence of the changing demographic composition of the population. New cohorts with different degrees of attachment to the parties enter the electorate and gradually replace the older cohorts with stronger traditions of political party loyalties. Evidence of major net changes of party loyalties *within* a cohort over time is found in only one cohort, and that change is in the opposite direction than that predicted by the "life-cycle" hypothesis. Period effects—the short-term influence of election campaigns and other political events—do not appear to have a substantial impact in moving the level of Independent preference between elections in the same direction for each cohort.

One way to measure the impact of demographic succession on the change in aggregate level of Independent preference is to ask what the rate would have been in 1972 if the proportion of birth cohorts in the population had not changed over twenty years. By applying the proportions for 1952 to the percentages of Independent identifiers in 1972, and adding up the predicted rates across cohorts (in effect, assuming that the post-1944 cohort had never been born), one would expect to find a mean level of 24.5 percent Independent instead of the observed rate of 35.3 percent. This expected level is not substantially different from the observed rate in 1952. Similarly, the expected rate in 1968 using observed proportions from the 1952 population is also 24.4 percent. Clearly, the increases in Independent preference for the electorate as a whole in 1968 and 1972 are traceable to two sources: (1) the slightly higher Independent preference in the 1925–44 cohort during this period; and (2) the appearance of the first waves of the Vietnam-era cohort with its very high level of Independent preference. Since the proportion of the electorate contributed by the third cohort is already beginning to decline, its disappearance will be offset by the substantial increases in the proportion of Independent identifiers contributed by the younger cohort.

The prognosis, based upon projections of the rates of demographic change through the 1970's and 1980's, and the assumption that there will be no major downward shifts in the currently observed percentages of Independents in each cohort, is for even higher mean levels of Independent preference in the electorate. This aggregate trend is backed by expected increases in many of the factors associated on the individual level with

Independence; there will be increases in the number of college-educated voters and white-collar occupations, an expansion in suburban living, and greater geographic mobility. As Independents continue to grow in number —and they have already surpassed the self-proclaimed Republicans as the second largest political grouping—they will pose increasingly difficult challenges to parties competing for their support. Although the data in the second panel of Table 7.1 did not demonstrate markedly decreasing levels of partisan inclination among Independents, such persons are less certain to back a party's candidates down the line.

Presidential Vote Changing

Identification with one or the other party does not automatically entail voting for that party's presidential and other candidates. The connection is more complex, involving the mediating processes of "perceptual adjustment by which the individual assembles an image of current politics consistent with his partisan allegiance" (Stokes, 1962). Although many researchers have focused upon partisan attitudes as psychological orientations intervening between party preferences and the pulling of a voting lever (Campbell et al., 1960; Goldberg, 1966), party identification appears to be the strongest single net correlate of the partisan choice for president (Knoke, 1974c).

The hypothesis of political disaggregation in the electorate implies that the party-vote correlation is diminishing. Even nominal Republican and Democratic partisans are increasingly disinclined to back their party's candidates. The growing number of self-proclaimed Independents, who have tendencies to split their ballots more evenly among both parties and to swing erratically between elections, will further reduce the possibility of predicting the vote from knowledge of the distribution of party preferences. The contrasting hypothesis of a persistent party alignment asserts that despite the shift in the marginal distributions of partisans, the predictive association of party and vote remains high.

The first measure of the association between party identification and voting behavior considers self-reports of past presidential voting. In the pre-election interview, respondents were asked whether, in the past elections in which they had been eligible to vote, they had always or almost always voted for the presidential candidates of one party or had changed their vote across parties between elections. These self-reports are displayed for the three major party groupings in Table 7.4. Consistent voting for Democratic presidential candidates by Democrats was exceptionally high (84.9 percent) in 1952, demonstrating the high degree of partisan commitment evoked by the New Deal and the Fair Deal. Republican support for Republican candidates during this era was much lower; about two out of three 1952 Republicans reported always or usually voting for a Republican candidate.

TABLE 7.4. PRESIDENTIAL VOTING AMONG PARTY IDENTIFIERS WHO HAVE
            VOTED AT LEAST ONCE, 1952-1972

PARTY AND	YEAR					
USUAL VOTE	1952	1956	1960	1964	1968	1972
			Percentages			
Democrats for Democrats	84.9	71.2	64.5	69.9	71.6	54.7
Republicans for Republicans	65.6	67.4	66.4	61.6	52.5	49.4
Independents for Both Parties	57.9	71.3	76.5	71.6	68.5	74.5
			Frequencies			
Democrats	629	626	733	654	584	892
Republicans	410	441	497	344	324	544
Independents	318	303	332	257	324	615

Thus, there was considerable vote changing in presidential elections by Republicans during the Roosevelt-Truman candidacies. Also, as the previous chapter disclosed, in 1952 proportionately more self-identified Republicans had once been Democrats than the reverse. It may be, then, that the less consistent pattern of past presidential support among Republicans arose from a greater defection of marginal Democrats and Independents to the Republican party during the first Eisenhower election.

Among those calling themselves Independents in 1952, slightly more than half report voting for candidates of each party in previous elections. However, in subsequent elections this level rises to between two-thirds and three-quarters of all Independents. The other Independents are actually "closet partisans": despite their proclamation of nonattachment on the initial question, they admit having consistently favored one party over the other in past presidential elections. The psychological Independence among these persons may be a form of social desirability response, rather than true Independence in the usual meaning of the word.

By the second Eisenhower election, the proportion of current Democrats claiming to have voted consistently for Democratic presidential candidates plummets, and it continues to fall through 1960. The level of Republican loyalty is constant through this period. Many Democrats defected in 1952 and 1956 to vote for Eisenhower without relinquishing their psychological attachment to the Democratic party. But in doing so, they could no longer report a record of past consistent support for Democratic candidates. The same phenomenon is revealed on the Republican side of the ledger in 1968, when consistent support drops 9 percent as a result of Republican defections during the preceding Goldwater election. The level of Democratic consistency rises in 1964 and 1968 as a consequence of high levels of support for Kennedy and Johnson among Democrats. But in 1968 the unpopularity of Humphrey and the attraction of Wallace for partisans of both major parties, again pulls down the levels of 1972 consistent voters in both major parties, especially among the Democrats. In 1972, barely half of all Republicans and Democrats report always having supported their party's presidential candidates, a very substantial decline from the levels reported twenty years earlier.

The partisans of both parties have gained much experience in switching support between parties at the presidential level of balloting. Such behavioral disengagement from a party standard may precede the weakening of psychological ties discovered in Table 7.1. The decline of consistent support for Democratic candidates among Democrats is especially steep in the South. Electoral Republicanism on the presidential level among Southern Democrats has grown enormously in the post-Roosevelt era. Five southern states gave their electoral college votes to Goldwater in 1964, while Wallace and Nixon together shut Humphrey out of the South in 1968. These aggregate ballot returns parallel the survey analysis for southern Democrats: in 1952 and 1956 the reported past consistency among Democrats in the southern and border states was above that of the national level, while in subsequent elections the rate was no higher than elsewhere in the country. An exception was the reportedly higher southern rate for 1968, which reflected Johnson's popularity among native southerners who still called themselves Democrats in that year. Goldwater's support in the South appears to have come from Independents and a growing number of southern Republicans, many of whom defected from the Democratic party before 1964.

State and Local Ticket-Splitting

Greater tendency to switch parties between presidential elections is not the only evidence of the evanescence of party loyalties over the past two decades. If we focus on state and local elections, the importance of party identifications in cuing voting behavior in less salient races can be gauged. In each survey's post-election interview, respondents reported whether they had voted a straight or split ticket for state and local elections (below the gubernatorial race) and, if straight, for which party they had voted. Although the form of the local ballot (single choice or multiple) may facilitate or impede ticket-splitting (Campbell and Miller, 1957), such causes of ticket-splitting are not expected to be a major contributor to change in aggregate rates over time. In their insightful book on ticket-splitting, DeVries and Tarrance (1972, p. 37) state that while they consider party identification less important in top races, it "probably still plays a major role in voting behavior, particularly for races below the level of Congress."

Table 7.5 reports the gross rates of straight-ticket voting on the state and local level and gives detailed breakdowns by party identification groupings. The total straight-ticket voting rate stabilizes between 71 and 73 percent in the first three elections but falls an average of 10 percent at each of the next three elections, ending in an orgy of ballot-dividing in 1972, when nearly three of every five persons cast votes for both parties. Clearly, the era of pulling the party lever has passed. The contributions of the three main partisan groups to this aggregate rate can be determined from the detailed breakdowns in Table 7.5. Independents are always considerably more likely to split their tickets for the lower political offices than are partisans. The rate of ticket-splitting among Independents grows from 40 percent in 1952 to 73 percent in 1972, and the increase is even more significant when one recalls that Independents constitute a greater proportion of voters at the later period.

Ticket-splitting among Democrats and Republicans is generally close to the average for all voters, although systematic differences in the relative levels of straight-ticket voting across parties can be observed. Landslide

TABLE 7.5. STRAIGHT-TICKET VOTING IN STATE AND LOCAL ELECTIONS,
            BY PARTY IDENTIFICATION, 1952-1972

PARTY AND VOTE	YEAR					
	1952	1956	1960	1964	1968	1972
Democrats for Democrats	65.5	72.6	73.0	65.4	52.3	42.6
Republicans for Republicans	76.2	71.0	71.1	49.1	56.7	50.8
Independents for Democrats	22.4	19.2	26.8	29.3	14.8	11.0
for Republicans	36.3	31.9	30.5	10.3	17.8	16.4
Total Straight- Ticket Voting	73.4	70.8	73.1	59.6	51.1	42.7

presidential votes occurred in four national elections: the two Eisenhower-Stevenson contests, Johnson-Goldwater, and Nixon-McGovern. In three of these, straight-ticket voting was highest among partisans of the victorious candidate's party by between 8 and 11 percent. Only in 1956 did a president's coattails fail to help his party's candidates further down the lists. The same relationship appears among those Independents who voted straight-party tickets. When Republican presidential candidates won big in 1952, 1956, and 1972, Independents voted for all state and local Republican candidates more often than they did for Democrats. When a Democratic presidential landslide materialized in 1964, its effects filtered down to the state and local contests; nearly three times as many Independents voted straight Democratic ballots as voted straight Republican. The two close national elections, 1960 and 1968, did not produce sizable differences in straight-ticket behavior either between partisan groups or within the Independent bloc. Thus, despite the erosion of consistent party support at even the state and local levels, ticket-splitting is not insensitive to events at the national level during presidential years. A popular presidential candidate is still worth several percentage points' advantage to his fellow candidates down the list, both in terms of retaining support within the party's voters and in attracting the Independent vote.

Another indicator of southern incorporation into the national electoral system is the rate of state and local straight-ticket voting among Democrats relative to the national levels. In the two Eisenhower elections, the rate at which southern Democrats supported state and local candidates with straight-ticket voting was some 15 to 18 percentage points higher than the rate for Democrats as a whole. But by 1972 the southern Democratic advantage in straight-ticket behavior exceeded the national average for all Democrats by only 3 percent. The great increase in the efforts of southern Republicans to contest state and local office races was largely responsible for this convergence.

National Elections—Congressional and Presidential

In the search for evidence of realignment, disaggregation, or perpetuation, voting behavior in national elections provides crucial data. Presidential election returns are the statistics most frequently cited to demonstrate the demise of one or the other party or to support contentions that the party system itself is coming unraveled. Congressional contests provide an essential baseline against which to measure presidential voting behavior. While a candidate's personality and campaign platform are influential in presidential balloting, the party label holds primacy in House races. If defection from one's party's presidential candidate is only one aspect of general change, similar patterns should be manifest on the level of congressional voting.

Although each district fields a different set of candidates, and cross-party voting may occur for highly particular reasons in some districts, such disturbances should be randomly distributed by time and space. Most voters know very little about the congressional candidates for whom they vote, often not even correctly recalling their names. Thus, party identification should be of paramount importance in these contests, and signs of increasing cross-party congressional voting would support the disaggregation thesis.

Figure 7.1 displays the rates of voting for Democratic congressional candidates among the three main party identification groupings from 1952 to 1972. There are no great differences in the extent to which Democrats and Republicans support candidates of the opposing party. In only two instances do fewer than 80 percent of partisans vote for candidates of their own party, and both involve Republicans (1964 and 1972). Independents have been fairly evenly divided in their support for congressional candidates, fluctuat-

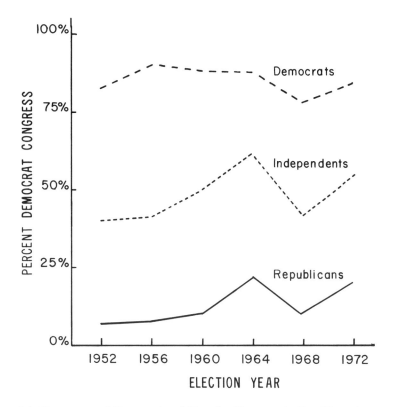

Figure 7.1. Percentage of Congressional Vote for Democratic Candidates by Party Identification, 1952–1972

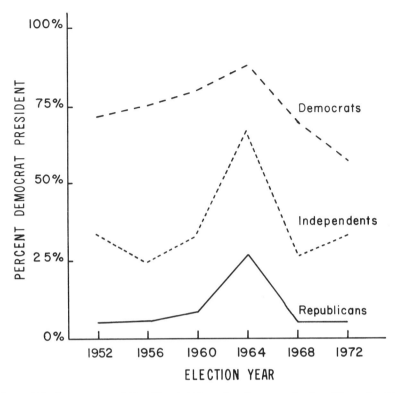

Figure 7.2. Percentage of Presidential Vote for Democratic Candidates by Party Identification, 1952–1972

ing within a band between 40 and 60 percent without apparent trend toward either party.

The effects of specific elections are noticeable in the last three elections. In 1964, when Goldwater headed the Republican ticket, the increase in Democratic congressional voting among both Independents and Republicans jumps above the previous election, while the Democratic rate holds constant at about 90 percent. In 1968, the drop-off in Democratic congressional support at all three levels of party identification is precipitous, especially among Independents. Curiously, in 1972, while Nixon is forging the largest majority of any Republican president since Harding, the level of Democratic congressional voting *increases* within each partisan group. Republican support for Democratic candidates rises nearly 10 percent over 1968. The result is a narrowing of the gap between Democrats and Republicans, from an 82 percent difference in congressional voting in 1956 to a 65 percent difference in 1972. The decreased difference is less dramatic if 1952 is taken as the origin of the trend, since the difference then was only 76 percent.

This inter-party convergence in congressional voting implies a diminution of the party identification-vote correlation. The 1972 differences are still quite substantial and are probably larger than some during the early years of the New Deal.

A better case for the convergence of voting behavior across party lines can be made with the data from presidential races. Figure 7.2 presents these results. The trends are considerably more volatile than are those for the congressional elections. Democratic votes for Republican candidates exceed Republican votes for the Democrats in the 1952, 1956, and 1960 contests. But the trend within both parties is towards greater support of the Democratic candidates, and it culminates in LBJ's rout of Goldwater in 1964, with substantial upsurges of Democratic presidential balloting at all three levels, especially among Independents. Among Independents, the 1964 election was a reversal of the other contests, in which these nonpartisans usually split two-to-one for the Republican candidate. But Johnson's landslide was not built solely upon captured Independents and stay-at-home Republicans. LBJ attracted more than a quarter of the Republican vote, a proportion exceeding even the usual Republican support for Democratic congressional candidates and rivaling Eisenhower's pull among Democrats in 1952 and 1956.

The figures for 1968 are complicated by Wallace's presence. He took 11.5 percent of the Democratic vote, 5.3 percent of the Republicans, and 17.7 percent of Independents. The drop-off in Democratic voting was precipitous at all levels of party identification, particularly among Democrats. In 1972, while Democratic congressional voting increased across all party categories, Democratic support for the presidential candidate continued to plummet. Fewer than six of ten nominal Democrats voted for McGovern, opening up the largest difference in congressional and presidential votes among Democrats in the twenty years (27 percent). Republican-Democrat differentials in presidential voting converge much more rapidly than do congressional voting differences during the same period. From an average of 70 percent difference in 1952, 1956, and 1960, the presidential difference falls to 62 percent in 1964, 64 percent in 1968, and only 52 percent in 1972.

These rates imply a sharp diminution of the effectiveness of party identification as a predictor of the presidential vote, though it is much more useful in predicting the congressional vote. Yet a measure of association between party identification and each of these national votes reveals virtually no difference. The measure of association, gamma, takes on a value of +1.00 if all partisans vote for the candidate of their party and 0 if votes are equally distributed across parties. The association of party identification with congressional vote is only slightly higher than for presidential vote in each year, and it is actually lower in 1968, when the presence of a third candidate alters the pattern. The twenty-year trend in party-vote association is definitely downward in both series, but the descent is very gradual. The

TABLE 7.6.   PERCENTAGE OF VOTERS CASTING PRESIDENTIAL AND CON-
             GRESSIONAL VOTES FOR SAME PARTY, BY PARTY IDENTIFICATION,
             1952-1972

| PARTY | YEAR | | | | | |
IDENTIFICATION	1952	1956	1960	1964	1968 **	1972
Democrat	69.2	74.1	78.8	83.8	71.6	54.9
Republican	91.9	91.1	87.0	65.8	82.6	66.9
Independent*	86.8	77.5	78.2	83.1	76.9	77.6
Total	87.5	84.5	86.0	84.9	82.2	70.4

*Consistent for Democrats or Republicans
**Excludes Wallace voters

congressional series drops from +.88 to +.78, while the presidential statistics
go from +.86 to +.75. Neither of these measures indicates a severe disruption of the capacity of party identifications to shape national voting choices
within the electorate.

One last piece of evidence on the party-vote correlation for national
elections is the national ticket-splitting between presidential and congressional candidates by party identification, illustrated in Table 7.6. The
percentage of all respondents voting for both presidential and congressional
candidates from the same party holds fairly steady from 1952 to 1964, then
drops slightly in 1968 and enormously in 1972. Broken down by party, the
percentages for Democrats and Republicans represent consistent votes for
candidates of the respective parties, while for Independents the percentages
reflect consistent votes for either Democratic or Republican presidential and
congressional candidates. Defections among Democrats and Republicans
may occur in different races and in different elections. In 1952 and 1972,
Democrats defected to the Republican presidential candidates while continuing to support Democratic congressional candidates. The high 1964
Republican defection involved defection at both presidential and congressional levels, but in 1972 Republican defection consisted of high rates of
voting for Democratic congressional candidates. Independents have been
generally more consistent in voting for candidates from the same party over
the twenty years surveyed.

The Wallace Vote and Realignment

Third-party movements arising during crisis periods have been a significant factor in past critical realignments. The "politics as usual" orientation
of the major parties in a given historical system is unable to cope with the

exigencies of a crisis. Third-party leaders step into the vacuum and attempt
to aggregate the interests of the aggrieved citizens (see Burnham, 1970, pp.
27–30). As the major parties eventually confront the issues raised by the
protest movement, the issues may be incorporated by one or the other party
as a conscious strategem to gain or maintain electoral dominance under the
new party alignment. Frequently, third-party movements mobilize previously nonparticipating strata of society or act as "halfway houses" in the
transition of disaffected elements from one major party to the opposing
coalition.

The Wallace movement of the late 1960's and early 1970's articulated the
resentment of many white Americans over the perceived inequities of the
civil rights movement and the remoteness of the federal government from
effective political control. As an example of a classic third-party movement,
the Wallace phenomenon falls, as Burnham (1970, p. 143) writes, "almost
too easily into the historical pattern of abnormal phenomena associated with
the early stages of critical realignment." In primaries and in his one national
presidential campaign, Wallace appealed primarily to peripheral segments of
the electorate: rural and small-town, southern, blue collar, and unionized
(Converse et al., 1969, p. 1102). Although Wallace polled only 13 percent of
the total popular vote in 1968, his regional strength in the South was higher.
The much-touted Nixon "southern strategy" in the 1972 reelection campaign
sought to neutralize or woo to Republicanism the Wallace base within the
South and the border states. The capricious removal of Wallace from the
1972 race confronted his followers with the choice between a Republican
candidate espousing many of their issues and a Democratic candidate
standing for everything which had alienated many southern Democrats and
Independents from the national party for twenty years.

While many observers have noted the superficial similarity of the Goldwater and Wallace appeals—both are presumably on the ideological right
—detailed analyses have disclosed distinct bases of social support. Goldwater's partisans tended to be educated, urban, and white collar, while "Wallace
was a poor man's Goldwater" (Converse et al., 1969, p. 1102). However,
Table 7.7 presents evidence that a major source of Wallace's 1968 strength
nationwide was among voters who had backed Goldwater in the previous
election (the analysis excludes respondents not voting in both elections). In
1968 the percentage of Wallace votes among ex-Goldwater voters (14.2) is
nearly twice the percentage of such votes among ex-LBJ voters (7.7).
When the relationship is further specified by the 1968 party identification of
the respondent, revealing interactions occur. Johnson voters do not differ
much in their preference for Wallace across all three party groupings:
Independents and Democrats vote for Wallace only 6 percent more than
do Republicans.

TABLE 7.7.   PARTY ORIGINS AND DESTINATIONS OF THE 1968 WALLACE VOTE

	Percent Voting for Wallace in 1968	
1968 PARTY	1964 VOTE	
	Goldwater	Johnson
Democrat	50.0	8.4
Independent	22.8	8.7
Republican	6.3	2.8
Total	14.2	7.7
(N)	(282)	(557)

	1968 Wallace Voters in the 1972 Election		
1972 PARTY	1972 VOTE		
	Nixon	McGovern	(N)
Democrat	75	25	(59)
Independent	78	22	(45)
Republican	95	5	(20)
Total	79	21	(124)

However, Goldwater voters exhibit a very steep gradient when analyzed by party identification. Few of those Republicans who stuck to Goldwater through the disaster of 1964 turn to Wallace in 1968—they are solidly in Nixon's camp. But almost a quarter of Independent and half of all Democratic Goldwater backers turn to Wallace rather than to Nixon or Humphrey. The latter group is heavily southern and represents nominal Democrats defecting from the national ticket for the second election in a row. These doubly deviant Democrats provide only a tenth of Wallace's support, however. Altogether, nearly half (48 percent) of Wallace's vote among persons voting in both elections comes from Goldwater voters of all partisan stripes.

Given Nixon's 1972 smashing of McGovern not only in the South but everywhere, one would not expect to see many 1968 Wallace voters voting for a Democrat perceived by many as a liberal/radical with heavy black commitments. The bottom panel of Table 7.7 bears out this expectation. Nixon's margin of victory from all voters was 64 percent, but previous

Wallace voters vote for Nixon by nearly 80 percent. Only a small gradient appears across current party groupings, showing McGovern to be slightly more popular among Democratic and Independent Wallace voters of the previous election. The rate of 1972 nonvoting among 1968 Wallace voters is about equal to that of the rest of the electorate, demonstrating no tendency among Wallace's backers to sit out the 1972 election for lack of an acceptable candidate.

The analysis to this point has strongly implicated the Wallace political base in a lengthy history of flirtation with the Republican presidential ticket. However, no evidence exists that desertion of the Democratic national party over three or more elections brought about a substantial realignment of party identifications within the Wallace contingent. Forty-five percent of Wallace voters identify with the Democrats in 1968, and thirteen percent identify with the Republicans. Among 1972 voters who voted for Wallace in 1968, 48 percent report current Democratic affiliation and 16 percent report Republican affiliation. An exclusive focus upon the top of the ticket in these national election years obscures the continued commitment of Wallace voters to Democratic candidates on the congressional, state, and local levels. The Wallace movement was very much a personal phenomenon of the late 1960's; it lacked an institutionalized structure to hold and bind into a permanent coalition the protest votes garnered in a brief national campaign. The Republican southern strategy, aimed as much at a nationwide state of mind as at a particular geographic region, was similarly a personal triumph but a party failure. The upheavals of 1964–72 at the presidential level did not produce a drastic revision of the social composition of the major party coalitions.

Party Identification and the Presidential Vote: A Causal Model

Ladd and Lipset have claimed that the electorate is now "more issue oriented and more candidate oriented and, consequently, less party oriented." This tripartite division of factors affecting the selection of a president draws upon the Survey Research Center tradition first expressed by Campbell et al. (1954). In *The Voter Decides*, the analysis of the 1952 presidential contest focused upon psychological variables intervening between the external world and the voter's ultimate choice. Party identification, concern with issues of national government policy, and personal attraction to the presidential candidates were each shown to have strong positive correlations with the direction of the vote. While an attempt was made to assess the relative strength of these three motivations to vote, the crude method of cross-tabulation did not permit quantitative measures of net impact (Campbell et al., 1954, pp. 144–64).

A later multiple regression analysis pointed to the party identification variable as more important than either issues or candidate attractiveness (Campbell and Stokes, 1959). But a still later report, in *The American Voter* (Campbell et al., 1960), gave the impression that once the six partisan attitude variables measuring issues and candidate preferences were controlled, the addition of party identification to the regression equation would add less than 2 percent to the explained variance. The authors attributed this small residual effect of party identification mainly to "persons who are without a well-developed image of the things to which their vote relates."

Recently, Kelley and Mirer (1974) developed a "voter's decision rule" to predict the presidential vote using only candidate evaluations and party identifications. The rule assumes that the voter weights his likes and dislikes for each candidate and votes for the one for whom he has the greatest net favorable attitude, if there is one. If the voter has no "favorite," he votes on the basis of his party identification, if he has one. If neither condition is met, the voter reaches a null decision. Using this rule, the authors correctly predicted 88 percent of the voters' choices for president across five SRC surveys.

Recent years have seen a growing interest in "issue voting," and new ways of measuring the effect of policy preferences on choice among presidential candidates have been developed. RePass (1971), for example, employed an index of issues of national importance named by respondents as being of most concern to them. A multiple regression of the vote found that candidates, issues, and party identification ranked in that order of importance. Other studies used a "proximity measure," which assesses the distance between a voter's preferred policy on some political issue and the position he imputes to a candidate (Brody and Page, 1972; Page and Brody, 1972; Miller et al., 1973). In general, the more distance between a candidate's perceived stance and the voter's, the less likely the respondent is to cast his vote for that candidate. The strong relationship between issue proximity and vote may be, to some unknown extent, spuriously inflated by rationalization and persuasion (Miller et al., 1973, n. 21).

A multivariate analysis of the 1972 election, using a "feeling thermometer" evaluation of candidates, party identification, and proximity measures of several issue dimensions, found that issues had substantially higher direct effects on the vote than did party identification, but candidate evaluations accounted for most of the explained variance (Miller et al., 1973). However, the authors acknowledge that long-term effects of party identification on the vote may be indirect through the intervening candidate and issue variables in the regression equation. When indirect effects in an elementary path analysis were taken into account, candidate evaluations, issues, and party identifications had about equal importance in deciding the presidential vote.

The feeling thermometers and proximity ratings are not available in the SRC surveys prior to 1968, so a longitudinal comparison of the changes in the components of the vote cannot use them. Other strategies for measuring issues have involved fixed-choice indexes of responses to a series of policy questions (Knoke, 1974c) and an index combining the fixed-choice equivalents to open-ended likes and dislikes about candidates and parties (Schulman and Pomper, 1975). Neither method is entirely satisfactory, and both, like the proximity measures, may distort the impact of issues during a campaign. Fixed-choice items often confront the respondent with issues which are neither salient nor relevant to him, and these items may provoke a "nonattitude" response (Converse, 1970). Use of open-ended items improves the saliency of topics but also allows voters to select issues which may not be addressed by the candidates in the course of the campaign. The problem of measuring issue preferences is clearly a knotty one, and it needs much more, careful work. Unfortunately, a secondary data analysis cannot undertake this developmental research.

To enable us to use all six surveys, candidate evaluations and issue dimensions were measured only by the open-ended responses to queries on likes and dislikes about the two parties and the two major presidential candidates. To ensure that all six elections could be compared, only three responses to each question were counted. A presidential candidate evaluation item was constructed by totaling the number of pro-Republican and anti-Democratic responses and subtracting the number of anti-Republican and pro-Democratic answers to the candidate questions. The resulting value indicates the net favorable partisan direction of the respondent. (This index is also used by Stokes, 1966; Knoke, 1974c; Kelley and Mirer, 1974; and Schulman and Pomper, 1975.) Similarly, a "partisan issues" measure was constructed by finding the net partisan direction of questions concerning likes and dislikes about the two major parties (except when the candidates were mentioned). The partisan issues score is thus independent of specific content, treating any and all types of "issues" as valid. The crudeness of the issues measure may underestimate the impact of some specific issues in a given campaign.

To determine the relative impact of candidate evaluation, partisan issues, and party identification (five-point scale) on presidential voting, the major-party dichotomy (Republican = 1, Democrat = 0; excluding all nonvoters and minor-party voters) was regressed upon these three variables. The results are displayed in Table 7.8. The unstandardized b coefficients in the top panel show the change in the probability of voting Republican for each change of one unit in party identification, candidate evaluation, or partisan issues net of the other two independent variables. The b's for party identification fluctuate between .10 and .13 but peak at .15 in 1972. These

TABLE 7.8.   REGRESSION OF TWO-PARTY PRESIDENTIAL VOTE ON PARTY
              IDENTIFICATION, CANDIDATE EVALUATION, AND PARTISAN
              ISSUES, 1952-1972

VARIABLES	1952	1956	1960	1964	1968	1972
				YEAR		
			Unstandardized b's			
Party Identification	.10	.13	.12	.10	.13	.15
Candidate Evaluation	.05	.06	.06	.07	.07	.08
Partisan Issues	.05	.04	.03	.03	.03	.002
(Constant)	(.288)	(.156)	(.168)	(.207)	(.157)	(.181)
			Standardized β's			
Party Identification	.30	.36	.33	.28	.35	.40
Candidate Evaluation	.28	.28	.39	.50	.44	.34
Partisan Issues	.30	.22	.18	.13	.13	.007
Multiple R^2	.593	.575	.651	.626	.651	.379

coefficients indicate a net difference of from 40 percent to 60 percent
between the Republican voting of strong Republicans and that of strong
Democrats. The coefficients for candidates monotonically increase from
1952 to 1972, while those for issues decreased to insignificance by 1972.

Determination of the relative importance of the three factors in each year
relies upon the standardized β regression (path) coefficients in the lower
panel of Table 7.8. In 1952 the three factors are identical in magnitude. A
change in one standard deviation of party, candidate, or issues results in a
change of just under a third of a standard deviation (which is .49) of the
probability of voting for the Republican. Altogether, the three variables in
additive combination account for more than 59 percent of the variance in
voting behavior.

Over the first five elections, the total proportion of variance explained by
the three-variable model hovers consistently around the 60 percent mark.
But the relative importance of the three causal components undergoes
considerable alteration. Partisan issues plummet in their ability to influence
the vote, disappearing altogether by 1972. Candidate preference rises to a

peak in 1964, when Goldwater appears to have evoked great adverse personal reactions among voters (Converse et al., 1965; Stokes, 1966), then tapers off over the next two elections. The party identification variable is clearly less important than candidate preferences in 1960, 1964, and 1968, but it rebounds strongly in 1972.

Party identification did not erode by either standardized or unstandardized measures of its relative contribution to the presidential vote over the twenty years surveyed. Party identification shows no secular trend toward becoming less important than candidate preference, and it is definitely becoming more important than issues. However, the overall determinancy of presidential vote dips sharply in 1972. The multiple R^2 is only .379. While the slopes for party identification and candidates are somewhat steeper in that election than in 1968, the scatter of observations around the multiple regression line is greater in 1972. In this sense, the most recent presidential election is less dependent upon party identification than previous elections have been. The situational factors surrounding the McGovern campaign, which induced more Democrats to defect from the party at the presidential level than at any time in generations, may have been too idiosyncratic to prophesy a lasting disintegration of the party-vote relationship. Clearly, of the factors having the greatest predictive power, party identification ranks among the top.

Summary

This chapter has surveyed most of the available evidence in the SRC studies for signs of party realignment or disintegration. To review the findings briefly: the number of Independents grew sharply in the late 1960's, although many of these persons could be designated as leaning to one or the other party. The proportion of strong partisans dropped off sharply in both parties. Much of this change in aggregate party identification distributions appears to be the result of a cohort-succession process, with more Independent, younger birth cohorts replacing more partisan, older cohorts. No evidence supported the "aging" hypothesis, i.e., that Independent preference gives way to partisan commitment as cohorts mature. Indicators of consistent voting for president, congressmen, and state and local offices along party lines all took a nose-dive in the latter part of the series. Ticket splitting rose dramatically, indicating an unwillingness among voters to be constrained by their usual party affiliations in choosing candidates.

All these changes may signal growing voter dissatisfaction with the choices offered by political parties. As such, this evidence does not contradict the thesis that party disintegration has grown apace in recent years. However, the alternative thesis of party realignment, which suggests that the Republican party is assuming the dominant role either in the standing preferences or in the voting behavior of the electorate, received virtually no support. A dissection of the partisan origins and destinations of the 1968 vote for George Wallace indicated that while Nixon was the major beneficiary in 1972, Wallace voters were no less Democratic in party identification in 1972 than they had been in 1968. The predictions of an imminent Republican majority were overly optimistic projections based on the unique circumstances of the first Nixon election.

Finally, the importance of party identifications in stabilizing political behavior is seen in the regression analyses of the two-party presidential vote. Party preference and candidate evaluation were about equal in their impact, but the importance of issues declined markedly from 1952 to 1972. The declining impact of issues flies in the face of the widely held belief that voters are more issue-conscious than ever. While the insignificance of the issue component may lie partly in the crudeness of the measure, an alternative interpretation stresses the ambiguity of the parties' positions and their perceived inability to resolve the political problems of the era. The issues of the 1968 and 1972 elections, when disintegration of voter ties to the parties rose to a peak, may have been superseded in the economic crises which emerged with full force in 1974. As I will demonstrate, aggregated time series data support the argument that the American electorate still responds politically to downturns in the business cycle by rallying to the Democratic party.

Chapter VIII

Whither the Party System?

Until now, the empirical evidence on party identification and voting behavior has focused on the relationships among variables at the time of each survey and the changes that occur in these variables between surveys. In this final chapter, the analysis shifts from the level of individuals to the dynamics of the electoral system, in a discussion that spans the series of biennial national elections after World War II. Aggregate characteristics of the electorate at each election are used to estimate the impact of political and economic events on the distribution of party affiliations and voting choices. The resulting equations form a preliminary social indicators model of the electoral system which can predict the electoral outcome of changes in the economy. Since the current indicators all spell hard times ahead for the Republican party, I conclude by speculating on the implications for the forthcoming national election.

Time Series Analysis

Aggregated data is used extensively in social and political research, but the vast bulk are cross-sectional comparisons of ecological units such as states or nations at a given point in time. Surprisingly little research with aggregated time series data has appeared in political science or political sociology. The methodology for time series analysis was developed in statistics and econometrics, but other social sciences were slow to adopt it, perhaps in part because of the absence of high-quality data covering extended periods of time. Among the previous studies relevant and helpful to the present undertaking were Mueller's investigations of presidential popularity (1970, 1973) and Kramer's analysis of short-term fluctuations in voting (1971).

Mueller's study used some 300 Gallup polls spanning the administrations of Truman through Johnson in which a national sample was asked, "Do you approve or disapprove of the way President＿＿＿is handling his job?" After fitting a series of equations, Mueller found that the percentage approving was a linear function of five variables:

(1) the number of years since a "rally point," consisting of the beginning of a presidential term and all international events considered dramatic enough to boost the popularity rating
(2) an economic slump variable, measured as the increase in the unemployment rate over that prevailing when the incumbent's term began, but set to zero if the rate falls, since an improving economy does not boost popularity
(3) a coalition of minorities variable, measured as the number of years since inauguration or reelection, to capture the progressive alienation of approval among initial supporters
(4) a war variable to capture the negative impact of Korea and Vietnam
(5) dummy variables for each presidential term to capture the personality factors of the incumbent's term in office.

The resulting linear regression disclosed that these variables accounted for 86 percent of the variation in the Gallup poll approval ratings. (See Hibbs, 1974, for a reanalysis of the data using a different estimating technique, which led to somewhat different results.) Since explaining variation in presidential popularity is not a concern of this book, a detailed recapitulation of Mueller's equations is not warranted. But the study remains a major example of the way economic and political events can be incorporated into a model to explain over-time variation in mass political phenomena. The dependent variable of Mueller's analysis will be used as an independent factor in attempting to account for party identification and voting rates in the model developed below.

Kramer's study of United States congressional voting behavior covered a wider period than that under consideration here. Kramer conceptualized a major party's share of the two-party vote as a function of voter satisfaction with the incumbent party's performance while in office. Dissatisfaction results in votes against the incumbent "team." In operational terms, aggregate satisfaction was represented by annual changes in such economic indicators as monetary income, real income, price levels (cost-of-living), and the unemployment rate. For congressional elections from 1896 to 1964, Kramer fitted several equations involving different combinations of variables which accounted for between 48 and 64 percent of the variation in the two-party vote. Among the economic variables, real personal income was the most important, while the rate of inflation or changes in unemployment had no net effect. Presidential coattails were also important, with "as much as 30 percent of the extra votes attracted by a strong presidential candidate, who runs well ahead of his ticket, benefitting the congressional candidates of his party" (page 141). Since Kramer's analysis concerns one of the dependent variables used below (although I use it for only the post-World War II period), the same set of explanatory variables will be investigated, along with additional, specifically political causes of voting distributions.

One goal of my analysis is to develop an initial social indicators model of the American electoral system. Such models link output descriptive indicators, which are the end products of social processes (e.g., crime rates, school enrollments), to analytic indicators which produce the values of the output indicators (see Land, 1975, for a detailed programmatic statement). The output variables in the present study are the distributions of votes for national political candidates and the subjective party identifications in the population in elections from 1948 through 1974.

Previous chapters have focused on the relationships between individual attributes at each point in time, but the social indicators model used in this chapter focuses on variation in the relationships between highly aggregated measures over time. Because the levels of analysis differ, the causes of behavior may be markedly different in the cross-sectional and time-series analyses. For example, while social class and voting behavior are correlated in samples of individuals, the class composition of the society is basically constant over the time series. As a consequence, the correlation of the percentage of manual workers with congressional voting distributions across elections is virtually nil. These differential findings about the impact of class are not necessarily contradictory. Social class remains an important factor in the voting decisions of individuals. Since the relationship is largely invariant across time, class cannot account for changes observed in the distribution of votes between parties over elections. The party distribution of the total vote responds to other factors having an approximately equal effect on all social classes. The social indicators model of the electoral process thus complements the static cross-sectional analyses developed in the previous chapters by revealing the dynamics of the system.

A Social Indicators Model

A social indicators model of the American electoral system encounters the problem of a small number of observations on which to estimate equations. Only seven presidential and fourteen congressional contests took place from 1948 to 1974. The latter races may offer a better measure of the nation's political mood, since congressional contests, in the aggregate, are generally devoid of the emphasis on personality which dominates presidential campaigns. Congressional elections thus may be closer to being pure referenda on the effectiveness of the political parties as governmental managers. The dependent variable in the social indicators model is the percentage of all congressional votes cast across all districts which are received by the Republican candidates at each biennial election (RCONG). The correlation with the percentage received by all Democratic candidates is so high (–.97) that the two are almost perfect inverses.

A variety of political and economic measures were considered for inclusion in the models predicting the congressional vote. The percentages of the electorate identifying with the Republican (RPID) and Democratic (DPID) parties were obtained for each election year from SRC or Gallup polls. Another valuable indicator of political disposition is a Gallup poll question asking what the most important problem facing the nation is and which party could do a better job of handling it. The percentages of voters picking the Democratic (DPROB) and Republican party (RPROB) as most competent are available from surveys conducted prior to all elections except those in 1952 and 1954. The correlations between the problem measures and the other variables were calculated without these two observations. A third political variable is the average presidential popularity rating (PRESPOP) during the year. Since the political impact the president's job performance has upon the congressional vote is likely to differ according to the president's party, PRESPOP was measured as the approval rating if the incumbent was a Democrat and the disapproval rating if he was a Republican.

A large number of economic measures are available from government publications. These range from highly aggregated indicators like Gross National Product (GNP) to per capita measures of hourly wages in specific industries and may be expressed in current dollars or in constant dollars (the latter adjust for the effects of inflation). After much study and preliminary investigation, two economic measures were chosen for inclusion. The first is annual unemployment as a percentage of the civilian labor force (UNEMP). The second is the annual percentage change in the gross weekly earnings of nonsupervisory personnel in nonagricultural industries, measured in constant (1967 = 100) dollars (CGWE). While both indicators of economic performance may seem highly restricted, they represent two widely publicized economic behaviors with major political implications. The unemployment rates appear monthly in newspaper and television reports, and are widely interpreted as a sign of the national government's ability to sustain a full-employment economy. Similarly, the change in real wages reflects the relative prosperity and productivity of a major segment of the work force. The two measures are only moderately intercorrelated (–.25), indicating that they tap different dimensions of economic performance.

In the social indicators model of the congressional election system from 1948 to 1974, UNEMP, CGWE, PRESPOP, DPROB, and RPROB are considered predetermined variables. That is, their values are determined by processes outside the scope of this model, and therefore, they do not appear as dependent variables in any equation. Among the three endogenous variables, the party identification variables (DPID and RPID) are conceptualized as intervening between the exogenous variables and RCONG. In estimating the equations presented below, each regression was run twice, first including all antecedent variables, and then retaining only those with significant effects.

The first two equations are for the Republican and Democratic party identifications, respectively.

(1) $\text{RPID}_t = 11.82 + 0.75\ \text{RPID}_{t-1} + 0.47\ \text{CGWE}_t - 0.18\ \text{DPROB}_t.$
          (3.72)   (.10)   (.16)   (.06)

          $R = .963$ $SE = 1.18$ $N = 14$

(2) $\text{DPID}_t = 36.08 + 0.37\ \text{DPID}_{t-1} - 0.51\ \text{YOUNG}_t + 0.22\ \text{DPROB}_t.$
          (11.67)   (.14)   (.23)   (.06)

          $R = .953$ $SE = 1.15$ $N = 14$

The figures in parentheses below each equation are the standard errors for the regression constants and coefficients. Values larger than twice the standard errors may be considered highly significant. The SE is the standard error for the equation. The multiple R shows that each equation accounts for more than 90 percent of the variation in the percentages identifying with each party. Most of this variance, however, is due to the effect of the same variable lagged by one year. This lagged effect represents the persistence of party preferences over time. It is twice as large for RPID as for DPID, since a 1 percent difference in Republican support in the previous year accounts for .75 percent in the current year, while 1 percent of DPID_{t-1} produces only .37 percent in DPID_t.

The other predetermined variables have significant effects on party preferences. A 1 percent rise in those saying the Democratic party can handle national problems better than the Republicans (DPROB) cuts Republican party identification by .18 percent while increasing Democratic support by about the same amount. (RPROB had no significant effect.) Republican party identification responds to earnings changes: real growth raises it and real decline erodes it. Since real earnings fell or failed to advance in the highly inflationary period of the late 1960's and early 1970's, Republican party strength suffered greatly during this period. Neither economic variable has a significant effect on Democratic party identification, but a demographic variable, the percentage of the electorate aged twenty to twenty nine (YOUNG), has a negative impact. Each increase of 1 percent in the number of young voters reduces Democratic affiliation by half a percentage, primarily as a result of the greater Independent preference in the baby-boom generation, which was documented in Chapter VII.

Neither UNEMP nor PRESPOP appears in either party identification equation. The zero-order correlations reveal that higher levels of unemployment co-vary positively with Democratic support and inversely with Republican, as might be expected. Similarly, the simple r's between PRESPOP are positive with Democratic affiliation and negative with Republican. However, once the other variables are entered into the equation, neither variable has a net effect on the level of party identification.

The third dependent variable in the model is the percentage of votes cast for Republican congressional candidates.

(3) $RCONG_t = 51.64 + 0.08\ RPID_t + 0.59\ CGWE_t\ -0.17\ DPROB_t$
     (4.34)   (.11)   (.15)   (.06)
     $- 0.62\ UNEMP_t.$
     (.35)

     $R = .958$ $SE = 1.02$ $N = 14$

Again, the equation accounts for more than 90 percent of the variation in vote returns for the fourteen elections. Both economic variables affect Republican fortunes. Each percentage of unemployment (UNEMP) costs the Republican candidates more than ½ of a percent of the aggregate vote percentage, while each percent increase in CGWE raises the vote percentage by almost the identical amount. The effect of perceptions that the Democratic party is better able to handle national problems (DPROB) costs the Republican votes, just as in equation (1) it costs them subjective affiliation. For each additional 6 percent saying the Democrats can do a better job, Republican congressional candidates lose another 1 percent in the aggregate vote.

The effect of party identification (RPID) on the Republican congressional vote (RCONG) is very small and does not exceed the standard error. Nevertheless, it is retained in the equation since it is a theoretically important variable and since the sign of its coefficient is in the expected direction. A change of 1 percent in the level of party identification yields a rise of less than $1/10$ of a percent in the aggregate congressional vote for Republican candidates. The zero-order relationship between RPID and RCONG across the fourteen elections is substantial (+.60), but the insignificance of the net regression slope indicates that this relationship is largely a spurious consequence of the mutual dependence of these measures on CGWE and DPROB.

The constant term in equation (3) is revealing. Were all the independent variables to assume a value of zero, Republican candidates would win a solid majority of the votes for congressional candidates. And since the correlation between RCONG and the number of seats won by Republicans (r = +.91) is high, the party would gain control of the House of Representatives. Yet in the twenty-six years covered by this social indicators model, the Republican party gained control of the House only once, in 1952, when Eisenhower's coattails pulled in enough marginal candidates to edge out the Democratic majority. The interested reader may enter various values of the four independent variables in the equation to ascertain the combination of conditions necessary for the Republicans to gain a majority of the congressional ballots. Without low unemployment (under 5 percent) and high real earnings gains (3 to 4 percent) coupled with low confidence in the Democratic party and moderate levels of subjective Republican affiliation, the probability of success is extremely small.

The model demonstrates the great vulnerability of Republican congressional candidates to the economy's performance, regardless of which party occupies the White House. All current values of the indicators point in the direction of further Republican disaster at the polling places. The possible consequences of this disaster for survival of the two-party system in its current form must be considered in the next section.

What Future for Republicans?

Many analysts viewed the 1974 congressional election, in which the Republican party lost over forty House seats, as a referendum on the scandals of the Nixon administration. The analyses in the previous section reveal, however, that the vote for Congress still responds primarily to economic factors, in a manner reflecting the Great Depression's political cleavages. In hard economic times the voters turn to the Democratic party for a solution. This response was true even in 1974, despite nearly two years' progressively unfolding political corruption which led to the first presidential resignation in history barely three months before the election. While Watergate may have had some lingering impact on the congressional vote, it was not apparent in the Gallup poll on the most important national problems. In mid-August, 1974, just after Nixon's resignation, only 7 percent of the respondents cited distrust of government as the most important problem, while 77 percent named inflation. By almost two to one, voters felt the Democratic party could do a better job of handling the nation's problems. Using the prevailing values of the predictor variables at the time of election, the social indicators model yields a predicted vote for Republican candidates which was only $1/3$ of a percent off the mark.

The 1974 election occurred before the worst of the current recession-depression. With high unemployment and inflation expected to prevail through the 1976 contest, the outlook for Republican fortunes grows even dimmer. Reasonable values to expect at that time might be 7 percent unemployment, a 2 percent increase in real earnings, at least 50 percent of the voters believing the Democrats can do a better job of solving the nation's problems, and Republican party strength continuing at a low 23 percent. Plugging these values into equation (3) yields an expected RCONG of only

41.8 percent. (The 95 percent confidence interval for this estimate lies between 39.8 percent and 43.9 percent.)

Not only does the Republican party carry the handicap of a faltering economy into the 1976 election, but in the preceding year, the right wing of the party threatened to defect to a third-party movement. In appointing Nelson Rockefeller, the *bête noire* of the conservatives, vice president, and in pursuing budgetary deficit policies to combat recession, President Ford provoked savage attacks from the right. He was accused of selling out the conservative majority which had been assembled by Nixon in 1968 and 1972. With Ford firmly in control of the Republican party apparatus and all but sure of renomination, conservative opinion leaders have advocated serious consideration of a third-party challenge at the presidential level.

Proponents of a conservative party like to cite polls showing that if voters were given a choice, more of them would choose to join a new conservative party than a new liberal one. Indeed, a Gallup poll taken after the 1974 election found that 40 percent of all voters (including 64 percent of current Republicans) preferred the conservative label, while only 30 percent selected the liberal party and 30 percent had no opinion. But the same poll also asked whether "the time has come for a new political party arrangement in the United States, with the conservatives making up one party and the liberals making up the other." Voters overwhelmingly rejected such a realignment (56 percent to 27 percent, with 17 percent undecided). Even among Republicans, from whom the bulk of conservative party support would have to be drawn, only 30 percent agreed that realignment would be desirable (Gallup, 1975, p. 14). Although these poll findings represent subjective responses to a hypothetical situation, they imply that a conservative third-party movement would have the same tough sledding as past efforts have had in this country.

The major effect of a right-wing challenge to Ford, whether within the Republican party or outside it, would be the crippling of further Republican prospects in the national elections. As the Goldwater and McGovern candidacies showed, neither the right nor the left has the strength to put ideologically pure candidates into office. Current efforts to push the Republican party to the right can only saddle many congressional candidates with yet another obstacle to building the broad-based coalition of groups necessary to win elections. The chief danger of a concerted challenge to the Republican president lies in the long-term damage to the party. Although competitive at the presidential level, the Republican party for the past half century has been unable to put together and sustain a majority delegation in the Congress. A further decimation of Republican strength at a time when it is already at an all-time low may well push the party beyond the threshold of recovery. Defection of the right wing of either major party could spell the end of the two-party system which has prevailed for 150 years. The Republican and Democratic parties have, in the past, shown a remarkable ability to learn from defeats, to reabsorb dissident elements, and to rebuild their respective group coalitions. But projection of the past as the key to the future is always a risky business. Much of what happens to the attachments of the mass electorate depends upon action taken and not taken by political leaders. The conditions prevailing at the time of this writing have not been approximated in recent history. The next national election may spell the end of the political alignments which are the subject of this book, or it may be a continuation of the party identifications and voting patterns which have prevailed for decades. The only safe prediction which can be made is that the change and continuity in American politics will continue to provide an endless source of fascination.

Methods of
Data Analysis

The purpose of this appendix is to give the reader a brief orientation to the methods of data analysis used in the book. The presentations are not intended to be comprehensive, but they will assist persons unfamiliar with the techniques of regression, path analysis, and log-linear models in the interpretation of results. More detailed sources on each method are cited in the separate sections.

A. Regression Analysis

Regression is one form of the "general linear model" (Fennessey, 1968; Burke and Schuessler, 1973) in which variation in an interval-level dependent variable is linearly related to variation in one or more independent variables of either interval- or nominal-level measurement. An encyclopedic account of the various forms which regression analysis may assume is found in Kerlinger and Pedhazur (1974). The dependent measure is assumed to be linearly related to the independent, or predictor, variables. In standard notation

$$\hat{Y}_i = a + b_j X_j + b_k X_k + \ldots + b_n X_n$$

where $\hat{Y}_i$ is the predicted dependent score and the X's are independent measures. The constant, or intercept term, is a. Each b coefficient expresses the amount of change in units of the dependent variable for each change of one unit of the independent variable, with the effects of the other independent variables removed. In a multiple regression equation, the b's are thus *net*, or partial, regression coefficients.

Tests of significance of individual b coefficients require division of each parameter estimate by its standard error, resulting in a t-ratio which is evaluated at a prespecified level. Since, for a large sample, a 95 percent confidence interval requires a t-ratio of ± 1.96, the rule of thumb is that any b more than twice its standard error is probably significantly different from zero.

Throughout the text, the assumption is made that the five-point party identification measure (from strong Democrat through strong Republican) has interval properties and may be treated as a dependent variable in multiple regression analyses. Suppose this measure were regressed upon years of education and thousands of dollars of income, resulting in the following estimates of the regression coefficients:

$$\hat{Y}_P = 1.75 + .20\ X_E + .10\ X_I$$

where $\hat{Y}_P$ is expected party identification, X_E is education, and X_I is income. Both effects are positive, indicating that higher levels of either variable raise the party identification score in the direction of greater Republican preference. Each year of education raises the expected mean party identification by one-fifth of a point, and each thousand dollars raises it by one-tenth of a point.

In a multiple regression, one is usually interested in comparing the relative effects of the independent variables on the dependent variable. But since the variables are often measured on different metric scales, direct comparison of the b coefficients is impossible. However, if the "raw-score" b is multiplied by the ratio of the standard deviations of X to Y, the resulting standardized coefficient, β, reveals the proportionate change in a standard deviation of the dependent variable for each change of one standard deviation in the independent variable. The standardized β's are used to assess the relative effect of variables in the same regression analysis. When comparing two or more populations, or the same population at different points in time, however, the unstandardized b's are preferable, since the population variances may differ (Blalock, 1967; Schoenberg, 1972).

To continue the example, suppose that upon standardization, we find that $\beta_E = .30$ and $\beta_I = .09$. We may then conclude that the effect of education is more than three times the effect of income on party identification, since a one standard deviation change in education results in a change of .30 standard deviation in party identification, but a similar change in income will produce only a .09 shift in a standard deviation of party identification.

Another multiple regression statistic of great importance is the coefficient of determination, or Multiple R^2. It expresses the proportion of variance in Y which is "determined" by the linear combination of the X's. By comparing the R^2's for various regression equations with different sets of predictor variables, one can determine what proportion of the explained variance is due to each independent variable or set of variables. For example, suppose the R^2 for the regression of Y_P on X_E and X_I is .25, indicating that a quarter of the variance in party identification can be attributed to the joint additive effects of both variables. If the regression of Y_P on X_E alone is .20, then the difference, or 5 percent, is the amount of explained variance which is contributed uniquely by income, X_I. See Cohen (1968) for a detailed discussion of ways to partition the multiple R^2 among the components.

Frequently, independent variables cannot be considered interval measures, as education or income are. For example, religious group membership simply cannot be scaled. In such instances, the suitable form of regression analysis is "dummy variable" regression (Suits, 1957). A set of nominal-level variables are created, which are coded 1 if the attribute is present in an observation and 0 if it is absent. Four major religious dummy variables might be: Protestant, Catholic, Jew, and Other. Each respondent will be classified into only one of these categories and thus will have a score of 1 on one of the four dummy variables and scores of 0 on the remaining three dummies. If the entire set of dummy variables were entered into the regression equation, estimates could not be obtained, since the dummies are linearly dependent. One dummy is usually omitted from the analysis, with the resulting b's becoming deviations from the omitted category. However, to facilitate interpretation, the dummy regression coefficients in this study are transformed into "structural coefficients," which are deviations from the grand mean of the sample (see Melichar, 1966; Andrews et al., 1967). For example, if the structural coefficients for party identification regression on religious groups are as follows: Protestant, $+.35$; Catholic, $-.20$; Jew, $-.65$; Other, $-.05$, it is easy to see that Protestants are the most Republican group and Jews the most Democratic since they have the two largest deviations from the sample mean.

B. Path Analysis

Regression analysis does not require prior assumptions about the causal processes among the variables in the equation. The analyst may have some implicit notion of the temporal and causal ordering of the variables, or he may be simply trying to predict one variable's value from knowledge of the other variables. If the researcher takes the former approach, making explicit his assumptions about the causal ordering among independent variables in his theory, another powerful analytic tool is at his disposal—path analysis. Originally developed by the geneticist Sewell Wright, and later introduced to sociology by Duncan, path analysis has captured the imaginations of many scientists in recent years for its ability to organize and display coherently a complex pattern of cause and effect underlying a system of variables (Wright, 1960; Duncan, 1966b; Land, 1969; Heise, 1969b).

Underlying the path model is a set of recursive structural equations indicating the magnitude of effects from temporally and causally antecedent variables. A typical path equation is

$$X_i = {}_{Pij}X_j + {}_{Pik}X_k + {}_{Piu}X_u$$

where X_j and X_k are measured variables causing X_i and X_u is an unmeasured residual term representing effects not explicitly entered into the model. The path coefficients, Pij's, are estimated from observed correlations by a least-squares procedure and are identical with standardized regression coefficients (β's). The substantive interpretation of direct path coefficients is exactly the same as for standardized regression coefficients.

The advantage of path analysis over simple regression lies in the ability to trace the direct and indirect effects in a hypothesized causal model linking a system of variables. Since variables in a path model may serve both as dependent and independent variables, the effects of some causally prior variable may be transmitted indirectly, through an intervening variable, as well as directly. A causal diagram of relationships is often useful to represent these relationships. To resume the example with party, education, and income, suppose Figure A.1 represents a hypothesized path model in which income intervenes between education and party preference. The direct effects of both variables on party are the same as in the standardized regression analyses. Education is hypothesized to have an effect on income, which in turn has a direct effect on party, allowing one to calculate the indirect effect of education on party by multiplying the values of the compound path. This indirect effect, .036, is smaller than the direct effect, implying that only a small part of the correlation between party and education arises from the causal effect of education on income. (Of course, the numerical values in this example are purely illustrative.) In actual path analyses of party identification, the indirect effects are generally negligible, so the direct path coefficients transmit almost all the causal effects.

C. Log-Linear Models

For a substantial portion of the analyses, the assumption of interval scaling of party identification need not be made. Instead, tables of cross-

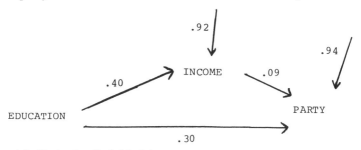

Figure A.1. Illustrative Path Model

tabulated nominal or ordinal variables will be analyzed. In recent years, important breakthroughs have been made in the quantitative analysis of contingency tables. Detailed discussion of the techniques appear in Goodman (1972a; 1972b; 1973a), Davis (1974), and Bishop et al. (1975). This section presents a basic approach to log-linear contingency table analysis using an illustrative example. The notation used is that found in Goodman's papers.

Table A contains the two-way cross-tabulation of dichotomous variables A and B. The observed cell frequencies (f_{ij}) and the row $(f_{i.})$, column $(f_{.j})$, and grand $(f_{..})$ totals are shown with example values. One way to show the association between variables A and B might be to percentagize either across rows or down columns and compare the differences. Instead of taking the ratio of a cell frequency to the marginal, however, log-linear models analyze the ratio of frequencies between two internal cells, the *odds*. The *conditional odds* for variable A vary according to the level of B within which the odds are calculated. For example, given that B is at level 1, the conditional odds for A are $f_{11}/f_{21} = 180/50 = 3.60$. The conditional odds for *A*, given level 2 of *B*, are $f_{12}/f_{22} = 90/80 = 1.125$. Similar odds for variable B could be formed conditional upon each level of A. If variables A and B are not associated with each other, then the conditional odds will be equal. Differences in the odds for the first variable across levels of the second variable imply that the two variables are related to each other, since variation in one variable is related to variation in the other.

By defining a bivariate association in terms of conditional odds, we obtain a new statistic to measure association in a 2 × 2 table, the *odds-ratio*. An odds-ratio is merely the ratio of two conditional odds. Upon rearrangement, it is seen to be the ratio of cross-product terms. For variable A, the ratio of conditional odds is:

$$\frac{\dfrac{f_{11}}{f_{21}}}{\dfrac{f_{12}}{f_{22}}} = \frac{f_{11}f_{22}}{f_{21}f_{12}}$$

TABLE A.   Example 2 x 2 Table with illustrative data.

VARIABLE B

		Level 1	Level 2	Total
	Level 1	f_{11}=180	f_{12}=90	$f_{1.}$=270
VARIABLE A				
	Level 2	f_{21}=50	f_{22}=80	$f_{2.}$=130
	Total	$f_{.1}$=230	$f_{.2}$=170	$f_{..}$=400

In the example, the ratio of 3.60 to 1.125 is 3.20. The reader may confirm for himself that this is the same value as the odds-ratio for variable B. Since equality of conditional odds, the criterion for independence between variables, would produce an odds-ratio exactly equal to 1.00, it is clear that the variables A and B in Table A.1 are strongly related. An odds-ratio larger than 1.00 indicates positive covariation, with level 1 of A tending to go with level 1 of B. An odds-ratio smaller than 1.00 indicates an inverse association.

One might hypothesize that in the population from which the two-variable relationship is sampled, variables A and B are not associated. Call this independence hypothesis H_1. One can determine what the *expected* cell frequencies (F_{ij}) would be if H_1 were true, then compare observed and expected frequencies to determine whether the probability of the discrepancy is greater than some chance level. Under H_1, the marginal frequency distributions and sample size are assumed to be fixed. The hypothesis says that the expected odds-ratio must equal 1.00. If this is true, then the conditional expected odds must also be equal, since their ratio is 1.00. Furthermore, the conditional expected odds will necessarily be equal to the marginal odds. Hence we calculate the expected cell frequencies in Table A so that the expected odds for A are:

$$\frac{F_{11}}{F_{21}} = \frac{F_{12}}{F_{22}} = \frac{f_{1.}}{f_{2.}}$$

the expected odds for B are

$$\frac{F_{11}}{F_{12}} = \frac{F_{21}}{F_{22}} = \frac{f_{.1}}{f_{.2}}$$

and the expected odds-ratio is

$$\frac{F_{11}}{F_{12}} \frac{F_{22}}{F_{21}} = 1.00.$$

Maximum likelihood estimates for the expected frequencies in an hypothesized log-linear model are obtained by a proportional-fitting algorithm which is too complex to be described in detail here. Interested readers should consult Goodman (1972b, pp. 1080–85), Davis (1974, pp. 227–31) and Bishop et al., (1975, pp. 57–122). The expected frequencies under H_1 are identical to those obtained in the usual chi-square test of independence in a two-way table. However, for multi-way tables the estimation procedure is more complex, and it is feasible only with a computer when many log-linear models must be tested.

H_1 constrains certain conditional odds in the expected table to be equal to certain marginals in the observed tables. We can designate model H_1 by the set of *fitted marginals*, that is, by the set of cross-tabulations formed by collapsing across certain dimensions of the observed full table. These marginal tables are constraints which must be satisfied in estimating the expected frequencies under the hypothesized model. For H_1, the set of fitted marginals are (A) and (B), the row and column marginal distributions in Table A. For more complex tables and hypotheses, the set of fitted marginals may involve several cross-tabulated variables. For example, an alternative hypothesis (H_2) about Table A.1 might be that variables A and B are not independent. H_2 is designated by the fitted marginals (AB) which indicate that the expected cell frequencies must equal those in the observed 2×2 table. H_2 also contains the fitted one-variable marginals (A) and (B), so it fits the same set as H_1 plus the two-way table (AB).

Other hypotheses can be made about the relationships in Table A: for example, H_3, which states that the distribution of B is equiprobable (the odds on B = 1.00), while the marginal on A is the same as that observed. This H_3 may be designated by the fitted marginal (A) only. Note that a hierarchical relationship exists between the three hypotheses. If H_3 correctly fits the observed data, then so will H_2 and H_1, since both the latter also fit the marginal table (A) as well. But neither H_2 nor H_1 imply H_3, since they both require additional marginals which the latter does not.

The hierarchical feature assures that if a simple set of marginals describes the data, so will a more complex model which simultaneously contains all the marginals included in the simpler one. The general strategy in log-linear model testing follows the rule of parsimony: locate an hypothesized model which fits the fewest set of complex marginals but which still produces expected frequencies close to the observed values. The fit of a model to the data is assessed by a likelihood-ratio chi-square test which compares the observed frequencies (f_{ij}) to the expected frequencies (F_{ij}) generated by the model

$$\chi^2 = 2 \sum_{i=1}^{2} \sum_{j=1}^{2} f_{ij} \; ln(f_{ij}/F_{ij}).$$

The degrees of freedom for evaluation depend upon the number of constraints imposed in calculating the expected frequencies. In general, the more marginals required to be fitted, the fewer the degrees of freedom. For systems of dichotomous variables, as in Table A, d.f. equal the number of cells minus one for the total (f..), minus one for each marginal table used in fitting the model. Multi-category variables contribute (k–1) degrees of freedom, where k is the number of categories.

To return to the data in Table A, the expected frequencies under H_1 yield chi-square = 28.5. Since there is only one degree of freedom (4 cells- 1 for (A) - 1 for (B) - 1 for f .. $= 1$ d.f.), the model must be rejected as providing a poor fit to the data. The procedure requires a model whose chi-square has a *high* probability of occurring by chance, since one wants to find a model whose expected frequencies *do not* differ significantly from the observed frequencies. Given the hierarchical nature of log-linear models, if H_1 fails to fit, then H_3 will not fit either, since it has only d.f. $= 2$ and the chi-square will not be lower. Therefore, the alternative H_2, which fits (AB), provides the best fit to the data. H_2 is not tested directly, since it has no degrees of freedom (4 cells- 1 for (AB) - 1 for (A) - 1 for (B) - 1 for f .. $= 0$ d.f.).

A model which fits expected frequencies to the full observed contingency table, and hence has no degrees of freedom, is called a "saturated" model, since all relationships in the observed data are present in the model. Models which omit some marginal tables are called "unsaturated." The only way a saturated model like H_2 can be tested is to compare it with an unsaturated model like H_1 which omits the most complex relationship, in this case (AB). Thus the test of H_1 not only showed that it did not provide a good fit, but also that H_2 gave the best fit. More generally, the significance of any relationship between variables can be tested by comparing two log-linear models, one which contains the fitted marginal table for the relationship and another which omits it. The difference in chi-squares for the two models is compared to the difference in d.f.'s to determine if the relationship is significant. Even though an unsaturated model may provide an acceptable overall fit to the data, some omitted terms may be significant and should be retained.

Besides significance tests and a notation system to describe the set of fitted marginals, log-linear methods provide explicit measures of the strength and direction of relationships among variables. Once a best-fitting model has been located, the expected cell frequencies may be written as either a set of multiplicative or additive effect parameters. For example, the expected frequencies in Table A under H_2 may be written as

$$F_{ij} = \eta \; \tau_i^A \; \tau_j^B \; \tau_{ij}^{AB}$$

where η is a "grand mean" constant to ensure that the sum of the F_{ij}'s will equal the observed total, f ..; the single-superscripted τ's are effect parameters measuring the geometric mean of the expected odds for A or B; and τ_{ij}^{AB} reflects the expected odds-ratio of the two variables.

By taking natural logarithms of the terms in the multiplicative model, we have transformed the equation into an additive one which is linear in the logs of the expected cell frequencies (hence the name log-linear models):

$$G_{ij} = \theta \; + \; \lambda_i^A \; + \; \lambda_j^B \; + \; \lambda_{ij}^{AB}$$

where $G_{ij} = \ln F_{ij}$; $\theta = \ln \eta$; and $\lambda = \ln \tau$. Each λ represents a deviation from the grand mean, θ, so that in a system of dichotomies, each λ has only one absolute value, and is positive or negative depending upon the level of the variable:

$$\lambda_1^A = -\lambda_2^A \qquad \lambda_1^B = -\lambda_2^B$$

$$\lambda_{11}^{AB} = \lambda_{22}^{AB} = -\lambda_{12}^{AB} = -\lambda_{21}^{AB}$$

However, where some variables have three or more categories, separate effect parameters with unique values are estimated for each category.

For the data in Table A, the following set of additive coefficients were obtained under H_2:

$$\theta = 4.496 \qquad \lambda_1^B = .056$$

$$\lambda_1^A = .350 \qquad \lambda_{11}^{AB} = .296.$$

While θ has no meaningful substantive interpretation, the λ parameters are relatively straightforward. The two positive values for λ_1^A and λ_1^B indicate that the odds for A and B, respectively, favor level 1 over level 2 and also that the distribution between categories is more unequal for A than for B. The positive value for λ_{11}^{AB} shows that the association between the two variables is positive; that is, level 1 on A tends to go with level 1 on B, and similarly for level 2 on both variables. A value for λ_{11}^{AB} of 0 would indicate that the two variables are unrelated; and a negative value would indicate that the co-variation is inverse.

In the text, the λ's are transformed to standardized values by dividing by the standard error. For large samples, if the expected value of a parameter is zero, the standardized λ is approximately normally distributed with zero mean and unit variance. Hence, as in ordinary linear regression, a standardized value at least 2.00 or larger may be said to be significant. While this standardization strictly applies only to saturated models, it provides an estimate of the lower bound of the standardized parameters in an unsaturated model (Goodman, 1972b, p. 1049). The formula for the standard error is

$$\hat{S}_\lambda = \sqrt{\frac{\sum_i \sum_j \left(\frac{1}{f_{ij}}\right)}{I^2}}$$

TABLE B.   Example 2 x 2 x 2 Table with Illustrative Data.

VARIABLE C

	Level 1 VARIABLE B			Level 2 VARIABLE B		
	Level 1	Level 2	Total	Level 1	Level 2	Total
Level 1	$f_{111}=70$	$f_{121}=20$	$f_{1\cdot1}=90$	$f_{112}=50$	$f_{122}=30$	$f_{1\cdot2}=80$
VARIABLE A Level 2	$f_{211}=30$	$f_{221}=30$	$f_{2\cdot1}=60$	$f_{212}=60$	$f_{222}=110$	$f_{2\cdot2}=170$
Total	$f_{\cdot11}=100$	$f_{\cdot21}=50$	$f_{\cdot\cdot1}=150$	$f_{\cdot12}=110$	$f_{\cdot21}=140$	$f_{\cdot\cdot2}=250$

where I is the number of cells in the contingency table. For data in Table A, $\hat{S}_\lambda = .055$. Thus, the odds on B do not differ significantly from equiprobability, but the odds on A do, and the odds-ratio for (AB) is also significant.

More complex contingency tables, involving cross-tabulation by additional variables, including those with more than two categories, may be analyzed by log-linear methods, which extend the ideas illustrated above. To illustrate this generalization briefly, Table AB presents the association between variables A and B broken down by dichotomous variable C. The association between variables A and B varies according to the level of the third variable. When C is at level 1, the odds-ratio for (AB) is 3.50; but when C is at level two, the (AB) odds-ratio is 3.06, indicating a slightly stronger association between the two variables at the first level of C. A relationship between two variables which is conditional upon the level of other variables is known as an *interaction*, and detection of such significant interactions is a primary statistical goal of log-linear analysis. The saturated log-linear model for the three-way interaction hypothesis in equation form is

$$G_{ij} = \theta + \lambda_i^A + \lambda_j^B + \lambda_k^C + \lambda_{ij}^{AB} + \lambda_{ik}^{AC} + \lambda_{jk}^{BC} + \lambda_{ijk}^{ABC}.$$

Since the saturated model cannot be directly tested using the likelihood ratio χ^2, the only way to determine if the three-way interaction is significant is to fit another model which omits this effect parameter. In the fitted marginals notation, this model is (AB)(AC)(BC), which of course includes the three one-way marginal tables (A)(B)(C) automatically. With eight cells in the three-way table and seven degrees of freedom used up in estimating the six marginals and the grand mean, only one degree of freedom is available to test the hyothesis that the three-way interaction (ABC) is significant. The chi-square value for this hypothesis is 0.09, which is not significant at $p = .05$ for d.f. = 1. Therefore we may reject the saturated model and conclude that the observed differences in conditional odds-ratios, (ABC), are not significant. The association between A and B is essentially the same at both levels of C. In fact, the association between *any* pair of variables is identical at each level of the third.

One can proceed to delete additional sets of fitted marginals to test hypotheses about the two-way relationships in the full contingency table. For example, the hypothesis that variables B and C are not significantly associated in the three-way table requires one to fit only the (AB)(AC) marginals. With chi-square equal to 19.3 and d.f. = 2, the model must be rejected as giving a poor fit. Similarly, tests of log-linear models (AC)(BC) and (AB)(BC) fail to fit the observed data. Thus we must conclude that each of the three two-way relationships is significant and cannot be omitted. Hence, the best-fitting model fits the marginal tables (AB)(AC)(BC).

While the strategy illustrated above begins with a saturated model and deletes complex interactions until the best-fitting model is located, the reverse procedure is followed in this study. One starts with a "baseline" model in which a dependent variable is hypothesized to be independent of the other variables in the contingency table, but these independent variables are assumed to interact completely among themselves. This model, of course, never yields a good fit to the data. The model is then re-estimated by introducing two-way relationships between the dependent variable and each independent variable. Differences in the chi-square relative to the reduction in d.f. are observed to determine which associations are significant, typically at the $p = .05$ level. If all the significant two-way relationships located by this stepwise procedure still fail to provide an acceptable fit, the procedure continues with three-way and higher interactions until a satisfactory fit is obtained. This best-fitting model is then compared to others which may contain even more complex sets of relationships, to determine whether any significant terms have been omitted. The final model located by this method will be the simplest explanation of the data, involving the fewest complex associations and interactions. To conserve space, the effect parameters from the final model are seldom presented in tabular form, but a summary interpretation is provided in the text.

Bibliography

Abramson, Paul R.
   1974   "Generational change in American electoral behavior." *American Political Science Review* 68 (March):93–105.

Adamany, David
   1964   "The size-of-place analysis reconsidered." *Western Political Quarterly* 17 (September):477–87.

Alexander, Franz
   1959   "Emotional factors in voting behavior." In *American voting behavior*, edited by E. Burdick and A. Brodbeck, pp. 300–307. New York: Free Press.

Alford, Robert R.
   1963   *Party and society*. Chicago: Rand McNally.

Allensmith, Westley, and Beverly Allensmith
   1948   "Religious affiliation and politico-economic attitude." *Public Opinion Quarterly* 12 (Fall):377–89.

Anderson, Charles H.
   1974   *The political economy of social class*. New York: Wiley.

Anderson, Donald N.
   1966   "Ascetic Protestantism and political preference." *Review of Religious Research* 7 (Spring):167–71.

Andrews, Frank; James N. Morgan; and John Sonquist
   1967   *Multiple classification analysis*. Ann Arbor, Michigan: Institute of Social Research.

Baltzall, E. Digby
   1964   *The Protestant establishment*. New York: Random House.

Bandura, Albert
   1971a   *Psychological modeling: Conflicting theories*. Chicago: Aldine.
   1971b   *Social learning theory*. Morristown, N.J.: General Learning Press.

Berelson, Bernard; Paul Lazarsfeld; and William McPhee
   1954   *Voting: A study of opinion formation in a presidential election*. Chicago: University of Chicago Press.

Bishop, Yvonne M. M.; Stephen E. Fienberg; and Paul W. Holland
   1975   *Discrete multivariate analysis: Theory and practice*. Cambridge, Mass.: M.I.T. Press.

Blalock, Hubert M., Jr.
1961   *Causal inference in nonexperimental research.* Chapel Hill, N. C.: University of North Carolina Press.
1967   "Causal inference, closed populations, and measures of association." *American Political Science Review* 61 (March):130–36.

Blau, Peter M., and Otis D. Duncan
1967   *The American occupational structure.* New York: Wiley.

Boudon, Raymond F.
1968   "A new look at correlation analysis." In *Methodology in social research*, edited by H. M. Blalock and A. B. Blalock, pp. 199–235. New York: McGraw-Hill.

Broder, David S.
1972   *The party's over: The failure of politics in America.* New York: Harper and Row.

Brody, Richard A., and Benjamin I. Page
1972   "Comment: The assessment of policy voting." *American Political Science Review* 66 (June):450–58.

Buchanan, William
1968   "Political identification." edited by D. L. Sills, pp. 57–61, in *The international encyclopedia of the social sciences*, Vol. VII. New York: Macmillan.

Burke, Peter J., and Karl F. Schuessler
1973   "Alternative approaches to analysis-of-variance tables." In *Sociological methodology, 1973–1974.* Edited by H. L. Costner, pp. 145–88. San Francisco: Jossey-Bass.

Burnham, Walter Dean
1968   "American voting behavior and the 1964 election." *Midwest Journal of Political Science* 12 (February):1–40.
1970   *Critical elections and the mainsprings of American politics.* New York: Norton.
1974   "Theory and voting research: Some reflections on Converse's 'Change in the American Electorate'." *American Political Science Review* 68 (September):1002–23.

Butler, David, and Donald Stokes
1969   *Political change in Britain: Forces shaping electoral choice.* New York: St. Martin's Press.

Campbell, Angus
1966   "A classification of the presidential elections." In A. Campbell et al., *Elections and the political order*, pp. 63–77. New York: Wiley.

Campbell, Angus; Philip E. Converse; Warren Miller; and Donald E. Stokes
1960   *The American voter.* New York: Wiley.
1966   *Elections and the political order.* New York: Wiley.

Campbell, Angus, and Homer C. Cooper
   1956   *Group differences in attitudes and votes.* Ann Arbor, Mich.: Institute
           for Social Research.

Campbell, Angus; Gerald Gurin; and Warren E. Miller
   1954   *The voter decides.* Evanston, Ill.: Row, Peterson.

Campbell, Angus, and Warren E. Miller
   1957   "The motivational basis of straight and split ticket voting." *American
           Political Science Review* 21 (June):293–312.

Campbell, Angus, and Donald E. Stokes
   1959   "Partisan   attitudes   and   the   presidential   vote."   In   *American
           voting behavior,* edited by E. Burdick and A. Brodbeck, pp. 353–71.
           Glencoe, Ill.: Free Press.

Centers, Richard
   1949   *The psychology of social classes.* Princeton, N. J.: Princeton University
           Press.

Cohen, Jacob
   1968   "Multiple regression as a general data analytic system." *Psychological
           Bulletin* 70 (December):426–43.

Converse, Philip E.
   1958   "The shifting role of class in political attitudes and behavior." In *Read-
           ings in social psychology* (3d ed.), edited by E. Maccoby, T. Newcombe,
           and E. Hartley, pp. 388–99. New York: Holt, Rinehart and Winston.
   1963   "A major political realignment in the South?" In *Change in the con-
           temporary South* edited by A. P. Sindler, pp. 195–222. Durham, N. C.:
           Duke University Press.
   1964   "The nature of belief systems in mass publics." In *Ideology and dis-
           content,* edited by D. E. Apter, pp. 206–61. Glencoe, Ill.: Free Press.
   1966a "Religion and politics: The 1960 election." In A. Campbell et al., *Elec-
           tions and the political order,* pp. 96–124. New York: Wiley.
   1966b "The concept of the normal vote." In A. Campbell et al., *Elections and
           the political order,* pp. 9–39. New York: Wiley.
   1968   "Some priority variables in comparative electoral research." Survey
           Research Centre, Occasional Paper Number 3. University of Strath-
           clyde, Glasgow.
   1970   "Attitudes and non-attitudes: Continuation of a dialogue." In *The quan-
           titative analysis of social problems,* edited by E. R. Tufte, pp. 168–89.
           Reading, Mass.: Addison-Wesley.
   1971   "Social cleavages in the 1964 election." In *Political parties and politi-
           cal behavior,* edited by W. J. Crotty, D. M. Freeman and D. S. Gatlin,
           pp. 420–22. 2d. ed. Boston: Allyn and Bacon.
   1972   "Change in the American electorate." In *The human meaning of social
           change,* edited by Angus Campbell and Philip E. Converse, pp. 263–337.
           New York: Russell Sage.
   1974a "Comment: The status of non-attitudes." *American Political Science
           Review* 68 (June):650–60.

1974b   "Comment on Burnham's 'Theory and Voting Research'." *American Political Science Review* 68 (September):1024–27.

Converse, Philip E.; Angus Campbell; Warren E. Miller; and Donald E. Stokes
1961   "Stability and change in 1960: A reinstating election." *American Political Science Review* 55 (June):269–80.

Converse, Philip E.; Aage R. Clausen; and Warren E. Miller
1965   "Electoral myth and reality: The 1964 election." *American Political Science Review* 59 (June):321–36.

Converse, Philip E.; Warren E. Miller; Jerrold G. Rusk; and Arthur C. Wolfe
1969   "Continuity and change in American politics: Parties and issues in the 1968 election." *American Political Science Review* 63 (December): 1083–1105.

Cooper, Homer C.
1959   "Social class identification and political affiliation." *Psychological Reports* 5:337–40.

Cosman, Bernard
1966   *Five states for Goldwater.* University, Ala.: University of Alabama Press.

Dahl, Robert
1961   *Who governs?* New Haven: Yale University Press.

Dahrendorf, Ralf
1959   *Class and class conflict in industrial society.* Stanford: Stanford University Press.

Davis, James A.
1974   "Hierarchical models for significance tests in multi-variate contingency tables: An exegesis of Goodman's recent papers." In *Sociology methodology 1973–1974*, edited by H. L. Costner, pp. 189–231. San Francisco: Jossey-Bass.

Devine, Donald J.
1972   *The political culture of the United States.* Boston: Little, Brown.

DeVries, Walter, and V. Lance Tarrance
1972   *The ticket-splitter: A new force in American politics.* Grand Rapids, Mich.: Eerdmans.

Diamond, William
1941   "Urban and rural voting in 1896." *American Historical Review* 46 (January):281–305.

Dobson, Douglas, and Duane A. Meeter
1974   "Alternative Markov models for describing change in party identification." *American Journal of Political Science* 18 (August):487–500.

Dreyer, Edward C.
1973   "Change and stability in party identification." *Journal of Politics* 35 (August):712–22.

Dulce, Berton, and Edward J. Richter
   1962   *Religion and the presidency: A recurring American problem.* New York: Macmillan.

Duncan, Otis Dudley
   1961   "A socioeconomic index for all occupations." In *Occupations and social status*, edited by A. J. Reiss, Jr., pp. 109–31. New York: Free Press.
   1966a "Methodological issues in the analysis of social mobility." In *Social structure and mobility in economic development*, edited by N. Smelser and S. M. Lipset, pp. 51–97. Chicago: Aldine.
   1966b "Path analysis: sociological examples." *American Journal of Sociology* 72 (July):1–16.

Duncan, Otis Dudley; David L. Featherman; and Beverly Duncan
   1972   *Socioeconomic background and achievement.* New York: Seminar Press.

Epstein, Leon D.
   1956   "Size of place and the division of the two-party vote in Wisconsin." *Western Political Quarterly* 9 (March):138–50.

Eulau, Heinz
   1962   *Class and party in the Eisenhower years.* Glencoe, Ill.: Free Press.

Featherman, David L., and Robert M. Hauser
   1973   "On the measurement of occupation in social surveys." *Sociological Methods and Research* 2 (November):239–51.

Fennessey, James
   1968   "The general linear model." *American Journal of Sociology* 74 (July): 1–27.

Flanigan, William H.
   1972   *Political behavior of the American electorate.* 2d ed. Boston: Allyn and Bacon.

Fuchs, Lawrence H.
   1956   *The political behavior of American Jews.* Glencoe, Ill.: Free Press.

Gallup, George
   1975   *The Gallup report.* Number 116, February. Princeton, New Jersey: American Institute for Public Opinion.

Glenn, Norval D.
   1972   "Sources of the shift to political independence: Some evidence from a cohort analysis." *Social Science Quarterly* 53 (December):494–519.
   1973   "Class and party support in the United States: Recent and emerging trends." *Public Opinion Quarterly* 37 (Spring):1–20.
   1975   "Class and party support in 1972." *Public Opinion Quarterly* 39 (Spring): 117–22.

Glenn, Norval, and Michael Grimes
   1968   "Aging, voting, and political interest." *American Sociological Review* 33 (August):563–75.

Glenn, Norval D., and Ruth Hyland
  1967   "Religious preference and worldly success: Some evidence from na-
          tional surveys." *American Sociological Review* 32 (February):73–85.

Gockel, Galen
  1969   "Income and religious affiliation: A regression analysis." *American
          Journal of Sociology* 74 (May):632–47.

Goldberg, Arthur S.
  1966   "Discerning a causal pattern among data on voting behavior." *American
          Political Science Review* 60 (December):913–22.
  1969   "Social determinism and rationality as bases of party identification."
          American Political Science Review 55 (March):5–25.

Goodman, Leo A.
  1972a   "A modified multiple regression approach to the analysis of dichoto-
          mous variables." *American Sociological Review* 37 (February):28–46.
  1972b   "A general model for the analysis of surveys." *American Journal of
          Sociology* 77 (May):1035–86.
  1973a   "The analysis of multidimensional contingency tables when some vari-
          ables are posterior to others: A modified path analysis approach."
          Biometrika 60:178–92.
  1973b   "Causal analysis of panel study data and other kinds of survey data."
          American Journal of Sociology 78 (March):1135–91.

Gordon, Robert A.
  1968   "Issues in multiple regression." *American Journal of Sociology* 73
          (March):592–616.

Gosnell, Harold F.
  1927   *Machine politics: Chicago style*. Chicago: University of Chicago Press.

Greenstein, Fred I.
  1965a   "Personality and political socialization: The theories of authoritarian
          and democratic character." *The Annals of the American Academy of
          Political and Social Science* 361 (September):81–95.
  1965b   *Children and politics*. New Haven: Yale University Press.

Hamilton, Richard F.
  1972   *Class and politics in the United States*. New York: Wiley.

Hartz, Louis
  1955   *The liberal tradition in America*. New York: Harcourt, Brace and
          World.

Havard, William C. (ed.)
  1972   *The changing politics of the South*. Baton Rouge: Louisiana State
          University Press.

Heise, David R.
  1969a   "Separating reliability and stability in test-retest correlation." *American
          Sociological Review* 35 (February):93–101.

1969b "Problems in path analysis and causal inference." In *Sociological Methodology 1969,* edited by E. F. Borgatta, pp. 38–73. San Francisco: Jossey-Bass.

Herberg, Will
1955 *Protestant—Catholic—Jew: An essay in American religious sociology.* Garden City, N. Y.: Doubleday.

Hess, Robert D., and Judith V. Torney
1967 *The development of political attitudes in children.* Chicago: Aldine.

Hibbs, Douglas A., Jr.
1974 "Problems of statistical estimation and causal inference in time-series regression models." In *Sociological methodology 1973-1974,* edited by H. L. Costner, pp. 252–308. San Francisco: Jossey-Bass.

Hikel, Gerald Kent
1973 *Beyond the polls: Political ideology and its correlates.* Lexington, Mass.: Heath.

Hodge, Robert W.
1970 "Social integration, psychological well-being, and their socioeconomic correlates." *Sociological Inquiry* 40 (Spring):182–206.

Hodge, Robert W., and Paul M. Siegel
1968 "Social stratification: Measurement." In *The international encyclopedia of social science,* Vol. 13, edited by D. L. Sills, pp. 316–25. New York: Macmillan.

Hodge, Robert W.; Paul M. Siegel; and Peter H. Rossi
1964 "Occupational prestige in the United States, 1925-63." *American Journal of Sociology* 70 (November): 286–302.

Hodge, Robert W., and Donald J. Treiman
1968 "Class identification in the United States." *American Journal of Sociology* 73 (March): 535–47.

Hyman, Herbert H.
1959 *Political socialization: A study in the psychology of political behavior* Glencoe, Ill.: Free Press.

Jackman, Mary R., and Robert W. Jackman
1973 "An interpretation of the relation between objective and subjective social status." *American Sociological Review* 38 (October):569–82.

Jencks, Christopher, et al.
1972 *Inequality: A reassessment of the effects of family and schooling in America.* New York: Harper and Row.

Jennings, M. Kent, and Kenneth P. Langton
1969 "Mothers versus fathers in the formation of political orientations among young Americans." *Journal of Politics* 31 (May):329–58.

Jennings, M. Kent, and Richard G. Niemi
1966 "Party identification at multiple levels of government." *American Journal of Sociology* 72 (July):86–101.

1968   "The transmission of political values from parent to child." *American Political Science Review* 62 (March):169–84.

1974   *The political character of adolescence.* Princeton: Princeton University Press.

Jensen, Richard F.

1970   "The religious and occupational roots of party identification: Illinois and Indiana in the 1870's." *Civil War History* 16 (December):325–43.

1971   *The winning of the Midwest: Social and political conflict, 1888-1896,* Chicago: University of Chicago Press.

Johnson, Benton

1962   "Ascetic Protestantism and political preference. *Public Opinion Quarterly* 26 (Spring):35–46.

Kelley, Jonathan

1973   "Causal chain models for the socioeconomic career." *American Sociological Review* 38 (August):481–93.

Kelley, Stanley, Jr., and Thad W. Mirer

1974   "The simple act of voting." *American Political Science Review* 68 (June):572–91.

Kerlinger, Fred N., and Elazar J. Pedhazur

1974   *Multiple regression in behavioral research.* New York: Holt, Rinehart and Winston.

Key, V. O., Jr.

1949   *Southern politics in state and nation.* New York: Random House.

1955   "A theory of critical elections." *Journal of Politics* 17 (February):3–18.

1966   *The responsible electorate: Rationality in presidential voting, 1936-1960.* Cambridge: Harvard University Press.

Key, V. O., Jr., and Frank Munger

1959   "Social determinism and electoral decision: the case of Indiana." In *American voting behavior,* edited by E. Burdick and A. Brodbeck, pp. 281–99. Glencoe, Ill.: Free Press.

Kleppner, Paul

1972   "The political revolution of the 1890's: A behavioral interpretation." In *Voters, parties, and elections,* edited by J. H. Silbey and S. T. McSeveney, pp. 184–94. Lexington, Mass.: Xerox College Publishing.

Knoke, David

1972   "A causal model for the political party preferences of American men." *American Sociological Review* 37 (December):679–89.

1974a   "Religious involvement and political behavior: A log-linear analysis of white Americans 1952-1968." *Sociological Quarterly* 15 (Winter): 51–65.

1974b   "Religion, stratification, and politics: America in the 1960's." *American Journal of Politics* 18 (May):31–45.

1974c   "A causal synthesis of sociological and psychological models of American voting behavior." *Social Forces* 53 (September):92–101.

Knoke, David, and Richard B. Felson
  1974   "Ethnic stratification and political cleavage in the United States, 1952-
          1968." *American Journal of Sociology* 80 (November):630–42.

Knoke, David, and Michael Hout
  1974   "Social and demographic factors in American political party affilia-
          tions, 1952–1972." *American Sociological Review* 39 (October):700–713.

Knoke, David, and David E. Long
  1975   "The economic sensitivity of the American farm vote." *Rural Sociology*
          40 (Spring):7–17.

Korpi, Walter
  1972   "Some problems in the measurement of class voting." *American Jour-
          nal of Sociology* 78 (November):627–42.

Kramer, Gerald H.
  1971   "Short-term fluctuations in U. S. voting behavior, 1896-1964." *Ameri-
          can Political Science Review* 65 (March):131–43.

Ladd, Everett Carll, Jr.
  1970   *American political parties: Social change and political response.* New
          York: Norton.

Ladd, Everett Carll, Jr., and Seymour Martin Lipset
  1973   *Academics, politics, and the 1972 election.* Washington, D. C.: Ameri-
          can Enterprise Institute for Public Policy Research.

Land, Kenneth C.
  1969   "Principles of path analysis." In *Sociological methodology 1969*, edited
          by E. F. Borgatta, pp. 3–37. San Francisco: Jossey-Bass.
  1975   "Social indicator models: An overview." In *Social indicator models*,
          edited by K. C. Land and S. Spilerman, pp. 5–36. New York: Russell
          Sage.

Lane, Robert E.
  1959   "Fathers and sons: Foundations of political belief." *American Socio-
          logical Review* 24 (August):502–11.

Langton, Kenneth P., and M. Kent Jennings
  1969   "Mothers versus fathers in the formation of political orientations."
          In *Political socialization*, edited by K. P. Langton, pp. 52–83. New
          York: Oxford University Press.

Laumann, Edward O., and David R. Segal
  1971   "Status inconsistency and ethnoreligious membership as determinants
          of social participation and political attitudes." *American Journal of
          Sociology* 77 (July):36–61.

Lazarsfeld, Paul F.; Bernard Berelson; and Hazel Gaudet
  1948   *The people's choice.* New York: Columbia University Press.

Lenski, Gerhard E.
  1963   *The religious factor.* Garden City, N. Y: Anchor Books.

Lewinson, Paul
  1965   *Race, class and party*. New York: Grosset and Dunlap.

Lipset, Seymour Martin
  1960   *Political man: The social bases of politics*. Garden City, N. Y.: Double-
          day.
  1968a   "Class, politics and religion in modern society: The dilemma of the
          conservatives." In *Revolution and counterrevolution*, edited by S. M.
          Lipset, pp. 246–303. New York: Basic Books.
  1968b   "Social class." In *The international encyclopedia of the social sciences*.
          Vol. 15, edited by D. L. Sills, pp. 296–316. New York: Macmillan.

Lubell, Samuel
  1970   *The hidden crisis of American politics*. New York: Norton.

McClosky, Herbert, and Harold E. Dahlgren
  1959   "Primary group influence on party loyalty." *American Political Science
          Review* 53 (September):757–76.

MacRae, Duncan, Jr., and James A. Meldrum
  1960   "Critical elections in Illinois: 1888-1958." *American Political Science
          Review* 54 (September):669–83.

McSeveney, Samuel T.
  1972   "Voting in the northeastern states during the late nineteenth century."
          Pp. 195–202 in J. H. Silbey and S. T. McSeveney (eds.), *Voters, parties
          and elections*, Lexington, Mass.: Xerox College Publishing.

Mann, Michael
  1970   "The social cohesion of liberal democracy." *American Sociological
          Review* 35 (June):423–39.

Marx, Karl
  1956   *Selected writings in sociology and social philosophy*, edited by T. B.
          Bottomore. New York: McGraw-Hill.
  1962   *Capital*. Vols. I-III. Moscow: Foreign Languages Publishing House.

Mason, Karen Oppenheim; William M. Mason; H. H. Winsborough;
and W. Kenneth Poole
  1973   "Some methodological issues in cohort analysis of archival data."
          American Sociological Review 38 (April):242–58.

Masters, Nicholas, and Deil S. Wright
  1958   "Trends and variations in the two party vote: The case of Michigan."
          American Political Science Review 52 (December):1078–90.

Matthews, Donald R., and James. W. Prothro
  1966   *Negroes and the new southern politics*. New York: Harcourt, Brace,
          Jovanovich.

Mayhew, Leon
  1968   "Ascription in modern societies." *Sociological Inquiry* 38 (Spring):
          105–20.

Melichar, Emanuel
    1966   "Least-squares analysis of economic survey data." *1965 Proceedings of the Business and Economic Statistics Section*, Washington, D.C.: American Statistical Association, 373–85.

Merelman, Richard M.
    1970   "Electoral instability and the American party system." *Journal of Politics* 32 (February):115–39.

Miller, Arthur H.; Warren E. Miller; Alden S. Raine; and Thad A. Brown
    1973   "A majority party in disarray: Policy polarization in the 1972 election." Paper presented at the American Political Science Association Meetings.

Mueller, John E.
    1970   "Presidential popularity from Truman to Johnson." *American Political Science Review* 64 (March):18–34.
    1973   *War, presidents and public opinion*. New York: Wiley.

Niemi, Richard G.
    1967   "A Methodological Study of Political Socialization in the Family." Ph.D. dissertation, University of Michigan.
    1973   "Collecting information about the family: A problem in survey methodology." In *Socialization to politics: A reader*, edited by J. Dennis, pp. 469–90. New York: Wiley.

Ollman, Bertell
    1972   "Toward class consciousness next time: Marx and the working class." *Politics and Society* 3 (Fall):1–24.

Oppenheim, Karen
    1970   "Voting in recent American presidential elections." Ph.D. dissertation, University of Chicago.

Page, Benjamin I., and Richard A. Brody
    1972   "Policy voting and the electoral process: The Vietnam war issue." *American Political Science Review* 66 (September):979–95.

Parkin, Frank
    1971   *Class inequality and political order*. New York: Praeger.

Phillips, Kevin P.
    1969   *The emerging Republican majority*. New Rochelle, N. Y.: Arlington House.

Pierce, John C., and Douglas D. Rose
    1974   "Non-attitudes and American public opinion: The examination of a thesis." *American Political Science Review* 68 (June):626–49.

Pomper, Gerald
    1967   "Classification of presidential elections." *Journal of Politics* 29 (August):535–66.
    1972   "From confusion to clarity: Issues and American voters, 1956-1968." *American Political Science Review* 66 (June):415–28.

Reiss, Albert J. (ed.)
1961   *Occupations and social status.* New York: Free Press of Glencoe.

RePass, David E.
1971   "Issue salience and party choice." *American Political Science Review* 65 (June):389–400.

Rice, Stuart A.
1928   *Quantitative methods in politics.* New York: Knopf.

Riecken, Henry W.
1959   "Primary groups and political party choice." In *American voting behavior*, edited by E. Burdick and A. Brodbeck, pp. 162–83. New York: Free Press.

Riker, William H., and Peter C. Ordeshook
1968   "A theory of the calculus of voting." *American Political Science Review* 62 (March):25–42.
1973   *An introduction to positive political theory.* Englewood Cliffs, N. J.: Prentice-Hall.

Rusk, Jerrold G.
1974   "Comment: The American electoral universe: Speculation and evidence." *American Political Science Review* 68 (September):1028–49.

Ryder, Norman B.
1965   "The cohort as a concept in the study of social change." *American Sociological Review* 30 (December):843–61.

Schoenberg, Ronald
1972   "Strategies for meaningful comparison." In *Sociological methodology, 1972*, edited by H. L. Costner, pp. 1–35. San Francisco: Jossey-Bass.

Schulman, Mark A., and Gerald M. Pomper
1975   "Variability in electoral behavior: Longitudinal perspectives from causal modeling." *American Journal of Political Science* 19 (February): 1–18.

Sellers, Charles
1965   "The equilibrium cycle in two-party politics." *Public Opinion Quarterly* 29 (Spring):16–38.

Shapiro, Michael J.
1969   "Rational political man: A synthesis of economic and social psychological perspectives." *American Political Science Review* 63 (December):1106–19.

Siegel, Paul M.
1971   "Prestige in the American Occupational Structure." Ph.D. dissertation, University of Chicago.

Siegel, Paul M., and Robert W. Hodge
1969   "A causal approach to the study of measurement error." In *Methodology in social research*, edited by H. M. Blalock and A. B. Blalock, pp. 28–59, New York: McGraw-Hill.

Simmel, Georg
    1964   "The web of group affiliations." In *Conflict and the web of group affiliations*, edited by K. Wolff and R. Bendix, pp. 125–95. New York: Free Press.

Sorauf, Frank J.
    1972   *Party politics in America.* 2d ed. Boston: Little, Brown.

Stokes, Donald
    1962   "Party loyalty and the likelihood of deviating elections." *Journal of Politics* 24 (November):689–702.
    1966   "Some dynamic elements of contests for the presidency." *American Political Science Review* 60 (March):19–28.
    1968   "Voting," In *The international encyclopedia of the social sciences*, Vol. XVI, edited by D. L. Sills, pp. 387–95. New York: Macmillan.

Stokes, Donald E.; Angus Campbell; and Warren E. Miller
    1958   "Components of electoral decision." *American Political Science Review* 52 (June):367–87.

Stokes, Donald, and Gudmund Iversen
    1962   "On the existence of forces restoring party competition." *Public Opinion Quarterly* 26 (Summer):159–71.

Suits, Daniel B.
    1957   "Use of dummy variables in regression equations." *Journal of the American Statistical Association* 52:548–51.

Summers, Gene F.; Richard L. Hough; Doyle P. Johnson; and Kathryn A. Veatch
    1970   "Ascetic protestantism and political preference: A reexamination." *Review of Religious Research* 12 (Fall):17–25.

Sundquist, James L.
    1973   *Dynamics of the party system.* Washington, D.C.: The Brookings Institution.

Toennies, Ferdinand
    1957   *Community and society.* Translated by Charles Loomis. East Lansing, Mich.: Michigan State University Press.

Vaillancourt, Pauline, and Richard G. Niemi
    1974   "Children's party choices." In *The politics of future citizens*, edited by Richard G. Niemi, pp. 126–48. San Francisco: Jossey-Bass.

Warren, Bruce L.
    1971   "Socioeconomic achievement and religion: The American case." *Sociological Inquiry* 40 (Spring):130–55.

Weber, Max
    1966   "Class, status, party." In *Class, Status, and Power.* 2d. ed. edited by R. Bendix and S. M. Lipset, pp. 21–28. New York: Free Press.

Weir, Blair T.
    1975   "The distortion of voter recall." *American Journal of Political Science* 19 (February):53–62.

White, Theodore H.
    1961   *The making of the president 1960*. New York: Atheneum

Wilensky, Harold L.
    1966   "Class, class consciousness, and American workers." In *Labor in a changing America*, edited by W. Haber, pp. 12–28. New York: Basic Books.

Wiley, Norbert
    1967   "America's unique class politics: The interplay of the labor, credit and commodity markets." *American Sociological Review* 32 (August): 529–41.

Wilson, James Q.
    1960   *Negro politics: The search for leadership*. New York: Free Press.

Wright, Sewell
    1960   "The treatment of reciprocal interaction, with or without lag, in path analysis." *Biometrics* 16 (September):423–45.

Zeitlin, Irving M.
    1967   *Marxism: A re-examination*. Princeton, N. J.: Van Nostrand.

Index